W9-AXF-079

MORAL PROBLEMS IN CONTEMPORARY SOCIETY

edited by PAUL KURTZ
Department of Philosophy
State University of New York at Buffalo

Prometheus Books, Buffalo
Pemberton Books, London

MORAL PROBLEMS IN CONTEMPORARY SOCIETY

ESSAYS IN HUMANISTIC ETHICS

MORAL PROBLEMS IN CONTEMPORARY SOCIETY:
ESSAYS IN HUMANISTIC ETHICS

edited by Paul Kurtz

Printed in the United States of America

ISBN 0-87975-022-7

PB *Prometheus Books*
923 Kensington Ave.
Buffalo, N. Y. 14215

EDITOR'S PREFACE

In a world of unending and frightful problems, it is important that the humanist point of view be presented. Are there common ethical values that humanists maintain? Would the examination of them be helpful in clarifying the problems of society today? This is the impetus for a volume in humanistic ethics dealing with the moral problems in contemporary society; and it is the task to which the humanist writers in this volume have addressed themselves.

My special thanks in preparing this work go to Herbert Feigl, who first suggested that I undertake a volume devoted to humanistic ethics. I also wish to thank Lloyd Morain, Robert McCoy, Howard Radest, Edwin Wilson, Arnold Sylvester, and Tolbert H. McCarroll —leaders in the humanist movement in America—who have provided stimulus and support for this project. I am grateful to my colleagues, John Anton, Marvin Zimmerman, and Peter Hare in the Department of Philosophy at the State University of New York at Buffalo, who have read portions of this manuscript and offered useful suggestions in its development.

This volume is dedicated to humanists—past, present, and future —who, like the contributors to this volume, are committed to the vision of humanity as a whole. Only by a continuing dedication to the preservation and enhancement of humanistic values can mankind hope to prevail in the future.

Paul Kurtz
Buffalo, New York

CONTENTS

III

THE INDIVIDUAL: LAW, MORALITY, AND SOCIAL ORGANIZATION

IV

JUSTICE AND SOCIETY

V

DEATH

WHAT IS HUMANISM?

Paul Kurtz

Humanism has had a distinguished, though checkered, career in the history of Western thought. There have been many varieties of humanism, each appropriate to the age in which it appeared; though perhaps the moments of its highest brilliance can be seen in the Hellenic civilization of classical Greece and Rome, the Renaissance, the Enlightenment, and during the scientific revolution of modern times. In a very real sense the present age may be characterized as predominantly humanistic, for humanistic concepts and values pervade contemporary life. Indeed, a great number of diverse and often contending intellectual and philosophical movements may be said to be basically humanistic in character: naturalism, materialism, positivism, analytic philosophy, Marxism, phenomenology, existentialism, even Zen Buddhism and behavioristic and humanistic psychology.

Humanism has had a remarkable resurgence in the past decade. Intellectuals who have been atheists, agnostics, and skeptics and have attacked the inconsistencies of orthodox religion have been startled by the great success of their critiques. Large sections of the population are unaffiliated with any organized religious sect, and are humanist in outlook and belief. The "God is dead" movement has brought the sudden realization that humanism has been far more influential upon the mainstream of religion than has been imagined. Many Protestant theologians now accept humanistic premises: religion must be regarded essentially as a form of human experience, an expression of human values; it is empty if it substitutes a dead God for a living ideal of human justice. Most surprising, the Roman Catholic Church for the first time in modern times begins to show humanist strains: a sterile dogma and an outworn Thomism are increasingly questioned. It is the human church and its mission in human society that is beginning to be emphasized. Even Marxian socialists of Eastern Europe are rediscovering strong humanistic and existentialist foundations in the early Marx: not the destruction of the old society, or ownership of the means of production are the ends of socialism, but the full development of humanity and of the human individual.

As a result of these tendencies, humanism today is in a situation of challenge and crisis. It is one thing to reject orthodoxy, dogma, and creed as superstitious mythology irrelevant to the contemporary world; however, it is quite another thing to suggest in positive terms what humanism can offer in their place. Many humanists, who now believe that the battle against orthodoxy has been won, and who applaud the fact that many or most educated people are humanists in one form or another, also are convinced that humanists must replace the outworn symbols and clichés of an earlier age of protest with more meaningful and concrete principles of action. Many insist that humanists must overlook any differences that they had had in the past and instead emphasize their common assumptions.

Although humanists share many principles, there are two basic and minimal principles which especially seem to characterize humanism. First, there is a rejection of any supernatural conception of the universe and a denial that man has a privileged place within nature. Second, there is an affirmation that ethical values are *human* and have no meaning independent of human experience; thus humanism is an ethical philosophy in which man is central.

ANTI-SUPERNATURALISM

This first humanist principle, the rejection of the supernatural world view, humanism shares with materialism and naturalism.

Many humanists, however, who vehemently deny that ultimate reality is spiritual or divine, are not necessarily prepared to accept a materialistic or naturalistic framework. What is essential to all humanisms is the refusal to accept a simplistic cosmic purpose or teleology—to accept, that is, the view that God is the ultimate source of all existence and value, or that there is a bifurcation between nature and super-nature. The humanist does not exclude a transcendental reality on *a priori* grounds, nor does he necessarily deny that there may be aspects of the universe which perhaps are beyond investigation now or in the future. He only wishes to maintain that claims to a non-natural realm have not been confirmed by adequate evidence or supported on rational grounds. Moreover, attempts to prove the existence of God (ontological, cosmological, teleological, etc.) are unconvincing, unverified, and even meaningless. The humanist does not callously dismiss the reports of mystical or revelatory experience. But he looks upon these reports as events to be explained and interpreted in natural terms, much the same as any other data of experience. Such events he finds can be parsimoniously accounted for without reference to an alleged transcendental reality. In any case, he asks that all claims to knowledge be open to a responsible examination of the grounds by which they are supported; and he does not consider the evidence referred to by the mystic as conclusive.

Most humanists take man as a part of nature. There is no break between the human mind or consciousness on the one hand and the body on the other, no special status to personality or "soul," and no privileged or special place for human existence in the universe at large. All claims to unique human immortality or eschatological theories of history thus are held to be an expression of wish fulfillment, a vain reading into nature of human hope and fancy. Nature, for the humanist, is blind to human purposes and indifferent to human ideals.

VALUE IS RELATIVE TO MAN

The second basic humanist principle is the ethical concern for man and his works. The humanist says that a theory of value cannot be derived from a metaphysics of divinity, that value is relative to man and to what human beings find to be worthwhile in experience. Ethical standards thus are to be found not outside of life but within it. Most humanists have some confidence in the dignity and power of man to discover for himself the sources of the good life. Thus the humanist is an uncompromising critic of the established ethical codes and commandments of orthodox and authoritarian religion. Theistic religions have often suppressed the best human instincts; they have often been dishonest and immoral concerning man's right to truth; and they have frequently censored and blocked free and responsible intellectual inquiry. The humanist, on the contrary, asks that we, as human beings, face up to the human condition as it is. Humanists accept the fact that God is dead; that we have no way of knowing that he exists; or even of knowing that this is a meaningful question. They accept the fact that human existence is probably a random occurrence existing between two oblivions, that death is inevitable, that there is a tragic aspect to our lives, and that all moral values are our own creations.

To be sure, there have been some humanists who have, in the face of the rejections of the theistic universe of values, become pessimistic. Yet most humanists have found a source of optimism in the affirmation that value is related to man. Life is not hopeless, and with a proper recognition of the human estate there must also be an awareness of the challenges and of the possibilities that await us. This awareness may be a basis for genuine confidence, not despair and cynicism. For while there is death and failure, there is also life and success. And with life come great and bountiful promises: these are the joys of human love and shared experience, the excitement of creativity, the power of reason, the possibilities that we as human beings have some control over our destinies. If we grant that not all human sorrows and evils can be avoided, still the human situation is not totally irremediable; and with some confidence in our powers, particularly of thought and intelligence, we may help to build a good life.

The theist has not always allowed man to be himself. He has looked outside of nature or human nature, and has created idolatrous religions, worshiping graven images. He has often frustrated and thwarted independent self-assertion. He has thus contributed to the alienation of man from himself and nature. Man is made to feel himself dependent upon God, a "sinner" who must renounce and suppress his pride. But the more he exalts God, as the father image, the more he demeans himself. Surely man is dependent upon external forces, some of which are beyond his control (such as death), but why worship or submit to them, and why weaken or belittle man, asks the humanist. Why exacerbate his guilt complex, and his sense of sin, and why exalt acquiescence? Man needs to be himself. He needs to affirm his manhood, to develop the courage to persist in spite of all the obstacles that would destroy him, indeed to exceed himself by creating a new life for himself. The challenge for the free man is to realize his possibilities, and to create new ones, not to cower in masochistic denial, not to withdraw in anxiety, fear, and trembling, not to look outside of himself for help that is not there.

Humanism today can look to the ennoblement and enrichment of human life as an end, whether in individual terms, as each man satisfies his ideals and dreams, or in social terms, where we seek to develop rules and norms of justice. Humanism claims that man is rooted in the soil (nature), that it is the flesh (life) that gives him satisfaction, but that it is in social harmony and creative fulfillment (the "spirit") that he finds his deepest significance.

Is humanism a religion or an ethic? There are many humanists who agree that humanism often functions as a religion, though they emphasize the *human* qualities in religious experience. There are others who deny this, who do not wish to stretch the term "religion" beyond the belief in some "divine and unseen power," which they reject, and who therefore maintain that humanism is primarily a philosophical or scientific point of view. For those who consider humanism a religion, "God" is only a symbol of man's aspirations, the ideals which stimulate him to devotion and action (Dewey and Braithwaite). One who takes "God" to be a hidden or transcendental being only confuses the issues of life, and does not face death. Some humanists (Tillich) seek to retain the classical symbols of theistic religion, but they wish to demythologize them and to reinvigorate them with new meaning appropriate to our age of science and world revolution. Thus the symbols of mythological and miraculous revelation are to be reinterpreted to arouse concern for man *as man.* "God," then, is not a symbol of one who speaks to man from on high, but an expression of man's deepest longings, man speaking to himself. Those humanists who are dubious of this effort to translate religious symbols into naturalistic and humanistic terms, which they consider to be hypocritical and dishonest, would seek to build a new set of symbols and beliefs appropriate to the present age, symbols better able to dramatize the aspirations of humanity.

All humanists agree, however, that humanism involves, at a minimum, an ethical posture and that it expresses normative values. And this in the case whether we choose to call humanism a nontheistic religion (that is, whether we wish to emphasize the fact that humanistic ethics may be enhanced and supported by feeling, devotion, and commitment to a set of ideal values), or whether we wish to insist that humanism is primarily a rational philosophical or scientific outlook (in which feeling and commitment recede into the background and reason dominates). Accordingly, humanism involves an ethics in the sense that it has a set of normative values and prescriptive ideals.

What is important, as Sartre has said, is that there are no absolute values or norms independent of what man individually and socially chooses. Instead, man is condemned to make man; we alone are responsible for what we are and what we do. Perhaps this is an overstatement of the case for freedom; at least the humanist asks that man begin to shed the chains of illusion that bind him, and assert himself. What man needs is not renunciation, but affirmation; not resignation, but confidence; above all, not blind piety and faith, but honesty and truth.

The humanist in ethics is usually cautious and tentative in his judgments, and he may even be skeptical about his humanism, recognizing its limitations. He knows that it is difficult to find absolute standards, or categorical imperatives. Yet he suggests that the human animal, who finds himself thrust into existence without having asked to be put there, can to some extent define himself and determine who he is and what he shall be. Man can achieve a satisfying and authentic existence here and now. But the first essential for this is that he cease deluding himself about what is and is not in store for him. The humanist recognizes the rich diversity and relativity of value, and the fact that there are alternate paths which man may take to achieve the good life. He merely claims that it is we who are to choose, whatever we choose, and that we should not shirk our responsibility to so choose, or escape to a world of dogma and myth.

RELEVANCE OF REASON

Some humanists add to the above two principles still a third, which they think is essential to any definition of humanism. They claim that ethical principles are open to rational criticism, that value judgments are capable of some empirical warrant, and that scientific knowledge can be applied to the solution of the problems of man. Such humanists are frequently committed to situational ethics—to the view that ethical principles are not *a priori* or universal, but only general guides to be applied and modified in the light of empirical circumstances and conditions, in terms of means and consequences. This point of view is sometimes known as scientific humanism.

Not all humanists, however, share this faith in the power of reason; nor do they all have confidence in the possibility of ethical objectivity. For example, some existential humanists and positivists, pointing to the basically emotive character of philosophical theories of value, have emphasized the subjective ingredients in human values. Though all humanisms share the critique of theistic ethics as full of vain hope and illusion, humanistic ethics at the very least involve a rejection of absolutistic ethics as unfounded in reason or evidence, and hence unreasonable.

The whole question of the empirical objectivity and testability of ethical judgments has been vigorously discussed in twentieth-century ethics, particularly by analytic philosophers. Such philosophers have devoted the lion's share of their attention to technical meta-questions rather than to practical matters. Many humanists (for example, utilitarians and pragmatists) had accepted some version of naturalistic ethics, i.e., the view that ethical judgments are empirical or may be supported by scientific knowledge; and they also have had some confidence that philosophy might provide some help in solving moral and social problems. This point of view, however, has been subjected to a strong criticism by many analytic philosophers.

The key questions that have been raised in meta-ethics are epistemological, and they concern the definition of our basic moral terms and the methods by which we justify moral principles. G. E. Moore denied that we could define basic moral terms or derive moral conclusions from nonmoral premises without committing the "naturalistic fallacy." The intuitionists agreed that ethical terms are unanalyzable properties and not amenable to empirical test. And later the logical positivists and emotivists claimed that all ethical terms are expressive and imperative, that attempts to define them are persuasive, and that attitudes, being divorced from beliefs, could not be supported scientifically. Many existentialists went in a different direction, though they claimed that our basic values are commitments, absurd and nonrational, and not amenable to any kind of objective treatment. The upshot of the matter was that until very recently many humanistic philosophers seemed reluctant to say anything positive about man's moral life or to recommend any prescriptive ideals—skepticism and despair seemed the only alternatives.

There are those who have been pleased with the results, likening what has occurred to a "revolution" in ethics. Others have considered this state of affairs scandalous. One can agree that a powerful advance has been made by developing useful analytic tools, but one can decry the fact that philosophers have ignored the practical moral problems of life. We seem today to be witnessing within philosophy a strong reaction away from the extreme skepticism in meta-ethics which existed only a few years ago. There is now a recognition that ethical language, after all, does make some sense, that there is a kind of logic of decision-making, and that *reason applies to some extent to practice.* Analytic philosophers have had second thoughts about the emotivists' critique, and naturalistic philosophers in rejoinder have attempted to provide revised and more carefully framed theories. It is now also recognized that philosophers had best not withdraw from the world to a linguistic sanctuary, that there are real problems that human beings face, and that philosophical analysis on the level of concrete experience and in relation to the actual problems of life may have some relevance. Still philosophers today disagree about the precise role of reason in ethics or the degree of objectivity.

What has been overlooked is that although philosophers may dispute on the technical meta level concerning linguistic and epistemological issues, they nonetheless may share certain moral principles. Thus many philosophers, including philosophical and logical positivists, are humanists in ethics proper, if not in meta-ethics. Though philosophers may differ in method and approach in meta-ethics, many accept in their *own* moral and political lives a general form of humanistic ethics.

HUMANITARIANISM

Many humanists also wish to add still a fourth principle to their definition of humanism—namely, that humanism involves some form of social humanitarianism. Such humanists have had a commitment to some form of the greatest happiness for the greatest number principle or to some other social justice principle; they have considered that the highest moral prescription is for *humanity* as a whole. This involves the view that since all men are members of the same human family it is our obligation to further the welfare of mankind. Now it is possible to be a humanist in the first two senses above—to reject supernaturalism and to claim that value is basically human—and not to accept the third and fourth principles above, that is, the commitment to reason or to humanitarianism. One can think of Epicurus or Nietszche as humanists in this sense. Many classical humanists have emphasized the achievement of human happiness and the perfecting of the individual as the highest human good. Yet today most humanists are in some way also dedicated to the ideal of social meliorism and a concern for their fellow man. Indeed, the challenge has been hurled at secular humanists by theistic theologians, that if man is the sole source of human values, what guarantee or safeguard will we have that humanists can develop a sense of responsibility to their fellow men and overcome subjectivism and relativism? Can humanism develop not only an ethic of the good life, applicable to individuals, but an ethic of moral responsibility and obligation appropriate to other human beings or to society at large? If God is dead and if there is no afterlife, does morality have meaning and does man have a basis for moral action? Yes, the present-day humanist insists. Indeed, the notion of a dead and risen God, of a last judgment day, and of the paradox of evil in a world of divine creation, is hardly a "rational" foundation of morality; and on the contrary seems to the humanist to be absurd. The *only* meaning man can find for morality is that which he makes for himself. At least, the humanist and secular view of the universe is more realistic and honest and avoids deception and false hope. Thus humanism, not being based on theistic illusion or obedience, provides man with a more secure foundation for the moral life.

Moral imperatives for the humanist are based upon human experience. They are grounded in an estimation of the consequences of our action: which moral rules, we ask, will, as a matter of fact, lead to the best possible life for all concerned, including myself. Humanist morality need not be grounded in unadulterated egoism—although considerations of self-interest are part of the justification that one gives for his moral beliefs. Rather, morality is rooted in a sensitivity to the interests and needs of others, a rational awareness that my good is tied up with the good of others, and a recognition that any happiness that I desire presupposes some conditions of order and rules, which would make it possible for other human beings beside myself to achieve their ends. If the humanist admits of no absolute foundation for moral sympathy or *a priori* justification of first principles, he does believe that a reasonable case for morality can be made, a case which all but the extreme skeptic will understand, since it is based upon the common moral experience of mankind.

There are a great variety of humanitarian humanisms, among the most important of which are utopian humanism, liberal humanism, democratic humanism, utilitarian humanism, and socialist humanism. There is a double humanist concern: in individual terms the ideal of the development of the potentialities of the individual, *and* in social terms the ideal of social harmony and justice. If liberal, Renaissance and Enlightenment humanisms emphasized the perfectability of the individual and had faith in the instrumentality of reason and education, utilitarian, democratic, and especially socialist humanisms have emphasized that many or most of the problems of man can only be resolved by social action, by changing the social system, the underlying economic structure, the forces and relationships of production. Humanists today attack all those social forces which seek to destroy man: they deplore the dehumanization and alienation of man within the industrial and technological society, the conflict and tension, poverty and war, racial discrimination and hatred, inequality and injustice, overpopulation and waste, the emphasis on the mere quantity rather than on the quality of life. In effect, they condemn all of the contradictions of modern life, and the failure of modern man to achieve the full measure of his potential excellence. The problem for the humanist is to create the conditions which would emancipate man from oppressive and corruptive social organization, and from the denigration and perversion of his human talents, which would liberate him from one-sided and distorted development, and which would enable him to achieve an authentic life. Humanists may not agree about the methods of achieving a just and equitable society. But they share a vision of the good life and the means of attaining it: a faith in freedom and reason, dignity and equality, social peace and harmony. And they are interested in creating a society in which the fruits of modern technology and automation can be enjoyed and leisure life enriched.

HUMANISTIC ETHICS AND PRACTICAL ISSUES

It is significant that humanists of different philosophical persuasions—whether they accept a materialist, or naturalist, or organicist view of the universe, whether they are committed to scientific method in nature and human life or are not, whether they accept dialectical materialism, or hedonism, phenomenalism, empiricism, pragmatism, or rationalism—nevertheless *do* share certain general ethical principles in common. Although there exists considerable agreement concerning these ethical principles, there has not been sufficient attention devoted to the explicit definition and elaboration of the principles in concrete terms. Here I am thinking of principles, not on the meta level, but on the substantive level of practical application. The crucial question to be asked of humanism today does not concern the status of its general outlook or ideal ends, but whether it has anything positive to say about the living moral alternatives that confront mankind. The solutions of moral problems are terribly difficult. One can argue that if one is to resolve paradoxes the first condition is freedom from the dogma of supernatural mythology or the attempt to impose an authoritarian code from without; and the second condition is vital concern with mankind itself. Humanists do not necessarily have greater wisdom than other human beings or greater sensitivity to human needs. They do not agree in all cases on what are the best policies to adopt or courses to follow. At least they are not weighed down by an alien morality, as are theists, nor do they have illusions about the universe and man's place in it. But it is essential that humanists be not simply negative in their rejection of nonhumanism, but positive, and that they turn their attention to the actual issues on the frontier of present-day concern.

With this in mind *The Humanist* magazine invited eighteen key thinkers, representing the major schools on the philosophical spectrum of contemporary thought, to contribute to this special volume on humanistic ethics. Ernest Nagel, Sidney Hook, Abraham Edel, Corliss Lamont, Rollo Handy, John Anton, Charles Frankel, and Paul Kurtz represent the naturalistic and pragmatic tradition in American thought. Marvin Farber is a key figure in the introduction of phenomenology to the United States, and Maurice Natanson is a phenomenologist and existentialist. Herbert Feigl is a classic figure in logical positivism. Kurt Baier, Kai Nielsen, and Nagel are analytic philosophers. John Somerville, Lamont, and Hook are Marxists. H. J. Blackham is former Chairman of the British Humanist Association. At a time when many contemporary philosophers have retreated from ethics for fear of committing the "naturalistic fallacy," many psychologists have maintained a vital interest in basic moral issues. Accordingly, we have invited three leading psychologists to contribute to this volume: A. H. Maslow and Carl Rogers, representing humanistic or phenomenological psychology and psychoanalysis, and B. F. Skinner, the most influential behaviorist in America.

We have asked our contributors to do either one or both of two things: first, to say what they consider humanist ethics to be (only some have chosen to do this); and second, to deal with a basic moral issue or moral problem, of their own choice, in order to illustrate humanism in concrete terms. Most, but not all, of the papers in this volume, were written specifically for this volume or have appeared in *The Humanist.* The papers conveniently divide themselves among several cognate topics: ethics, religion, and the meaning of life; the good life; the individual—law, morality, and social organization; justice and society; death. Although there are other live moral issues on the frontier of social concern with which our contributors have not dealt, they have managed to focus on a number of those which are of vital significance to modern man.

It is clear from the papers in this volume that humanistic ethics is not a dogma or a creed, that it does not have a specific platform or program that can be easily laid out, a "Thus saith the Humanist" to replace a "Thus saith the Lord." Rather, humanism expresses an outlook: the view of man not as a divine creation but as a product of nature, and the consideration of his moral values as thoroughly human in origin and meaning. But it also represents an attitude: to submit moral values to critical and reflective analysis and to view them from the standpoint of a humanitarian concern for mankind as a whole.

It is our hope that this volume will have something worthwhile to say not only to readers who are avowed humanists but also to those who are humanists though they may not be aware of it. Here we have in mind the considerable number of educated people who reject orthodox theisms and are committed to humanistic values, though they have been unable to define what their values are or to see how they apply to the concrete problems of life. And we also hope that this volume will have something to say to those who are not humanists, but ought to be.

This volume is predicated on the premise that both ethical philosophy and philosophically oriented psychology can take a new departure, and that in addition to the proper concern of philosophy for meta-questions or of psychology for experimental inquiry, both can show an interest in the basic moral questions that exercise mankind. In its original Socratic sense, ethical inquiry meant the development of practical wisdom. If humanistic ethics is to mean anything, then it must not only clarify our basic moral concepts, but also provide some normative guidance for the moral life.

I

ETHICS, RELIGION, AND THE MEANING OF LIFE

ETHICS WITHOUT RELIGION*

Kai Nielsen

1

There certainly are fundamental difficulties and perhaps even elements of incoherence in Christian ethics, but what can a secular moralist and humanist offer in its stead? Religious morality—and Christian morality in particular—may have its difficulties, but secular and humanist morality, religious apologists argue, has still greater difficulties. It leads, they claim, to ethical skepticism, nihilism, or, at best, to a pure conventionalism. Such apologists could point out that if we look at morality with the cold eye of an anthropologist we will —assuming we are clearheaded—find morality to be nothing more than the often conflicting *mores* of the various tribes spread around the globe. If we eschew the kind of insight that religion can give us, we will have no Archimedean point in accordance with which we can decide how it is that we ought to live and die. If we look at ethics from such a purely secular point of view, we will discover that it is constituted by tribal conventions, conventions which we are free to reject if we are sufficiently free from ethnocentrism. We can continue to act in accordance with them or we can reject them and adopt

* This paper was originally published in *The Ohio University Review*, VI (1964), 48–62. Reprinted by permission of *The Ohio University Review*.

a different set of conventions; but whether we act in accordance with the old conventions or forge "new tablets," we are still acting in accordance with certain conventions. Relative to them certain acts are right or wrong, reasonable or unreasonable, but we cannot justify these fundamental moral conventions themselves or the ways of life which they partially codify.

When these points are conceded, theologians are in a position to press home a powerful apologetic point. When we become keenly aware, they argue, of the true nature of such conventionalism and when we become aware that there is no overarching purpose that men were destined to fulfill, the myriad purposes, the aims and goals humans create for themselves, will be seen not to be enough. When we realize that life does not have a meaning—that is, a significance —which is there to be found, but that we human beings must by our deliberate decisions give it whatever meaning it has, we will (as Sartre so well understood) undergo estrangement and despair. We will drain our cup to its last bitter drop and feel our alienation to the full. Perhaps there are human purposes, purposes to be found *in* life, and we can and do have them even in a Godless world, but without God there can be no one overarching purpose, no one basic scheme of human existence, in virtue of which we could find a meaning for our grubby lives. It is this overall sense of meaning that man so ardently strives for, but it is not to be found in a purely secular world view. You secularists, a new Pascal might argue, must realize, if you really want to be clearheaded, that no purely human purposes are ultimately worth striving for. What you humanists can give us by way of a scheme of human existence will always be a poor second best and not what the human heart most ardently longs for.

The considerations for and against an ethics not rooted in a religion are complex and involuted; a fruitful discussion of them is difficult, for in considering the matter our passions, our anxieties, our (if you will) ultimate concerns are involved, and they tend to blur our vision, enfeeble our understanding, of what exactly is at stake. But we must not forget that what is at stake here is just what kind of ultimate commitments or obligations a man could have without evading any issue, without self-deception, or without delusion. I shall be concerned to display and assess, to make plain but also to weigh, some of the most crucial considerations for and against a purely secular ethic. While I shall in an objective fashion try to make clear what the central issues are, I shall also give voice to my reflective convictions on this matter. I shall try to make evident my reasons for believing that we do not need God or any religious conception to support our moral convictions. I shall do this, as I think one should in philosophy, by making apparent the dialectic of the problem (by bringing to the fore the conflicting and evolving considerations for and against) and by arguing for what I take to be their proper resolution.

2

I am aware that Crisis Theologians would claim that I am being naïve, but I do not see why purposes of purely human devising are not ultimately worth striving for. There is much that we humans prize and would continue to prize even in a Godless world. Many things would remain to give our lives meaning and point even after "the death of God."

Take a simple example. All of us *want* to be happy. But in certain bitter or skeptical moods we question what happiness is or we despairingly ask ourselves whether anyone can really be happy. Is this, however, a sober, sane view of the situation? I do not think that it is. Indeed we cannot adequately define "happiness" in the way that we can "bachelor," but neither can we in that way define "chair," "wind," "pain," and the vast majority of words in everyday discourse. For words like "bachelor," "triangle," or "father" we can specify a consistent set of properties that all the things and only the things denoted by these words have, but we cannot do this for "happiness," "chair," "pain," and the like. In fact, we cannot do it for the great majority of our words. Yet there is no great loss here. Modern philosophical analysis has taught us that such an essentially Platonic conception of definition is unrealistic and unnecessary.[1] I may not

[1] This is convincingly argued in Michael Scriven's essay "Definitions, Explanations, and Theories" in *Minnesota Studies in the Philosophy of Science,* III, ed. Herbert Feigl, Michael Scriven, and Grover Maxwell (Minneapolis, 1958), pp. 99–195.

be able to define "chair" in the way that I can define "bachelor," but I understand the meaning of "chair" perfectly well. In normal circumstances, at least, I know what to sit on when someone tells me to take a chair. I may not be able to define "pain," but I know what it is like to be in pain, and sometimes I can know when others are in pain. Similarly, though I cannot define "happiness" in the same way that I can define "bachelor," I know what it is like to be happy, and I sometimes can judge with considerable reliability whether others are happy or sad. "Happiness" is a slippery word, but it is not so slippery that we are justified in saying that nobody knows what happiness is.

A man could be said to have lived a happy life if he had found lasting sources of satisfaction in his life and if he had been able to find certain goals worthwhile and to achieve at least some of them. He could indeed have suffered some pain and anxiety, but his life must, for the most part, have been free from pain, estrangement, and despair, and must, on balance, have been a life which he has liked and found worthwhile. But surely we have no good grounds for saying that no one achieves such a balance or that no one is ever happy even for a time. We all have some idea of what would make us happy and of what would make us unhappy; many people, at least, can remain happy even after "the death of God." At any rate, we need not strike Pascalian attitudes, for even in a purely secular world there are permanent sources of human happiness for anyone to avail himself of.

What are they? What are these relatively permanent sources of human happiness that we all want or need? What is it which, if we have it, will give us the basis for a life that could properly be said to be happy? We all desire to be free from pain and want. Even masochists do not seek pain for its own sake; they endure pain because this is the only psychologically acceptable way of achieving something else (usually sexual satisfaction) that is so gratifying to them that they will put up with the pain to achieve it. We all want a life in which sometimes we can enjoy ourselves and in which we can attain our fair share of some of the simple pleasures that we all desire. They are not everything in life, but they are important, and our lives would be impoverished without them.

We also need security and emotional peace. We need and want a life in which we will not be constantly threatened with physical or emotional harassment. Again this is not the only thing worth seeking, but it is an essential ingredient in any adequate picture of the good life.

Human love and companionship are also central to a significant or happy life. We prize them, and a life which is without them is most surely an impoverished life, a life that no man, if he would take the matter to heart, would desire. But I would most emphatically assert that human love and companionship are quite possible in a Godless world, and the fact that life will some day inexorably come to an end and cut off love and companionship altogether enhances rather than diminishes their present value.

Furthermore, we all need some sort of creative employment or meaningful work to give our lives point, to save them from boredom, drudgery, and futility. A man who can find no way to use the talents he has or a man who can find no work which is meaningful to him will indeed be a miserable man. But again there is work—whether it be as a surgeon, a farmer, or a fisherman—that has a rationale even in a world without God. And poetry, music, and art retain their beauty and enrich our lives even in the complete absence of God or the gods.

We want and need art, music, and the dance. We find pleasure in travel and conversation and in a rich variety of experiences. The sources of human enjoyment are obviously too numerous to detail. But all of them are achievable in a Godless universe. If some can be ours, we can attain a reasonable measure of happiness. Only a Steppenwolfish personality beguiled by impossible expectations and warped by irrational guilts and fears can fail to find happiness in the realization of such ends. But to be free of impossible expectations people must clearly recognize that there is no "one big thing" or, for that matter, "small thing" which would make them permanently happy; almost anything permanently and exclusively pursued will lead to that nausea that Sartre has so forcefully brought to our attention. But we can, if we are not too sick and if our situation is not too precarious, find lasting sources of human happiness in a purely secular world.

It is not only happiness for ourselves that can give us something of value, but there is the need to do what we can to diminish the awful sum of human misery in the world. I have never understood those who say that they find contemporary life meaningless because they find nothing worthy of devoting their energies to. Throughout the world there is an immense amount of human suffering, suffering that can, through a variety of human efforts, be partially alleviated. Why can we not find a meaningful life in devoting ourselves, as did Doctor Rieux in Albert Camus' *The Plague*, to relieving somewhat the sum total of human suffering? Why cannot this give our lives point, and for that matter an overall rationale? It is childish to think that by human effort we will someday totally rid the world of suffering and hate, of deprivation and sadness. This is a permanent part of the human condition. But specific bits of human suffering can be alleviated. The plague is always potentially with us, but we can destroy the Nazis and we can fight for racial and social equality throughout the world. And as isolated people, as individuals in a mass society, we find people turning to us in dire need, in suffering and in emotional deprivation, and we can as individuals respond to those people and alleviate or at least acknowledge that suffering and deprivation. A man who says, "If God is dead, nothing matters," is a spoilt child who has never looked at his fellow men with compassion.

Yet, it might be objected, if we abandon a Judeo-Christian *Weltanschauung*, there can, in a secular world, be no "one big thing" to give our lives an overall rationale. We will not be able to see written in the stars the final significance of human effort. There will be no architectonic purpose to give our lives such a rationale. Like Tolstoy's Pierre in *War and Peace,* we desire *somehow* to gather the sorry scheme of things entire into one intelligible explanation so that we can finally crack the riddle of human destiny. We long to understand why it is that men suffer and die. If it is a factual answer that is wanted when such a question is asked, it is plain enough. Ask any physician. But clearly this is not what people who seek such answers are after. They want some *justification* for suffering; they want some way of showing that suffering is after all for a good purpose. It can, of course, be argued that suffering sometimes is a good thing, for it occasionally gives us insight and at times even brings about in the man who suffers a capacity to love and to be kind. But there is plainly an excessive amount of human suffering—the suffering of children in children's hospitals, the suffering of people devoured by cancer, and the sufferings of millions of Jews under the Nazis—for which there simply is no justification. Neither the religious man nor the secularist can explain, that is justify, such suffering and find some overall "scheme of life" in which it has some place, but only the religious man needs to do so. The secularist understands that suffering is not something to be justified but simply to be struggled against with courage and dignity. And in this fight, even the man who has been deprived of that which could give him some measure of happiness can still find or make for himself a meaningful human existence.

3

I have argued that purely human purposes—those goals that we set for ourselves, the intentions we form—are enough to give meaning to our lives.[2] We desire happiness, and we can find, even in a purely secular world, abundant sources of it. Beyond this we can find a rationale for living in seeking to mitigate the awful burden of human suffering. Given these two considerations we have enough to make life meaningful. But it might be objected that I have put far too great stress on the value of human happiness. There are other considerations in life; there are other values that are intrinsically worthwhile. We desire self-consciousness and some sense of self-identity as well as happiness. And we do not desire them for the enjoyment and happiness that will come from them but for their own sakes.

I am inclined to agree that this is so; human happiness and the desire to avoid suffering are central but not the only facets of morality. To acknowledge this, however, only complicates the secular picture of morality: it gives us no reason to bring in theistic concepts.

[2] I have argued this point in considerably more detail in my "Linguistic Philosophy and 'The Meaning of Life,'" *Cross-Currents*, XIV, No. 3 (Summer 1964), 313–34.

I admire human beings who are nonevasive and who have a sense of their own identity, and I regard an understanding of myself as something which is to be prized for its own sake. I do not need a deity to support this or give it value.

Philosophers, and some theologians as well, might challenge what I have said in a slightly different way. Even if we add consciousness as another intrinsic good, there is not the close connection between happiness and self-awareness on the one hand and virtue or moral good on the other that I have claimed there is. That men *do* seek happiness as an end is one thing; that they *ought* to seek it as an end is another. As G. E. Moore has in effect shown, we cannot derive "X is good" from "people desire X" or from "X makes people happy," for it is always *meaningful* to ask whether or not happiness is good and whether or not we ought to seek it for its own sake.[3] It will be argued that I, like all secularists, have confused factual and moral issues. An "ought" cannot be derived from an "is"; we cannot deduce that something is good from a discovery that it will make people happy. My hypothetical critic could well go on to claim that we first must justify the fundamental claim that happiness is good. Do we really have any reason to believe that happiness is good? Is the secularist in any more of a position to justify his claim than is the religionist to justify his claim that whatever God wills is good?

I would first like to point out that I have not confused factual and moral issues. One of the basic reasons I have for rejecting either a natural-law ethics or an ethics of divine commands is that both systematically confuse factual and moral issues. We cannot deduce that people ought to do something from discovering that they do it or seek it; nor can we conclude from the proposition that a being exists whom people call "God" that we ought to do whatever that being commands. In both cases we unjustifiably pass from a factual premise to a moral conclusion. Moral statements are not factual statements about what people seek or avoid, or about what a Deity commands. But we do justify moral claims by an appeal to factual claims,

[3] G. E. Moore, *Principia Ethica* (Cambridge, 1903), Chapters 1 and 2.

and there is a close connection between what human beings desire on reflection and what they deem to be good. "X is good" does not mean "X makes for happiness," but in deciding that something is good, it is crucial to know what makes human beings happy. Both the Christian moralist and the secular moralist lay stress on human happiness. The Christian moralist—St. Augustine and Pascal are perfect examples—argues that only the Christian has a clear insight into what human happiness really is and that there is no genuine happiness without God. But we have no valid grounds for believing that only in God can we find happiness and that there are no stable sources of human happiness apart from God.[4]

I cannot prove that happiness is good, but Christian and non-Christian alike take it in practice to be a very fundamental good. I can, in sum, only appeal to your sense of psychological realism to get you to admit intellectually what in practice you *do* acknowledge, namely, that happiness is good and that pointless suffering is bad. If you *will* acknowledge this, I can show, as I have, that man can attain happiness even in a world without God.

Suppose some Dostoyevskian "underground man" does not care a fig about happiness. Suppose he does not even care about the sufferings of others. How then can you show him to be wrong? But suppose a man doesn't care about God or about doing what He commands either. How can you show that such an indifference to God is wrong? If we ask such abstract questions, we can see a crucial feature about the nature of morality. Sometimes a moral agent may reach a point at which he can give no further justification for his claims but must simply, by his own deliberate decision, resolve to take a certain position. Here the claims of the existentialists have a genuine relevance. We come to recognize that nothing can in the last analysis take the place of a decision or resolution. In the end we must simply decide. This recognition may arouse our anxieties and stimulate rationalization, but the necessity of making a decision is

[4] I have tried to establish this in my "An Examination of an Alleged Theological Basis for Morality," *Iliff Review*, XXI, No. 2 (Fall 1964), 39–49.

inherent in the logic of the situation. Actually the religious moralist is in a worse position, for he not only needs to subscribe to the principle that human happiness is good and that pain and suffering have no *intrinsic* value; he must also subscribe to the *outré* claims that only in God can man find happiness and that one ought to do whatever it is that God commands. That man can find lasting happiness only if he turns humbly to his Saviour has the look of a factual statement and is a statement that most assuredly calls for some kind of rational support. It is not something we must or can simply decide about. But the assertion that one ought to do what is commanded by God, like the assertion that happiness is good, does appear *simply* to call for a decision for or against. But what it is that one is deciding for when one "decides for God or for Christ" is so obscure as to be scarcely intelligible. Furthermore, the man who subscribes to that religious principle must subscribe to the secular claim as well. But why subscribe to this obscure second principle when there is no evidence at all for the claim that man can find happiness only in God?

Morality is not science. Moral claims *direct* our actions; they tell us how we *ought* to act; they do not simply *describe* what we seek or explain our preferential behavior.[5] A secular morality need not view morality as a science or as an activity that is simply descriptive or explanatory. It can and should remain a normative activity. Secular morality starts with the assumption that happiness and self-awareness are fundamental human goods and that pain and suffering are never desirable in themselves. It may finally be impossible to prove that this is so, but if people will be honest with themselves they will see that in their behavior they clearly show that they subscribe to such a principle, and a philosopher can demonstrate that criticisms of such moral principles rest on confusions. Finally, I have tried to show that a man with secular knowledge alone can find clear and permanent sources of happiness such that whoever will avail him-

[5] This crucial claim is ably argued for by P. H. Nowell-Smith, *Ethics* (London, 1954), Chapters I–IV; by John Ladd, "Reason and Practice" in *The Return to Reason*, ed. John Wild (Chicago, 1953), pp. 235–58; and by A. E. Murphy, "The Common Good," *Proceedings and Addresses of the American Philosophical Association*, XXIV (1950–51), 3–18.

self of these sources of happiness can, if he is fortunate, lead a happy and purposeful life.

4

The dialectic of our problem has not ended. The religious moralist might acknowledge that human happiness is indeed plainly a good thing while contending that secular morality, where it is consistent and reflective, will inevitably lead to some variety of egoism. An individual who recognized the value of happiness and self-consciousness might, if he were free of religious restraints, ask himself why he should be concerned with the happiness and self-awareness of *others,* except where their happiness and self-awareness would contribute to his own good. We must face the fact that sometimes, as the world goes, people's interests clash. Sometimes the common good is served only at the expense of some individual's interests. An individual must therefore, in such a circumstance, sacrifice what will make him happy for the common good. Morality requires this sacrifice of us, *when it is necessary* for the common good; morality, any morality, exists in part at least to adjudicate between the conflicting interests and demands of people. It is plainly evident that everyone cannot be happy all the time and that sometimes one person's happiness or the happiness of a group is at the expense of another person's happiness. Morality requires that we attempt to distribute happiness as evenly as possible. We must be fair: each person is to count for one and none is to count for more than one. Whether we like a person or not, whether he is useful to his society or not, his interests, and what will make him happy, must also be considered in any final decision as to what ought to be done. The requirements of justice make it necessary that each person be given equal consideration. I cannot justify my neglect of another person in some matter of morality simply on the grounds that I do not like him, that he is *not* a member of my set, or that he is *not* a productive member of society. The religious apologist will argue that behind these requirements of justice as fairness there lurks the ancient religious principle that men are creatures of God, each with an infinite worth, and thus men are never to be treated only as means but as persons deserving of respect in their own right. They have an infinite worth simply as persons.

My religious critic, following out the dialectic of the problem, should query: why should you respect someone, why should you treat all people equally, if doing this is not in your interest or not in the interests of your group? No purely secular justification can be given for so behaving. My critic now serves his *coup de grâce:* the secularist, as well as the "knight of faith," acknowledges that the principle of respect for persons is a precious one—a principle that he is unequivocally committed to, but the religious man alone can *justify* adherence to this principle. The secularist is surreptitiously drawing on Christian inspiration when he insists that all men should be considered equal and that people's rights must be respected. For a secular morality to say all it wants and needs to say, it must, at this crucial point, be parasitical upon a God-centered morality. Without such a dependence on religion, secular morality collapses into egoism.

It may well be the case that, as a historical fact, our moral concern for persons came from our religious conceptions, but it is a well known principle of logic that the validity of a belief is independent of its origin. What the religious moralist must do is to show that only on religious grounds could such a principle of respect for persons be justifiably asserted. But he has not shown that this is so; and there are good reasons for thinking that it is not so. Even if the secularist must simply subscribe to the Kantian principle, "Treat every man as an end and never as a means only," as he must subscribe to the claim, "Happiness is good," it does not follow that he is on worse ground than the religious moralist, for the religious moralist too, as we have seen, must simply subscribe to his ultimate moral principle, "Always do what God wills." *In a way,* the religious moralist's position here is simpler than the secularist's, for he needs only the fundamental moral principle that he ought to do what God wills. The secularist appears to need at least two fundamental principles. But in another and more important way the religious moralist's position is more complex, for he must subscribe to the extraordinarily obscure notion that man is a creature of God and as such has infinite worth. The Kantian principle may in the last analysis simply require subscription, but it is not inherently mysterious. To accept it does not require a crucifixion of the intellect. And if we are prepared simply to commit ourselves to one principle, why not to two principles, neither of which involves any appeal to conceptions whose very intelligibility is seriously in question?

The above argument is enough to destroy the believer's case here. But need we even make those concessions? I do not think so. There is a purely secular rationale for treating people fairly, for regarding them as persons. Let me show how this is so. We have no evidence that men ever lived in a presocial state of nature. Man, as we know him, is an animal with a culture; he is part of a community, and the very *concept* of community implies binding principles and regulations—duties, obligations, and rights. Yet, by an exercise in imagination, we could conceive, in broad outline at any rate, what it would be like to live in such a presocial state. In such a state no one would have any laws or principles to direct his behavior. In that sense man would be completely free. But such a life as Hobbes graphically depicted, would be a clash of rival egoisms. Life in that state of nature would, in his celebrated phrase, "be nasty, brutish and short." Now if men were in such a state and if they were perfectly rational egoists, what kind of community life would they choose, given the fact that they were, very roughly speaking, nearly equal in strength and ability? (That in communities as we find them men are not so nearly equal in power is beside the point, for our *hypothetical* situation.) Given that they all start from scratch and have roughly equal abilities, it seems to me that it would be most reasonable, even for rational egoists, to band together into a community where each man's interests were given equal consideration, where each person was treated as deserving of respect.[6] Each rational egoist would want others to

[6] Some of the very complicated considerations relevant here have been subtly brought out by John Rawls in his "Justice as Fairness," *The Philosophical Review*, LXVII (1958), 164–94. I think it could be reasonably maintained that my argument is more vulnerable here than at any other point. I would not, of course, use it if I did not think that it could be sustained, but if anyone should find the argument as presented here unconvincing I would beg him to consider the argument that precedes it and the one that immediately follows it. They alone are sufficient to establish my general case. Since this essay was first prepared for publication, Georg von Wright's powerful book *The Varieties of Goodness*

treat him with respect, for his very happiness is contingent upon that; and he would recognize, if he were rational, that he could attain the fullest cooperation of others only if other rational egoists knew or had good grounds for believing that their interests and their persons would also be respected. Such cooperation is essential for each egoist if all are to have the type of community life which would give them the best chance of satisfying their own interests to the fullest degree. Thus, even if men were thorough egoists, we would still have rational grounds for subscribing to a principle of respect for persons. That men are not thoroughly rational, do not live in a state of nature, and are not thorough egoists does not gainsay the fact that we have rational grounds for regarding social life, organized in accordance with such a principle, as being objectively better than a social life which ignored this principle. The point here is that even rational egoists could see that this is the best possible social organization where men are nearly equal in ability.

Yet what about the world we live in—a world in which, given certain extant social relationships, men are not equal or even nearly equal in power and opportunity? What reason is there for an egoist who is powerfully placed to respect the rights of others, when they cannot hurt him? We can say that his position, no matter how strong, might change and he might be in a position where he would need his rights protected, but this is surely not a strong enough reason for respecting those rights. To be moral involves respecting those rights, but our rational egoist may not propose to be moral. In considering such questions we reach a point in reasoning at which we must simply *decide* what sort of person we shall strive to become. But, as I have said, the religious moralist reaches the same point. He too must make a decision of principle, but the principle he adopts is a fundamentally incoherent one. He not only must decide, but his decision must involve the acceptance of an absurdity.

It is sometimes argued by religious apologists that only if there is a God who can punish men will we be assured that naturally selfish men will be fair and considerate of others. Without this punitive

---

(London, 1963) has come into my hands. The point made above is argued for convincingly and in detail in Chapter X of that book.

sanction or threat men would go wild. Men will respect the rights of others only if they fear a wrathful and angry God. Yet it hardly seems to be the case that Christians, with their fear of hell, have been any better at respecting the rights of others than non-Christians. A study of the Middle Ages or the conquest of the non-Christian world makes this plain enough. And even if it were true (as it is not) that Christians were better in this respect than non-Christians, it would not show that they had a superior moral reason for their behavior, for in so acting and in so reasoning they are not giving a morally relevant reason at all, but are simply acting out of fear for their own hides. Yet Christian morality supposedly takes us beyond the clash of the rival egoisms of secular life.

In short, Christian ethics has not been able to give us a sounder ground for respecting persons than we have with a purely secular morality. The Kantian principle of respect for persons is actually bound up in the very idea of morality, either secular or religious, and there are good reasons, of a perfectly mundane sort, why we should have the institution of morality as we now have it, namely, that our individual welfare is dependent on having a device which equitably resolves social and individual conflicts. Morality has an objective rationale in complete independence of religion. Even if God is dead, it doesn't really matter.

It is in just this last thrust, it might be objected, that you reveal your true colors and show your own inability to face a patent social reality. At this point the heart of your rationalism is very irrational. For millions of people "the death of God" means very much. It really does matter. In your somewhat technical sense, the concept of God may be chaotic or unintelligible, but this concept, embedded in our languages—embedded in "the stream of life"—has an enormous social significance for many people. Jews and Christians, if they take their religion to heart, could not but feel a great rift in their lives with the loss of God, for they have indeed organized a good bit of their lives around their religion. Their very life-ideals have grown out of these, if you will, myth-eaten concepts. What should have been said is that if "God is dead" it matters a lot, but we should stand up like men and face this loss and learn to live in the post-Christian era. As Nietzsche so well knew, to do this involves a basic reorientation of one's life and not just an intellectual dissent to a few statements of doctrine.

There is truth in this and a kind of "empiricism about man" that philosophers are prone to neglect. Of course it does matter when one recognizes that one's religion is illusory. For a devout Jew or Christian to give up his God most certainly is important and does take him into the abyss of a spiritual crisis. But in saying that it doesn't *really* matter I was implying what I have argued for in this essay, namely, that if a believer loses his God but can keep his nerve, think the matter over, and thoroughly take it to heart, life can still be meaningful and morality yet have an objective rationale. Surely, for good psychological reasons, the believer is prone to doubt this argument, but if he will only "hold on to his brains" and keep his courage, he will come to see that it is so. In this crucial sense it remains true that if "God is dead" it doesn't really matter.

MEANING AND MORALS

Kurt Baier

Humanism attempts to provide individuals and societies with guidelines which try to make the life of every individual as good as his abilities and tastes allow. It insists on doing so without relying on any characteristically religious beliefs, such as the belief in God, an afterlife, or a divine moral government of the world. The reason for such austerity is that humanists have become convinced by philosophical argument that such beliefs cannot be known to be true. Humanists insist on an obvious corollary, not always admitted by those who admit that religious beliefs are incapable of being known, namely, that no individual or group of individuals should be permitted, on the basis of their necessarily unfounded religious hopes and beliefs, to impose any restrictions on the lives of others not sharing these beliefs.

Humanism is no longer a movement of antireligious thinkers. In fact, it has received its strongest support from "advanced theologians." The most widely discussed (though not perhaps the most widely followed) contemporary theologians embrace such sophisticated doctrines as that "God is dead" or that religion is "morality plus stories"; in their view of religion the supernatural is "demythologized," and immortality, salvation, and damnation are interpreted as somehow located in this earthly life.

All the same, we must not exaggerate the extent of the popularity of humanism. It remains true that large sections of our society reject these modern views in theology. And even those who accept them cannot altogether shake off the deeply ingrained conviction that a life without such supernatural beliefs must lack some of the most important and significant features of a truly good life. There are, in particular, three matters on which a humanist philosophy would seem to be inadequate. Can a humanist lead a happy life? Can he lead a meaningful life? Can humanism show that life *ought* to be governed by morality even if that morality has to be man-made?

Consider first the possibility of a happy life. Is it really true that a life which is not safe from accident, disaster, and final extinction cannot be a happy one? Is it true that only "by the hope of the future world, this life, which is miserably involved in the many and great evils of this world, is happy as it is also safe. For if not yet safe, how could it be happy?"[1] Admittedly, no one is guaranteed happiness, on the humanist view, but no one is certain of misery either. And if a man can hope for salvation and eternal bliss, he surely can equally hope to get through life without major disaster, as many people seem to do. It is in any case misleading to say that the belief in an afterlife can provide the element of "safety" whose absence from this life St. Augustine and others quite understandably deplore. For not only is there no guarantee that there is an afterlife, but even if there is one, there is no guarantee of salvation and eternal bliss. On the contrary, if there really is an afterlife, it may well be a lot worse than the worst sort of earthly life, and without the escape afforded by suicide. The belief in an afterlife thus involves the fear that one may well be among those whom God, as St. Augustine has it, "in His justice has predestined to punishment," and not among those "whom in His mercy He has predestined to Grace."[2] As far as safety is concerned, the believer in an afterlife is therefore worse off than the nonbeliever. For he must hope not only for an afterlife, but for Grace as well. But if believers can be happy because they have hope, why not unbelievers? Can they not hope to be lucky? Of course, when disaster strikes, the unbeliever

[1] St. Augustine, *The City of God,* Bk. XIX, Chapter 4.
[2] St. Augustine, *The Enchiridion,* Ch. C.

cannot hope for a future life but neither need he fear that he is one of those headed for damnation.

The most significant differences between believer and unbeliever have, however, not yet been brought to light. Those who see the world from a theistic perspective need not accept what many people find it very difficult to accept, namely, that the rewards which this life has to offer are the best we can hope for and are quite adequate for happy and meaningful lives; and that some individuals, through no recognizable fault of their own, cannot attain happy and meaningful lives. Seen from a theistic perspective—that is, a world history beginning with the creation by a divine person of a universe thereafter under His moral government—the grossly unequal distribution of happiness and unhappiness among different individuals appears to make sense and to give our lives meaning. But in the absence of such a perspective, it seems that life must be meaningless.

It must be admitted that there really is a sense of "meaning" in which this is true. In the absence of such a world history, men would have no "allotted purpose" in a divine scheme, as machines, domestic animals, or servants have an allotted purpose in human schemes. It would not then be true that our actions inevitably serve a purpose allotted to each of us. It would not be true that "He uses the very will of the creature which was working in opposition to the Creator's will as an instrument for carrying out His will, the supremely Good thus turning to good account even what is evil, to the condemnation of those whom in His justice He has predestined to punishment, and to the salvation of those whom in His mercy He has predestined to grace."[3] However, our lives need not be emptied of *all* meaning simply because no one is using us for his schemes. And if someone is so constituted that he craves being used for some great purpose, he can probably be accommodated in some large-scale organization or other. In short, humanism does not necessarily rob a life of its meaning, even in the sense of "allotted purpose." However, for a humanist, life does not *necessarily* have such a meaning—some lives do and some do not. It all depends on whether a person has come to have a purpose allotted to him by

[3] *Ibid.*

someone else. Some people may not consider it a loss but a gain for their lives not to have meaning in this sense.

Humanists have of course no difficulty in attributing meaning to individual lives, in another related sense, namely, "having significant or meaningful goals." The life of a philanthropist, a scientist, an explorer has goals the pursuit of which, with whatever degree of success, makes that life meaningful, significant, valuable.

Implied in these senses of "meaning," however, is the idea that what is meaningful is not human life as such, the existence of human beings, but the lives of individual human beings, not necessarily all of them. If we want a guarantee that no life is meaningless, insignificant, futile, vain, then a life's meaning must not depend on that life's particular course, on what life holds for the person living it. The meaning of life, in this sense, must be something guaranteed by mere membership in the human race. Such a guarantee would be provided by the participation of every human being in the cosmic drama of Creation, Paradise, the Fall, Redemption, and the Eternal Life, whether Salvation or Damnation. On that theory, meaning is guaranteed to every life, just as meaning is guaranteed to every role in a play, however humble or small a part it may be. But is a guarantee of this sort of meaning really a comfort? Is not the analogy with a play seriously misleading? Could Cain and Judas, for instance, find any consolation in the guaranteed significance of their lives? Perhaps they could. After all, they played important roles, and that is no doubt deeply satisfying, even if one's role is that of the villain. Significance is found, self-respect established, identity determined by leading a life which commands attention, no matter whether the response is applause or hatred and condemnation. But even here the guarantee does not work equally well for every man. Cain and Judas sinned in the limelight, Lucifer is more celebrated than Gabriel. But what about those unknown and unsung sinners whom God in His justice has predestined to damnation? Can they find any more meaning in their lives if they think of them as damned than those who do not believe in this guaranteed significance? It seems clear that such a guarantee of significance does little to compensate for the insignificance, futility, or misery of a particular role in the vast drama.

Still, many will feel that the question of whether there is an after-life is more important to the meaning of life than has so far been explained. One need not agree with Tolstoy in virtually identifying the question of meaningfulness with the question of immortality to have doubts about the view of those humanists who claim that death is entirely irrelevant to questions of worthwhileness and hence to meaningfulness. These further doubts are well expressed in a recent paper by Ronald Hepburn.[4]

> A person [he says] may heed the argument that mortality and value are compatible, and yet may be burdened with a sense of futility that the argument cannot dispel. His malaise may range from occasional vague misgivings over the worthwhileness of his activities, to a thoroughgoing arrest of life. We can most usefully consider this sort of malaise at a still more general level. A complaint of meaninglessness can be a complaint about a felt disproportion between preparation and performance; between effort expended and the effect of effort, actual and possible. Yeats expressed the complaint in well-known words: "When I think of all the books I have read, wise words heard, anxieties given to parents, . . . of hopes I have had, all life, weighed in the balance of my own life, seems to me *a preparation for something that never happens.*" [Compare . . . Tolstoy's question, "What does it *lead* to?"] [5]

The tenor of these complaints is that the things life can hold for us are not worth their price. Hepburn uses an analogy from musical composition. Some musical passages have "introduction quality," others "exhibition quality." The first is felt as preparation, the other as fulfillment. A piece of music is disappointing, perhaps worthless, if it consists solely of passages with introduction quality.

We can think of lives which are similarly disappointing, perhaps worthless. Young men struck down before the prime of their lives by accident, war, or an incurable disease. These lives are pointless, futile, senseless. The efforts made and the sufferings endured are in vain, for they are not necessary preparations, training, or simply conditions for something worthwhile. These lives have only introduction and not exhibition quality. This point must, I think, be granted.

[4] "Questions about the Meaning of Life," *Religious Studies*, I, 125–40.

[5] *Ibid.*, pp. 132–33.

Just because some lives (one hopes, by wise social arrangements, most lives) can have both introduction and exhibition quality, and therefore can be meaningful, significant, rewarding lives, so other lives can and unfortunately do lack exhibition quality, and are to that extent futile lives.

This is a familiar line of argument. Humanists must acknowledge its legitimacy. For humanism cannot pretend that every life must hold enough of "exhibition quality" to justify everything in it that had merely "introduction quality." Humanism cannot deny the possibility of lives containing much that is futile, vain, senseless. Worse still, it cannot deny the possibility that a person, say during the terminal stages of an incurable illness, can have overwhelming reason for thinking that the remainder of his life will be senseless, its suffering futile, its heroism in vain, and therefore deliberate death the most rational course.

So much must be granted. But now theists may attempt an extension of this line of argument. They may contend that, from the perspective of natural science—which is also the perspective of humanism—no lives at all can have meaning. As Hepburn formulates it, "to the naturalist, human endeavour viewed *sub specie aeternitatis*, may seem to shrivel, frighteningly. (Compare Sartre's troubled musings on the heat-death of the sun, in his autobiographical essay, *Les Mots*, p. 208.) He may nonetheless judge as entirely worthwhile some social reform, viewed against the backcloth of a dozen years, or months, of social abuse." [6] And he sums up the argument by saying,

> There must in fact remain, with the naturalist, an uncomfortable tension or conflict between the "close-up," anthropocentric view or perspective that can sustain his sense of meaningfulness and worthwhileness, and on the other hand his sense of intellectual obligation to the objective, scientific and anti-anthropocentric view —*which tends to vilify, if not logically, then psychologically*. The Christian is not exposed to this tension in the same way or to the same extent. The doctrines of divine creation and of incarnation combine to rule out the judgment that, in leaving the arena of the human, one is leaving simultaneously the theatre of mind and pur-

[6] *Ibid.*, p. 135.

> pose and value. For the theist, that is, there is the implicit promise of a *harmony* of perspectives.[7]

Hepburn seems to me to point clearly to the main discomfort we feel in regard to the scientific world picture: its depiction of the realm of mind, purpose, value, and meaning as confined to the human arena. Assuming that our earthly lives *are* preparations for something beyond them, then indeed the scientific world picture must incline us to the view that they are futile or in vain, for it tells us that nothing of exhibition quality can be expected by us. However, as soon as the point is spelled out, its illegitimacy is transparent. We can formulate our disappointment only by surreptitiously reintroducing the anthropocentric point of view. If our life really ends with death, then it cannot be any sort of preparation: what comes afterward cannot give sense to but neither can it make futile what has happened in an individual life. Social reform is not made any the less meaningful when we consider it against the backcloth of the eventual heat-death of the sun. Such considerations are simply irrelevant to the question of the worthwhileness or futility of a contemplated reform. The significance of my bishop's game-winning move is not "vilified" (logically or psychologically) by the fact that I have used a pebble to replace the missing piece, and that I shall toss that pebble back on the beach where I found it. If contemplating the eventual heat-death of the sun does seem to some people to vilify our lives, they must be confused about what considerations can be relevant to the nobility or vileness of our lives. It is unfortunate that Hepburn seems to underwrite this confusion by dignifying it with the expression "psychological vilification." For if the scientific world view does not "logically" (i.e., when you consider the matter logically) "vilify" our lives, as Hepburn seems to admit, then to say that it tends to do so "psychologically" can only be a polite (though confusing) way of calling it "illogical," something our religiously conditioned "psyches" understandably tend to do but for which they have no rational warrant.

By far the most important challenge to a humanist philosophy, however, is that coming from the field of ethics. For the belief in

[7] *Ibid.* [Italics added.]

an afterlife, in which a person's moral performance in this life is infallibly judged and brought to justice, provides impressive supernatural backing for a society's conventional morality. The decline of this belief exposes the merely conventional character of such a morality. Its various restrictions are then no longer accepted as inescapable and the question why they should not be evaded when this is advantageous begins to loom large. And since it seems impossible to distinguish the eliminable flaws of a given conventional morality from the essential flaws of any morality whatever, it is difficult to resist the conclusion that now the devil is dead, we can do what we like. In the absence of adequate reasons for accepting such a conventional morality, and of an indubitable method for arriving at moral precepts which everyone can see to be compelling, the natural response is skepticism, cynicism, hypocrisy, and the unbridled pursuit of what makes a life worth living. If humanism is to meet this challenge, it must show whether and why moralities are necessary, what benefits they confer on us and what harm they prevent, how their content must be determined, and why a person should be moral even when that runs counter to his best interest.

Our first problem is this. If, in the absence of supernatural beliefs, the voice of conscience, of the moral sense, and of intuition are only the impressively dressed-up demands of our society, then these voices cannot tell us what is right and what is wrong in a sense which provides an adequate reason for doing what is right and refraining from doing what is wrong. How then can we find out what is really right and what is merely supposed so by our society? The only alternative to theories based on intuition, it seems, are theories which base our knowledge of right and wrong on some form of calculation. The two most popular candidates are egoism and utilitarianism. The former maintains that each individual can tell what it would be right for him to do by calculating what would be in his best interest. This is, at first sight, an attractive view. It is internally consistent, rational, and brutally honest. It does not enmesh us in the problems of why a person should be moral when being so is contrary to his best interest. On this theory that problem can never arise: no agent is ever confronted by the choice between doing what is in his best interest and doing what is right. The answer he gives to one question is *ipso facto* also the answer to the other question. However, despite its attractions, this theory is open to the following completely decisive objection. To qualify as a moral theory, it must hold for everybody. But if everybody accepts that theory, the result is wholly undesirable. For in the world as we know it, the best interests of one person often conflict with the best interests of another. Hence if one person *succeeds* in promoting his best interests, he will thereby often *prevent* another from promoting his. In such a situation, the competitors will often waste much ingenuity and effort on getting the better of each other, perhaps in the process even harm each other, without in the end being able to accomplish more than they would have accomplished if they had abandoned their efforts to gain an advantage for themselves and had settled the conflict by tossing a coin; and frequently they will accomplish less. As an universal method of determining what each person *should* do, egoism is not therefore the best policy. In social contexts, such a mode of behavior does not yield the results it was ostensibly designed to yield: the greatest possible good for each person.

Utilitarianism provides a formula intended to meet the main shortcomings of egoism. On the utilitarian theory, each individual tells what it would be right for him to do by working out what would be in the best interest of the greatest number. Now, this theory is in many respects superior to egoism. It can, for instance, deal with the problem which we saw to be insoluble for egoism. For if in the case of a conflict of interest between two persons, the interest of one is greater than that of the other, then the utilitarian formula directs *both* persons to do what is necessary to promote *the greater* of the two interests. However, this theory (and also its many other subtler versions which have recently been propounded) has one serious weakness: it deals less satisfactorily than egoism with the question of *why one should do* what is right and refrain from doing what is wrong. For egoism, that question holds no difficulties. If an egoist asks it, another egoist can point out to him that the moral course is identical with the course most profitable to him, and this will normally satisfy the questioner. And, if perchance it does not satisfy him, no other egoist need be concerned. If one egoist does not want to do what is in his best interest, why should any other egoist worry? It will usually be in a person's interest if others are *not* egoists. The situation is quite different in the case of utilitarianism. In the first place, the answer, "it is in the best interest of the greatest number," will not always, or even normally, be acceptable to a person when it conflicts with his own best interests, or even with the best interests of those, normally fewer, people about whom he actually cares, or when it includes the best interests of those whom he hates. But if he continues to press for an answer to the question, "Why should I be a utilitarian?" or "Why should I do what is in the best interest of the greatest number?" other utilitarians cannot shrug this question off, as egoists can shrug off the corresponding question by an egoist. The reason for this is, of course, that whereas egoists have no interest in other people's being egoists, utilitarians have an interest in other people's being utilitarian. In this respect utilitarianism resembles our everyday conception of morality, egoism does not.

These inadequacies of egoism and utilitarianism point the way to a tenable humanist ethics. We are seeking a rational principle of behavior which can be recommended to everybody. We must reject egoism because in social contexts the single-minded *pursuit* by each of his own best interest does not lead to the desired result, the *successful promotion* of the interest of each, and through it to the best possible life for each. The reason why such a pursuit is unsuccessful is that the pursuers get in each other's way. Let it be granted, then, that principles of behavior can be recommended to everybody if they successfully promote the best possible life for everybody, and that the best possible life for everybody cannot be achieved in isolation but only in social contexts in which the pursuits of each impinge on the pursuits of others. Then we acknowledge that egoism, the single-minded pursuit of one's own best interest, irrespective of how this affects others, cannot be the supreme rational principle of behavior. This does not mean that we must reject self-interest altogether, but it does mean that we must accept suitable modifications, i.e., those modifications which if generally adopted would improve everybody's life.

The considerations so far advanced illuminate the genesis of a rational morality. I have shown the need (for purposes of attaining the best possible life for everybody) to adopt general modifications of the principle of egoism. This explains four essential features of a morality: (1) that its precepts should be capable of coming into conflict with the precepts of self-interest; (2) that its precepts should be thought of as overriding those of self-interest; (3) that each man should have an interest in other people being moral, since other people's immorality will affect his interest; and (4) that each person should have an interest in the effective enforcement of the principles and precepts of morality.

The last point requires elucidation. We have seen that a group of interacting self-seekers can improve their lives by adhering to certain restrictions on the precepts of egoism. However, the improvements in each person's life are not the result of his own adherence to these restrictions, but the result of others adhering to them. Each person, in observing these restrictions, is promoting not his own interest but that of another. To improve his own life, such a self-seeker should therefore be "of good will," i.e., prepared to abide by these restrictions if and only if he has some hope that others will also abide by them. He should be prepared to pay his share of the price of an improvement in the life for all, but only if the others are prepared to pay their share. But since his own readiness to pay his share of the price is quite independent of other people's readiness, he may pay his share when others are not willing to pay theirs. (In that case his sacrifice is in vain.) It is, therefore, in his interest to support any social device which would ensure that his sacrifice is paralleled by that of others. The enforcement of social rules by various forms of social sanctions is such a device. If effective, such social sanctions ensure that in cases of conflict members of the society follow the sanctioned rules rather than the rules of self-interest.

In a perfect society there would thus be a complete coincidence between morality and self-interest. For in such a society everyone could be sure that by following the moral principles and precepts he would contribute his necessary share of the price of the best possible life. He would not be tempted to do better for himself by not paying his share because the effective sanction would always outweigh the gain he could make in this way. And he need have no fear of being "a sucker" (i.e., the only one or one of the few who are paying the price) because he knows that it would no more pay others to cheat on their share than it would pay him to do so.

It is worth pausing here for a moment to compare the humanist picture of the ideal moral order with the traditional picture. There is one striking similarity: in both ideals there is complete coincidence between the courses prescribed by morality and self-interest. In each case this coincidence is due to the existence of a *perfect* system of sanctions. A second, but merely superficial similarity, is that in both cases morality permits, indeed requires, the individual moral agent to aim at the best *possible* life for himself. And in each case, the precepts of morality are other than, in conflict with, and superior to the precepts of self-interest.

Nevertheless, the similarity is only superficial. For in the traditional view, the best possible life is the perfect afterlife, virtue being not the individual's share of the price of the best possible life on earth, but the price of the entrance ticket to the next. Thus, on this view, eternal bliss in the afterlife plays two roles, that of the best possible life for the sake of which we make the morally required sacrifices in this life, and the reward we reap for having made these sacrifices. By contrast, the eternal torments play only one role, the punishment we have to endure if we do not make the morally required sacrifices in this life. On this view, there is not a clear rational connection, but a contrived incomprehensible one, between the sacrifices morally required in this life and the eternal bliss or torment in the next. By omitting the causal connection between the morally required sacrifices and the best possible life for all, and by identifying the rational goal of each individual (the best possible life) with the reward for making the morally required sacrifices (which on this theory cannot be shown necessary), the traditional theory makes a mystery of morality and moreover portrays the divine moral government of the world as a monstrous system of chicanery. For that theory offers no explanation why the morally required sacrifices should be a condition of eternal bliss or why failure to make these sacrifices should be punished with eternal torments.

On the humanist view of morality, the precepts of both self-interest and morality are guidelines to the same goal, the best possible life for each individual. The difference between them lies simply in this: the former are "reflexively," the latter "distributively" advantageous. That is to say, the precepts of self-interest formulate guidelines designed in such a way that an individual following them thereby promotes his own interest, regardless of how that affects others. The precepts of morality formulate guidelines designed in such a way that an individual following them promotes the advantage of another, and that *all* those governed by a given morality derive the greatest possible advantage only if *all* follow these guidelines.

Unlike the traditional ideal, the humanist ideal can therefore explain why the best possible life for all requires the existence of a moral order, i.e., a system of rules and precepts which function as curbs on self-interest, and which are enforced as far as desirable. The explanation is, of course, that the best possible life can be lived only in societies, but that in social contexts the inconsiderate (egoistic) pursuit of the best possible life for oneself leads to what Hobbes called "the war of all against all," a state falling far short of the best possible life.

The humanist conception of morality can moreover explain the fact that the basic moral precepts are regarded as obligatory, i.e., absolutely binding. It can do so, moreover, without involving itself in dubious philosophical doctrines, such as Kant's synthetic *a priori* judgments. The explanation of this "categorical" bindingness (to give it its Kantian title) is simply this: the question whether a given person follows moral precepts, unlike the question whether he follows the precepts of self-interest, is a matter which is not solely that person's business (since other people's interests are deeply affected by it); therefore it is justifiable to institute *adequate* sanctions, that is, techniques by which a person can if necessary be *compelled* to follow the sanctioned precepts. Moral precepts are therefore not merely rightly regarded as overriding those of self-interest, but also rightly regarded as obligatory, that is, as justifiably enforced and not left to an individual's own discretion. This view is therefore superior to both egoism and utilitarianism. For unlike egoism, it provides precepts which promote the best possible life for each, and it offers an explanation of why the question "Why should one be moral?" is rightly thought to require a telling answer. For though egoism can give an answer which will normally be telling, it will not matter to any egoist if it is not. And unlike utilitarianism, this theory can give a telling answer. The utilitarian answer, "Being moral promotes the greatest good of the greatest number," will often not be telling, namely, when a person does not happen to desire the greatest good of the greatest number, or does not desire it as much as his own good. The theory here expounded does not depend on the psychological contingency that a person's greatest desire should be the promotion of the greatest good of the greatest number. It can answer the query, "Why should one be moral?" whatever one's desires may be. For it can tell him that by being moral he contributes his share to the best possible life for all, always including himself.

But the greatest merit of such a humanist ethics as I have sketched is its capacity to generate an unchallengeable method for determining what is morally right and wrong. Unlike other theories, this theory does not have to base its method for determining what is right and wrong on the generally accepted views of what is so. It does not have to plead for credibility by the proof that its results will be acceptable to all right-thinking men. On the contrary, it determines who the right-thinking men are, and what are sound and what unsound moral convictions in a given community. For this theory starts from an explanation of why a certain sort of modification of the precepts of egoism is necessary for the best possible life for everyone, and why these necessary modifications must have the status of categorical imperatives, that is, of absolutely binding obligations. Such an explanation provides a justification for a system of such modifications, and so also for the precepts constituting such a system. This is not the place to battle with the difficulties of a detailed casuistry derived from the general principles of such a humanist ethic, but it may be in order to conclude this essay with a few words about the generative principle of a sound humanist morality.

The inadequacy of egoism, we saw, lay in the fact that in social contexts its precepts cannot lead to success because the unflinching pursuers of their own interest will get in each other's way. The first task of a morality is therefore to set down overriding precepts for those cases in which success by one person in the pursuit of his interest would mean failure by another in the pursuit of his. The moral precept "Thou shalt not kill" can be interpreted as such a rule. It says that whenever success in the pursuit of one's interest involves taking the life of another, one ought to desist from that pursuit. Such a view does not rest on any prior and unsupported intuition that life or even human life is sacred. The killing of animals does not come under this precept because they are not included in the goal of providing the best possible life for each human being and because killing them for food is thought (I think rightly) to contribute to the best possible life. Suicide does not fall under it either because one's taking one's own life does not necessarily constitute preventing someone else from promoting his interest. For the same reason mercy killing by request of the sufferer does not come under this precept. And because sperm or even a fetus cannot as yet be said to have an interest, contraception and even abortion do not fall under this precept either.

There are many other principles which can be derived from our outline of the ideal of morality. Their derivation and application to the complexities of a modern society are of course extremely difficult tasks. Even so, they are among the most important tasks facing us. Given the injustices prevailing in our society defended often by reference to moral precepts which lack all rational justification, can we really be surprised by the much-deplored despair and the resulting alienation and anomie of large sections of our society?

ETHICS, RELIGION, AND SCIENTIFIC HUMANISM*

Herbert Feigl

The kind of world we are facing nowadays is one of deep concern. There are so many horrible things going on that it is psychologically understandable that a kind of moral disillusionment has set in, particularly among the younger generation. In my own feeble way I hope to retain some moral backbone in spite of all of the developments that might make one skeptical, if not completely disheartened. The ethical outlook that I represent is, if you want a label for it, *scientific humanism.* What I wish to present is more along the lines of a sober philosophical analysis rather than mere preachment. The present generation doesn't like to be preached at any more than I do. I think that there is a fundamental difference between the analytic clarification of ideas and the communication of scientific knowledge claims on the one hand, and the edification, exhortation, and consolation that belongs to religious language on the other.

Traditional religions in their orthodox forms breed in their own way more problems than they solve, and people who might originally have had open minds, close them and never open them again. There

* A shorter version of this article was published originally as "Scientific Humanism" in *The Humanist,* XXVIII, No. 5 (1968), 21–25. Reprinted by permission of *The Humanist.*

is a difference between the scientific attitude and the dogmatic theological attitude. We have two extremes as far as intellectual attitudes are concerned. On the one hand there is dogmatism, and on the other hand extreme skepticism. The dogmatic attitude is the attitude of the closed mind; the extreme skeptic has his mind open on both ends; everything flows through and nothing sticks. Clearly the critical approach that is so typical of the scientific attitude is the attitude of the open mind, but not open on both ends. In other words, no scientist in his right mind will doubt everything equally strongly. He will have doubts on some things; and while he might admit that in principle all scientific knowledge is open to revision, that does not mean that he is questioning everything all of the time or some of the things all of the time. So I do think that the critical attitude exemplified by some of our greatest scientists proves that they observe the golden mean between the dogmatic attitude that often goes with theological fixations and the extreme skepticism that philosophers sometimes cook up for their own amusement. Actually you cannot live as an extreme skeptic because you then would have to doubt every step you take in any and all of your activities.

We all live by "faith" or "belief" of some kind, but it is vitally important to distinguish different kinds of belief. Before I go into the various meanings of the word "belief," let me illustrate by means of an allegory: Religious faith is like a cane, a walking stick. Some carry the cane because they could not walk without it; it serves them as a crutch; that is, religion in their case upholds them. They could not live without an orthodox kind of religious faith, and such people should not be deprived of it if that is what they need. Other people carry the cane because father did and father must have known what was right. Then there are those who carry the cane because it is a sort of personal ornament. It gives them admission to the kind of club and social organization that they want to be in. There are still others who use the cane as a magic wand—in faith-healing, for example. And some carry the cane only to use it in steep places of the road. (I'm not sure whether God will pay attention to people who turn to him only in their distress.) Finally there are some people who carry the cane to whack other people over the head with it. Now this allegory is cheap and crude. I realize this, and I want to say immediately that if we want to be broad-minded and open-minded philosophers we have to understand the psychology of religion much better. In our age this is facilitated by new developments in psychology and also by such developments in our philosophical outlook as have resulted from the clarifications of ideas carried on by empiricists, logicians, and linguistic analysts.

As I see it, we are living in a new age of enlightenment in which we ask persistently, and we hope with good results, two major questions: "What do you mean?" and "How do you know?" What do you mean by the words that you use, and how do you know your assertions to be true or probable, i.e., on the basis of what evidence, grounds, or reasons? In asking these questions—especially the first question—we go beyond the so-called warfare between science and theology that had been written about many years ago—for example, by Andrew White. The major concern then was the incompatibilities of the best established results of science with the dogmas contained in the Scriptures. On the whole we feel today that this is not the most prominent issue. We are no longer primarily concerned with the discrepancies between the modernists and theologians, nor to revise theological doctrines in such a fashion as to make them compatible with science and to reconstrue them in the light of the best knowledge available in astronomy, geology, biology, theory of evolution, etc. Rather, the question, "What do you mean?" really is the central issue; namely, the meaning of the word "belief" or of any cognate terms. I'll put it in quotes because I'm now talking about the word "belief," and it seems to me that it has at least three different meanings. Unless you recognize this you will never get clear in your discussion of science versus theology or theologically framed religious faith.

Now taking our start from everyday language we find, first, that each of us is perfectly clear that we use the word "belief" in a sense that we could call empirical, on the lowly level of common life, as when I say I believe that there might be a rainstorm tonight (I may be right, I may be wrong, but this is my belief); or when I say I believe that I have two dollars in my pocket. It has been pointed out that even the best established scientific theories are objects of belief in the sense that whatever evidence speaks for them does not do so conclusively or with finality. This is very simple logic, in that any scientific theory that has been formulated is in the form of a universal proposition: under these circumstances, no matter where and when, such and such conditions will follow. In the more developed sciences this is expressed in mathematical language such as in differential equations. In science we tentatively put forth knowledge claims which have a universal range, and which are in principle refutable by bona fide instances to the contrary. So whether it is on the elementary level of common life or whether it is on the level of scientific theorizing, as in recent theoretical physics, we are dealing with beliefs that are capable of tests; and we know what we are talking about because we can tell what kind of difference it would make. This principle is well known in American philosophy due to the work of Charles S. Peirce and William James. I think that it was William James who said that a difference must make a difference if there is to be a difference—meaning that if there is no difference between the affirmation and the denial of a certain proposition, that proposition did not really have scientific significance because it is completely removed from any test.

Now some forms of theology have precisely built into their conceptual structure the idea of absolute untestability. Since I am referring to *some* forms, but by no means to all, I will call this second kind of belief simply "trans-empirical." Usually people in this connection speak of the "supernatural," but that is a cloudy notion because you never know how to draw the line when something has not as yet been scientifically explained. The boundary between the supernatural and the natural and between what can be explained scientifically and what cannot is often unclear. However, if you take some typical examples from traditional theology, then very often, after a lot of discussion and many dialectical moves, the final answer is that "this is a matter of faith." "There is nothing that can be proved or disproved"; at least, that is what the man in the street will tell you. I'll wager that if you took a Gallup poll of the opinion of the man on the street on theological matters, he would say, "Don't confuse this with science." In science you can prove or disprove, in the sense of confirming or disconfirming, at least indirectly and incompletely, no matter how strongly or weakly. But it requires an act of faith to uphold the theological dogma, and this is entirely different from belief in the empirical sense. Thus testability is ruled out because in the end we are told that there are mysteries that are unfathomable to the human mind.

William James tried to help us in this connection with his famous story about the cat in the library. A cat in the library that knows all the cozy nooks and corners and knows how to get in and out might "think," "I know all about the library!" But the cat wouldn't have the slightest idea what people are doing there: taking down books, making notes, scanning the indexes, etc. Those things would escape the cat completely. Now the conceited scientist, says William James, is like that conceited cat in the library. He might say, "Here is the universe with its regularities described in our scientific laws, there are no mysteries any more. Well, there may be a few open questions and a few obscure corners in the universe, but by and large we know the hang of it all because of the basic laws we have found in physics, biology, etc.; by and large we have learned what most of our natural universe is like." There actually was an article a few years ago by an outstanding Harvard scientist who said that we had the main problems solved; the rest required a little mathematical refinement and experimental clarification, but by and large science is near its end. Contrast this with what Newton said when he compared himself with a boy who was picking up shells at the seashore and thinking of the tremendous ocean of the unknown and unclarified thinking before him. True, Newton lived three centuries ago, when science was just beginning to formulate its first great synthesis. But surely we cannot decide by *a priori* reasoning between those two views, because all we have to go by is inductive reasoning. New facts crop up in observations and experiments over and over again as the scientists test their theories. A humble attitude like Newton's is more commendable than the attitude of that scientist who was smug enough to think that science was about to come to an end. If you want my personal opinion, I think that science is an endless quest: the universe has many more aspects than we are aware of or that we have formulated in our science thus far.

Now a few more words about the trans-empirical aspects of belief. Take the famous problem of evil. As I see it in the Judeo-Christian tradition we have trans-empirical faith in a God who is all-knowing, all-powerful, who is all-good or benevolent. If there is such a God, then there should be no evil. There should be no evil in the world because, if there is, He would certainly know about it. If He is benevolent, He would want to eliminate evil; and if He is all-powerful, He has the ability to do so. However, unless you are a Christian Scientist, you will admit that there is evil in the world, for it stares you in the eye. After all, there is much that is unfortunate. There are wars, racial tensions, poverty, deprivation, injustice, suffering, misery, and disease in the world. All this we call evil; and it takes a lot of verbal juggling to talk yourself out of it. Elementary logical reasoning directly reveals that, if there is a God, then He could not be all three: benevolent, omniscient, and omnipotent. This, of course, does not disprove the existence of God: it just disproves that at least one of the three attributes of God would not be fulfilled because the conjunction holds only if all members of the conjunction are true. It was William James who attempted to resolve the paradox of evil by arguing that God is surely omniscient, and He is surely benevolent, but not all-powerful. And James thought that was an inspiring message for all human beings, because then we have to help the good Lord with our own efforts.

But James was by no means attached to any kind of orthodox religion. And the *usual* answer to the problem of evil that we get from theologians is that there are things (as there are for the cat in the library) that are absolutely "beyond our understanding"; that we simply must have "faith" in the existence of God and His goodness and greatness and power, and that ultimately the problem is an "unsolvable mystery."

Now here you have a sharp difference between the scientific attitude and the theological one. Modest scientists will admit that of course there are unsolved problems, but if they are faced with a problem that they can recognize and analyze as unsolvable, then they get suspicious that they may not even have a good question. Let me briefly illustrate the point by an example that is partly off the track, but it will help us to see that borderline questions of this sort have occasionally come up, even in science. Take, for instance, Newton's doctrine of absolute space. For those of you who know the details, I should add that I am talking merely about the kinematics of absolute space and not about the dynamical arguments of Newton. Newton was influenced by Platonic doctrines, according to which space is a reality in and by itself, existing independently, and whatever exists in the world has its place in absolute space. In fact there was a basis for Newton's thinking this because he considered space a sense organ of God. God, as it were, has a finger in every pie and is omnipresent because space is his sense organ. During Newton's lifetime, this doctrine was attacked by Leibniz, Newton's great contemporary in Germany, who challenged not Newton himself but Samuel Clarke, Newton's faithful disciple. Leibniz asked questions that are very close to the kind of questions that later pragmatists and positivists were to ask: "What is the difference that makes the difference?" For instance, Leibniz asked in his correspondence: Suppose we take all of the particles in the universe, stars, atoms, etc., in their momentary orientation and distances, etc., and leave everything intact while moving all the contents of the universe two miles to the east. Would that make a difference that makes a difference? Obviously not. There would be nothing testable about that difference. So, as long as space is considered as an absolutely independent reality, it could not possibly be testable. The critique by Leibniz of absolute space and time is similar to the one that I think has influenced some of the "God is dead" theologians in recent time. They are bothered not so much by the conflict between the best scientific evidence and the Scriptural dogmas and assertions about Genesis, and so on, as by the question, "Do we still mean anything if we remove our assertions entirely from empirical testability?"

We will return to this in a moment. The third meaning of the word "belief" is perhaps best called "commitment." If I got up before you on a soap box and said, "I believe in human equality," you would immediately realize that I am not trying to tell you that we are all equal, because we are all more or less unequal, physically, intellectually, etc. Clearly what I was expressing was my commitment to a doctrine of human rights, human equality before the law, equality of opportunity, and so on. In other words, the statement involves taking a firm attitude and is itself not a knowledge claim at all; it is a matter of putting yourself on record and vowing a certain attitude.

Now it seems to me that some of the humanly more valuable elements in religion come precisely from the connection of trans-empirical faith with a commitment. Do we have to have trans-empirical faith in order to have the kind of moral and social commitment that normal, sane, and humane human beings generally have, at least, as a standard of criticism? Quite true, we do not always behave according to the ideals to which we have committed ourselves, and we may sometimes feel guilty about it; but when it comes to criticism of others, or even to criticism of ourselves, we do use moral standards which we all have to some extent in common, at least at a given stage in human development and civilization.

Implicit in what I am saying here is, of course, the controversial philosophical conviction that moral principles are essentially in the imperative form, and that we are deluding ourselves if we give them a purely descriptive, declarative form. To be sure this is an often-used device in the scientific age; people are often so fact-minded that they insist on statements that are couched in the form of declarative statements capable of empirical evidence. But I ask you, could you, for instance, provide any kind of empirical evidence for a doctrine of human rights? You can talk about human nature. As long as you merely state the facts about human nature, individually, psychologically, anthropologically, or socio-psychologically, you will not get an imperative out of it that would be the expression of a commitment of how we ought to think or act. In other words I do not see how you could arrive from premises, that contain only statements concerning what *is* the case, or what happens under what circumstances, to moral imperatives that tell you what *ought* to be done or what we ought to strive for.

Hence, we have commitments of this sort. I wish to stress immediately how tremendously important they are in the whole business and art of living together and what terrible blunderers we are still in this art of living together, as witness all the upheavals, riots, and wars that are going on. I will later try to show you in what way we can come to a philosophical understanding of commitments.

At this point I wish to insert a brief discussion of some theological arguments that try to show that just as there is a kind of experience that supports the statements of everyday life, or the factual knowledge claims of the scientist, so there is a kind of experience that similarly supports the religious beliefs. There are some theologians who do not pay much attention to this kind of argument, but you often hear it from philosophers that empiricists are too narrow-minded. They pay attention only to sensory experience, we are told. It is fairly obvious that scientific knowledge, as well as the knowledge of everyday life, is based on evidence that comes to us through the senses—seeing, hearing, touching, smelling, etc. But there are other forms of experience; and many of us know from first hand that there is such a thing as religious experience, as in the actual act of worship or prayer. There is the experience which the mystics refer to as the "mystical experience," and which seems exceptional. But still in extreme forms of religious experience the mystics usually tell us that they cannot really describe these experiences or give us a clear-cut interpretation of them. They can circumscribe them, they can hint at them, they can allude to them. But we are told by some philosophers that you cannot be so narrow-minded as to say that trans-empirical faith has no factual meaning, nor can it have any factual truth because it cannot be based on sensory experience. This is the complaint.

Now here I have to be very brief. It seems to me that you don't have to subscribe to any dogmatic Freudian psychoanalytic theories in order to see that the human situation is such that we do not have to explain mystical experience in the way which the mystic himself or the religious person takes it; namely, as given by the grace of a deity. We can have a perfectly natural explanation, just as we have a perfectly natural explanation about the origins of our sensory experiences that serve as evidence for our knowledge claims in everyday life and the factual knowledge claims of the advanced scientist. Now it seems to me that the human situation being what it is, and human childhood and infancy being what they are, it should not be surprising that the notion of a superior power would arise; and if it is available in the culture, it would be readily adopted by the person growing up through adolescence. In other words, the greater power of parents, educators, and elders in comparison with the helpless infant brings about an image of a superior being to which he can appeal, which may forgive, or which may punish. Accordingly, in some of the monotheistic religions the idea of a personal God is usually couched in terms of the father image. We then are told we must not take this too literally. But then the question is what does demythologizing leave over if it is carried to the bitter end? The situation of the infant is such that his very physical existence depends upon the sustenance and assistance rendered by the father and mother. Very soon the "do's" and "don't's" of education take over—in other words, imperatives reinforced by rewards or punishments. What could be more natural than that the infant would develop the idea that perhaps there is a superior power of the paternal or maternal type, somewhere but invisible, who watches over us, to whom we are morally responsible for our actions, and with regard to whom we may feel proud or guilty, as we do toward our natural parents. Now this is a piece of psychology that I don't wish to present dogmatically. It is just to show that the usual argument from mystical religious experience claims to find an explanation analogous to but different from scientific explanation, that it is the alleged result of grace coming down upon us from the deity, and that it is not accessible to sensory observation.

I'm usually told at this juncture of the argument that one had better not explain the issues psychologically. One could say in reply that, according to the Freudians, a person who rejects God is a typical father-killer with a strong Oedipus complex and that accounts for his attitude. So they say that what is sauce for the goose is sauce for the gander. I don't see that this reply is to the point of the original argument because the question was as to whether we need a trans-empirical explanation of mystical experience; and I have suggested what I consider to be at least a beginning or blueprint or promissory note for a negative answer. Of course, I would also want an explanation of the behavior of the raging atheist. All I wanted to show is that we do not need the theistic kind of reasoning in order to account for the phenomenon of religious experience. The influence of the cultural and moral traditions as well as psychology can provide a very plausible naturalistic explanation of religious experience. As Voltaire once put it, if God didn't exist, he would have to be invented.

In our age of scientific enlightenment we often ask ourselves what kind of foundation we can give to morality, to our basic commitments, to human rights and human equality? This is, of course, not an easy question to answer. It seems to some people much more convenient to appeal to trans-empirical authority. Often the question is raised, "What lends authority to the ethical principles without which we could not survive?" I believe that the cynicism and anarchism we see in so many young people today represents a danger not only for the survival of civilization and for human well-being, but even for the psychological well-being of the individual concerned. Now what can we say in this connection? Philosophers have been in a quandary for centuries as to how to justify fundamental principles of morality.

This invites a little logical analysis to find out what it is that we mean by justification. If we justify knowledge claims in mathematics it is done by proof; that is, by deductive derivation. If we justify knowledge claims in empirical science, it is done by observation, experimentation, statistical design, call it inductive, or what you will. There are also principles that at least pragmatically have proven their worth and that is the very reason why we keep them around and live in accordance with them. In the ethical domain it is more difficult to derive what you want to derive, and I find that it is easier to beg the question by putting an ethical or moral accent in your principles. Perhaps we are all suffering from the philosophical demand for demonstration. There are limits to demonstration. From this point of view I am quite inclined to say that you won't get any place with ethical justification unless you start with certain commitments. The adoption of those commitments can be made palatable, but there is nothing that we can prove or disprove about them. To be sure, utilitarians and hedonists try to show that if we are to have the greatest happiness for the greatest number, then these moral precepts commend themselves for adoption; but of course this idea presupposes already that the major aim, the greatest good of the greatest number, is itself morally desirable.

Some clarification would help here. Kant, the German philosopher of the eighteenth century, introduced the distinction between hypothetical and categorical imperatives, in plainer language, conditional and unconditional imperatives. If your doctor tells you that *if* you want to improve your health, you'd better take the following medicines or change your diet or stop smoking, then this is a conditional imperative. It assumes that you accept the end and that he with his professional knowledge can give you the kind of advice that you can adopt in order to attain this end. This is the purpose of the applied sciences, such as technology, engineering, medicine, and so on. It is the technological sciences that give us information about the best means that will most economically conclude the attainment of those ends. These are hypothetical or conditional imperatives. *If* you want this end, you'd better avail yourself of the following means. You'd better do such and such, in order to gain what you most deeply desire. By contrast, ethical imperatives must be based upon a fundamental or supreme ethical imperative that is unconditional; that is, if your intuitions are correct, because somewhere in the analysis of moral behavior and moral experience we do come upon certain terminal values. We are not talking about absolute values, but some that furnish the basis to the rest of our values. And these are the ones to which we commit ourselves, at least as principles of criticism, even if we do not always obey them. Just remember a situation when you are dealt with unjustly or unfairly. You cry, "Unfair! Unjust!" Whenever we are in danger, we appeal to such principles. We find them even on the highest levels: for example, in the Supreme Court and in the Congress of the United States and the United Nations, where one appeals to fairness and justice.

Now it is true that practically all of these ethical terms are emotionally laden and are open to persuasive definitions. Charles L. Stevenson's remarkable book *Ethics and Language* gives an example of such a definition which illustrates the point better than an abstract explication. A liquor advertisement, for instance, says "that true temperance is a cocktail before dinner, a glass of wine with dinner and a cordial or brandy after dinner!" Thus, you can see what goes on in persuasive definitions. Words have a certain emotive appeal. "Freedom" and "slavery," for instance, have certain opposite emotive appeals. It is quite characteristic that in international discussions we deal out to each other labels that have emotive appeals. The totalitarian countries say, "Capitalism in America is pure slavery; look at the poor, exploited worker." We look at the fellow in the totalitarian countries and we say, "You think you have freedom? My goodness, with all those restrictions!" and so on and so forth. It is necessary that we look below the surface of the verbal games that people play and penetrate to the definitions that tamper with the factual meaning of words but retain their emotive appeal.

Accordingly when I claim that there are ethical ideals that seem to be fairly basic in human concerns, I allow for a little latitude that of course can be exploited by "persuasive" definitions. Nevertheless, I think that there is a tenable middle ground between the relativists and the absolutists in morals. The relativists, for instance the anthropologists of the last century, have left their mark by maintaining a pluralism of moral values. On the other side, the absolutists, for instance theologically or metaphysically inclined philosophers, have given us a dogmatic monism in claiming that there is only one set of moral standards common to all mankind. The relativists hold an empirically discernible idea, namely that human values are relative to human needs, interests, and desires. Whereas some of the absolutists, including Kant, say that basic human values are independent of human interests and needs in that we may have to act even against our interests to do the morally right thing. This latter point has been exaggerated I think.

In my view we may well reject extreme relativism. The relativist, especially the anthropologist, has confused mores and folkways with morality. If we dig deeper into human nature we find that in some social contexts certain moral ideals inevitably work themselves out. So I think that a unified set of supreme moral values can be empirically discerned as inherent in the conscience of man, even if it is not always displayed in his behavior. We cannot, however, get away from the fact that human needs and interests and human nature in general are highly relevant for human values or moral ideals. I assume a sort of synthesis between a "nothing but" and a "something more" view of morality; namely, morality on the one hand is relative to human interests, and moral values neither come down from on high nor are dictated by the deity. There is a golden mean that combines the valid element of monism—i.e., that ethical principles are universally applicable—with the empiricism of relativism which teaches that human values are related to human nature. If you want a label for this call it "scientific humanism."

Now what are these moral values that we share in common? Very likely they have had a development. It is perfectly clear, for instance, that the ancient enlightened philosophers were perfectly satisfied to exploit men as slaves and had no particular compunction about it since they distinguished between "superior" and "inferior" human beings. In this regard a tremendous transformation has occurred. And we can certainly be thankful to the great religions for their ethical contributions. We do not have to accept their trans-empirical method in order to support their commitment to the ideals of the brotherhood of man or equality before the law. I have already said we cannot demonstrate anything in this field because all such demonstrations would ultimately be a matter of a vicious circle. But what we can show is that in the development of human civilization certain transformations have taken place. There are certain activities and abilities of the human animal that are essential for his survival. But when civilization takes over, something else supervenes in addition to what was a purely biological function in the first place. For example, our eyes are clearly outposts in the preservation of existence. We recognize dangers, we recognize our food by eyesight; but seeing can become "beholding" the beautiful in nature and art. So here a certain sublimation has taken place. Similarly, hearing, a similar biological function in the first place, may become a means to listening to great music; walking may become hiking or dancing. The original functions, you understand, do not fade out but are supervened by the further functions that represent our higher cultural activities. Speech as a means of communication for very practical purposes is indispensable, but it also may become poetry and song. Sexuality may become love. I don't recommend that sexuality fade out, but love is something more than mere sexuality. Hard toil and burdensome work may become creative work, as we see it in the works of artists and scientists, and may be intrinsically enjoyable. Schopenhauer spoke of human intelligence as a lantern in the light of which we look for food and avoid dangers. Surely it has its biological and practical functions, but it may be sublimated into scientific activities. The great scientists pursue science for its own sake, not merely for its practical applications.

If human nature had been as bad as Hobbes believed, and everyone had been the enemy of everyone else, we would soon, in the natural necessities and exigencies of living together, arrive at least at what you might call "business reciprocity." "I'll do something for you because I expect you can do something for me." That's the lowest level. Of course, even beneath that level is the commitment not to do harm to anyone else, because if you do there are bound to be repercussions. So from these lowly origins we may learn and arrive at higher levels of morality. Take the Hippocratic oath, for example, which young medics have to swear. The oath is essentially the commitment not to do harm, but further it is the commitment to help patients. This is quite elementary. The knowledge that the doctor acquires in his study of anatomy, physiology and medicine would enable him to make his patient gravely ill and kill him. But he does not use his knowledge this way if he is an ethical medical man and an ethical human being. The Hippocratic oath is clearly a matter of commitment. One can, however, arrive at higher levels with the principles of justice and fairness. In spite of the fact that they are all subject to persuasive definitions, there is a core there that we understand and that we all appeal to when we are pressed.

I don't think that we have to go to the New Testament to find this. One can find it in the Old Testament, especially among the Jewish prophets: the principles of kindness, fairness, equality. And I think among all people, but in very diverse forms, you have ideals closely approximating these. Now these moral commitments, or principles, or whatever you wish to call them, may well have come out of the natural development of human beings in the social context. What I am trying to maintain is that in this age of scientific enlightenment, I think we can avoid regressing to a completely cynical, anarchistic view of the world. I think that there are scientifically evident features of the development of the human race and of individuals. Psychology points in the direction of human needs and interests that must be satisfied. And in the social context, certain traffic rules simply have to be obeyed if we are to survive as a society. Thus we have ideals of justice and equality.

What if you don't have such an ideal, as for instance in the case of what a clinical psychologist or psychiatrist calls a "psychopathic personality"? Here, unfortunately, there is nothing that you can do with such a person; not even therapeutic means have been found, and reeducation seems difficult or impossible. Psychopathic people, if they have any regrets (not repentance), regret only that they were not clever enough to avoid being found out. In regard to the person who is absolutely without conscience, I don't think that any logical or empirical demonstration would help. I think that all we can do in human society is to avoid the preaching of morality. Instead we should educate by example, and especially in regard to our children. Parents should show the children how things can be done, and in a very gentle way correct them.

If I had any reason to believe that orthodox religions would promote peace and justice in this world I wouldn't criticize them at all. The empirical evidence seems to speak against them. Much as I appreciate the deep moral concern of truly religious persons, I think that institutional religions have often encouraged wars and cruelty of one kind or another. The flame and sword of Islam is one example, the Crusades another. Preachers who bless the arms of their country have their counterparts in the preachers who bless the arms of the other country. All are examples of hypocrisy and injustice. If I had any evidence that traditional religion, implemented by a conceptual theological framework, was effective along the lines that every humanist would like to have effected, I would cease and desist in my criticism spoken from a logical point of view. My analysis has been addressed to those of our generation who are looking for the kind of clarity and intellectual responsibility in morality that we have achieved and continue to achieve in the sciences. From the point of view of the scientific humanist I think that there is still some hope that mankind will grow up. But whether or not mankind will actually learn to use scientific and untried intelligence in the treatment of moral problems depends upon the cooperative efforts of everyone.

The opportunity for the development of a scientific humanism is very great indeed. But the challenges of our day are so tremendous that unless mankind develops soon the ability to resolve his moral problems with clarity and intelligence, the consequences of his folly would be too terrible to contemplate.

II

THE GOOD LIFE

THE GOOD LIFE OF THE SELF-ACTUALIZING PERSON*

A. H. Maslow

Humanistic ethics have at times emphasized "self-actualization" as a desirable goal for man and as a source of happiness. This is an old idea in the history of thought. Plato and Aristotle were concerned with the concept. Recent psychological research has given support and a practical significance to the theory. Examining the characteristics of the "self-actualizing" person assists the continual humanist quest for the good life.

Self-actualizing people are gratified in all their basic needs embracing affection, respect, and self-esteem. They have a feeling of belongingness and rootedness. They are satisfied in their love needs, because they have friends, feel loved and love-worthy. They have status, place in life, and respect from other people, and they have a reasonable feeling of worth and self-respect.

Self-actualizing people do not for any length of time feel anxiety-ridden, insecure, unsafe; do not feel alone, ostracized, rootless, or isolated; do not feel unlovable, rejected, or unwanted; do not feel despised and looked down upon; and do not feel unworthy nor do they have crippling feelings of inferiority or worthlessness.

Since the basic needs had been assumed to be the only motivations

* This article appeared in *The Humanist,* XXVII, No. 4 (1967), 127–29, 139. Reprinted by permission of *The Humanist.*

for human beings, it was possible, and in certain contexts useful, to say of self-actualizing people that they were "unmotivated." This aligned these people with the Eastern philosophical view of health as the transcendence of striving or desiring or wanting.

It is also possible to say and to describe self-actualizing people as expressing rather than coping. They are spontaneous, natural, and more easily themselves than other people.

What motivates the self-actualizing person? What are the psychodynamics in self-actualization? What makes him move and act and struggle? What drives or pulls such a person? What attracts him? For what does he hope? What makes him angry, or dedicated, or self-sacrificing? What does he feel loyal to? Devoted to? What does he aspire to and yearn for? What would he die or live for?

These questions ask for an answer to the question: What are the motivations of self-actualizing people? Clearly we must make an immediate distinction between the ordinary motives of those people who are below the level of self-actualization and motivated by the basic needs, and the motivations of people who are sufficiently gratified in all their basic needs and are no longer primarily motivated by them. For convenience, call these motives and needs of self-actualizing persons "meta-needs." This also differentiates the category of motivation from the category of "meta-motivation."

Examining self-actualizing people, I find that they are dedicated people, devoted to some task outside themselves, some vocation, or duty, or job. Generally the devotion and dedication is so marked that one can correctly use the old words vocation, calling, or mission to describe their passionate, selfless, and profound feeling for their "work." We could even use the words destiny or fate in the sense of biological or temperamental or constitutional destiny or fate. Sometimes I have gone so far as to speak of oblation in the religious sense of dedicating oneself upon some altar for a particular task, some cause outside oneself and bigger than oneself, something not merely selfish, something impersonal. This is one way of putting into adequate words the feeling that one gets when one listens to self-actualizing people talking about their work or task. One gets the feeling of a beloved job, and further, of something for which the person is "a natural," that he is suited for, that is right for him, even something for which he was born.

In this kind of a situation, it is easy to sense something like a preestablished harmony or a good match like a perfect love affair in which it seems that people belong to each other and were meant for each other. In the best instances the person and his job fit together and belong together perfectly like a key and a lock, or resonate together like a sung note which sets into sympathetic resonance a particular string in the piano keyboard.

Often I get the feeling that I can tease apart two kinds of determinants from this fusion which has created a unity out of a duality, and that these two sets of determinants can, and sometimes do, vary independently. One can be spoken of as the responses to forces relatively within the person: e.g., "I love babies (or painting, or research, or political power) more than anything in the world." "It fascinates me." "I am inexorably drawn to . . ." "I need to . . ." This we may call "inner requiredness" and it is felt as a kind of self-indulgence rather than as a duty. It is different from and separable from "external requiredness," which is felt as a response to what the environment, the situation, the problem, or the external world calls for and requires of the person. A fire "calls for" putting out, or a helpless baby demands that one take care of it, or some obvious injustice calls for righting. Here one feels more the element of duty, of obligation, of responsibility, of being compelled helplessly to respond no matter what one was planning to do, or wished to do. It is more "I must," "I have to," "I am compelled" than "I want to."

In the ideal instance, "I want to" coincides with "I must." There is a good matching of inner with outer requiredness. The observer is overawed by the degree of compellingness, of inexorability, or preordained destiny, necessity, and harmony that he perceives. Furthermore, the observer, as well as the person involved, feels not only that "it has to be" but also that "it ought to be, it is right, it is suitable, appropriate, fitting, and proper." I have often felt a gestalt-like quality about this kind of belonging together, the formation of a "one" out of "two." I hesitate to call this simply "purposefulness" because that may imply that it happens only out of will, purpose, decision, or calculation; the word doesn't give enough weight to the subjective feeling of being swept along, of willing and eager surrender, or yielding to fate and happily embracing it at the same time. Ideally, one discovers one's fate; it is not made or constructed or decided upon. It is recognized as if one had been unwittingly waiting for it. Perhaps the better phrase would be "Spinozistic" or "Taoistic" choice or decision or purpose.

The best way to explain these feelings is to use the example of "falling in love." It is clearly different from doing one's duty, or doing what is sensible or logical. Also "will," if mentioned at all, is used in a very special sense. When two people fall in love with each other fully, each one knows what it feels like to be a magnet and what it feels like to be iron filings, and what it feels like to be both simultaneously. Very useful, also, is the parallel with the happy abandon of the ideal sexual situation. Here people resist and delay the inevitable climax, in a kind of fond self- and other-teasing, holding off as long as possible. Suddenly, in a single instant they can change to the opposite course of embracing eagerly and totally the end which they were moments ago delaying, as the tides suddenly change from going north to going south.

This example also helps convey what is difficult to communicate in words; the lovers' sense of good fortune, of luck, of gratuitous grace, of gratitude, of awe that this miracle should have occurred, of wonder that they should have been chosen, and of the peculiar mixture of pride fused with humility, of arrogance shot through with the pity-for-the-less-fortunate that one finds in lovers.

It can be said of the self-actualizing person that he is being his own kind of person, or being himself, or actualizing his real self. Observation would lead one to understand that "This person is the best one in the whole world for this particular job, and this particular job is the best job in the whole world for this particular person and his talents, capacities, and tastes. He was meant for it, and it was meant for him."

Accepting this premise, we move into another realm of discourse —the realm of being, of transcendence. Now we can speak meaningfully only in the language of being (the "B-language," communication at the mystical level described in my book *Toward a Psychology of Being*). It is quite obvious with such people that the ordinary or conventional dichotomy between work and play is transcended totally. Such a person's work is his play and his play is his work. If a person loves his work and enjoys it more than any other activity in the whole world and is eager to get to it, to get back to it, after any interruption, then how can we speak about "labor" in the sense of something one is forced to do against one's wishes?

What sense, for instance, is left to the concept "vacation"? For such individuals it is often observed that during the periods in which they are totally free to choose whatever they wish to do and in which they have no external obligations to anyone else, they devote themselves happily and totally to their "work." What does it mean "to have some fun"? What is the meaning of the word "entertainment"? How does such a person "rest"? What are his "duties," responsibilities, obligations?

What sense does money or pay or salary make in such a situation? Obviously the most beautiful fate, the most wonderful good luck, the most marvelous good fortune that can happen to any human being is to be paid for doing that which he passionately loves to do. This is exactly the situation, or almost the situation, with many self-actualizing persons. Of course, money is welcome, and in certain amounts is even needed. It is certainly not the finality, the end, the goal, however. The check such a man gets is only a small part of his "pay." Self-actualizing work or B-work, being its own intrinsic reward, transforms the money or paycheck into a by-product, an epiphenomenon. This is different from the situation of less fortunate human beings who do something that they do not want to do in order to get money, which they then use to get what they really want. The role of money in the realm of being is certainly different from the role of money in the realm of deficiencies.

These are scientific questions, and can be investigated in scientific ways. They have been investigated in monkeys and apes to a degree. The most obvious example, of course, is the rich research literature on monkey curiosity and other precursors of the human yearning for and satisfaction with the truth. But it will be just as easy in principle to explore the aesthetic choices of these and other animals under conditions of fear and of lack of fear, by healthy specimens or by unhealthy ones, under good choice conditions or bad ones, etc.

If one asks the fortunate, work-loving, self-actualizing person, "Who are you?" or "What are you?" he tends to answer in terms of his "call" . . . "I am a lawyer." "I am a mother." "I am a psychiatrist." "I am an artist." He tells you that he identifies his call with his identity, his Self. It is a label for the whole of him and it becomes a defining characteristic of the person.

If one confronts him with the question, "Supposing you were not a scientist (or a teacher, or a pilot), then what would you be?" or "Supposing you were not a psychologist, then what?" his response is apt to be one of puzzlement, thoughtfulness. He does not have a ready answer. Or the response can be one of amusement. It strikes him funny. In effect, the answer is, "If I were not a mother (lover, anthropologist, industrialist) then I wouldn't be *me.* I would be someone else, and I can't imagine being someone else."

A tentative conclusion is, then, that in self-actualizing subjects, their beloved calling tends to be perceived as a defining characteristic of the self, to be identified with, incorporated, introjected. It becomes an inextricable aspect of one's Being.

When asked why they love their work, which are the moments of higher satisfaction in their work, which moments of reward make all the necessary chores worthwhile or acceptable, which are the peak-experiences, self-actualizing people give many specific and *ad hoc* answers which to them are intrinsic reinforcers.

As I classified these moments of reward, it became apparent that the best and most natural categories of classification were mostly or entirely values of an ultimate and irreducible kind! Call them "B-values": truth, goodness, beauty, unity, aliveness, uniqueness, perfection, completion, justice, simplicity, totality, effortlessness, playfulness, self-sufficiency, meaningfulness.

For these people the profession seems to be not functionally autonomous, but to be a carrier of ultimate values. I could say, if I were not afraid of being misunderstood, that for example, the profession of law, is a means to the end of justice, and not a law to itself in which justice might get lost. For one man the law is loved because it is justice, while another man, the pure value-free technologist, might love the law simply as an intrinsically lovable set of rules, precedents, procedures without regard to the ends or products of their use.

B-values or meta-motives are not only intrapsychic or organismic.

They are equally inner and outer. The meta-needs, insofar as they are inner, and the requiredness of all that is outside the person are each stimulus and response to each other. And they move toward becoming indistinguishable, toward fusion.

This means that the distinction between self and not-self has broken down or has been transcended. There is less differentiation between the world and the person because he has incorporated into himself part of the world and defines himself thereby. He becomes an enlarged self. If justice or truth or lawfulness have now become so important to him that he identifies his self with them, then where are they? Inside his skin or outside his skin? This distinction comes close to being meaningless at this point because his self no longer has his skin as its boundary.

Certainly simple selfishness is transcended here and has to be defined at higher levels. For instance, we know that it is possible for a person to get more pleasure out of food through having his child eat it than through eating it with his own mouth. His self has enlarged enough to include his child. Hurt his child and you hurt him. Clearly the self can no longer be identified with the biological entity which is supplied with blood from his heart along his blood vessels. The psychological self can obviously be bigger than his own body.

Just as beloved people can be incorporated into the self, thereby becoming defining characteristics of it, so also can causes and values be similarly incorporated into a person's self. Many people are so passionately identified with trying to prevent war, racial injustices, slums, or poverty that they are quite willing to make great sacrifices, even to the point of risking death. Very clearly, they do not mean justice for their own biological bodies alone. They mean justice as a general value, justice for everyone, justice as a principle.

There are other important consequences of this incorporation of values into the self. For instance, you can love justice and truth in the world or in a person out there. You can be made happier as your friends move toward truth and justice, and sadder as they move away from it. That's easy to understand. However, suppose you see yourself moving successfully toward truth, justice, beauty, and virtue? Then you may find that, in a peculiar kind of detachment and objectivity toward oneself, for which our culture has no place, you will be loving and admiring yourself in the kind of healthy self-love that Fromm has described. You can respect yourself, admire yourself, take tender care of yourself, reward yourself, feel virtuous, love-worthy, respect-worthy. You may then treat yourself with the responsibility and otherness that a pregnant woman does whose self now has to be defined to overlap with not-self. So may a person with a great talent protect it and himself as if he were a carrier of something which is simultaneously himself and not himself. He may become his own friend.

These people, although concretely working for, motivated by, and loyal to some conventional category of work, are transparently motivated by the intrinsic or ultimate values or aspects of reality for which the profession is only a vehicle.

This is my impression from observing them, interviewing them, and asking them why they like doctoring, or just which are the most rewarding moments in running a home, or chairing a committee, or having a baby, or writing. They may meaningfully be said to be working for truth, for beauty, for goodness, for law and for order, for justice, for perfection, if I boil down to a dozen or so intrinsic values (or values of Being) all the hundreds of specific reports of what is yearned for, what gratifies, what is valued, what they work for from day to day, and why they work.

It is at this point in my theory that, quite fairly, both methodology and validity can be called into question. I have not deliberately worked with an *ad hoc* control group of non-self-actualizing people. I could say that most of humanity is a control group. I have a considerable fund of experience with the attitudes toward work of average people, immature people, neurotic and borderline people, psychopaths, and others. There is no question that their attitudes cluster around money, basic-need gratification rather than B-values, sheer habit, stimulus-binding, convention, and the inertia of the unexamined and nonquestioned life, and from doing what other people expect or demand. However, this intuitive or naturalistic conclusion is susceptible to more careful and more controlled and predesigned examination.

Secondly, it is my strong impression that there is not a sharp line between my subjects chosen as self-actualizing and other people. I believe that each self-actualizing subject more or less fits the description I have given, but it seems also true that some percentage of other, less healthy people are meta-motivated by the B-values also; especially individuals with special talents and people placed in especially fortunate circumstances. Perhaps all people are meta-motivated to some degree.

The conventional categories of career, profession, or work may serve as channels of many other kinds of motivations, not to mention sheer habit or convention or functional autonomy. They may satisfy or seek vainly to satisfy any or all of the basic needs as well as various neurotic needs. They may be a channel for "acting out" or for "defensive" activities rather than for real gratifications.

My guess, supported by both my "empirical" impressions and by general psychodynamic theory, is that we will find it ultimately most true and most useful to say that all these various habits, determinants, motives, and meta-motives are acting simultaneously in a very complex pattern which is centered more toward one kind of motivation or determinedness than the others.

If we can try to define the deepest, most authentic, most constitutionally based aspects of the real self, of the identity, or of the authentic person, we find that in order to be comprehensive, we must include not only the person's constitution and temperament, not only anatomy, physiology, neurology, and endocrinology, not only his capacities, his biological style, not only his basic instinctoid needs, but also *the* B-values which are also *his* B-values. They are equally a part of his "nature," or definition, or essence, along with his "lower" needs. They must be included in any definition of the human being, or of full-humanness, or of a person. It is true that they are not fully evident or actualized in most people. Yet, so far as I can see at this time, they are not excluded as potentials in any human being born into the world.

Thus, a fully inclusive definition of a fully developed self or person includes a value system by which he is meta-motivated.

What all of this means is that the so-called spiritual or "higher" life is on the same continuum (is the same kind of quality or thing) with the life of the flesh, or of the body, i.e., the animal life, the "lower" life. The spiritual life is part of our biological life. It is the "highest" part of it, but yet part of it. The spiritual life is part of the human essence. It is a defining-characteristic of human nature, without which human nature is not full human nature. It is part of the real self, of one's identity, of one's inner core, or one's specieshood, of full-humanness.

To the extent that pure expressing of oneself, or pure spontaneity is possible, to that extent will the meta-needs be expressed. "Uncovering" or Taoistic therapeutic or "Ontogogic" techniques should uncover and strengthen the meta-needs as well as the basic needs. Depth-diagnostic and therapeutic techniques should ultimately also uncover these same meta-needs because, paradoxically, our highest nature is also our deepest nature. They are not in two separate realms as most religious and philosophies have assumed, and as classical science has also assumed. The spiritual life (the contemplative, "religious," philosophical, or value-life) is within the jurisdiction of human thought and is attainable in principle by man's own efforts. Even though it has been cast out of the realm of reality by the classical, value-free science which models itself upon physics, it is now being reclaimed as an object of study and technology by humanistic science. Such an expanded science will consider the eternal verities, the ultimate truths, the final values, to be "real" and natural, fact-based rather than wish-based, legitimate scientific problems calling for research.

The so-called spiritual, transcendent, or axiological life is clearly rooted in the biological nature of the species. It is a kind of "higher" animality whose precondition is a healthy "lower" animality and the two are hierarchically integrated rather than mutually exclusive. However, the higher, spiritual "animality" is timid and weak. It is so easily lost, easily crushed by stronger cultural forces, that it can become widely actualized *only* in a culture which approves of human nature and, therefore, fosters its fullest growth.

NOTE: For a fuller and more detailed account of this investigation and the theorizing resulting, see A. H. Maslow, "A Theory of Metamotivation: The Biological Rooting of the Value-Life," *Journal of Humanistic Psychology*, VII (1967), 93–127.

TOWARD A MODERN APPROACH TO VALUES: THE VALUING PROCESS IN THE MATURE PERSON*

Carl R. Rogers

There is a great deal of concern today with the problem of values. Youth, in almost every country, is deeply uncertain of its value orientation; the values associated with various religions have lost much of their influence; sophisticated individuals in every culture seem unsure and troubled as to the goals they hold in esteem. The reasons are not far to seek. The world culture, in all its aspects, seems increasingly scientific and relativistic, and the rigid, absolute views on values which come to us from the past appear anachronistic. Even more important, perhaps, is the fact that the modern individual is assailed from every angle by divergent and contradictory value claims. It is no longer possible, as it was in the not too distant historical past, to settle comfortably into the value system of one's

* An earlier version of this article was originally published in the *Journal of Abnormal and Social Psychology*, LXVIII (1964), 160–67. Reprinted by permission of the *Journal of Abnormal and Social Psychology*.

forebears or one's community and live out one's life without ever examining the nature and the assumptions of that system.

In this situation it is not surprising that value orientations from the past appear to be in a state of disintegration or collapse. Men question whether there are, or can be, any universal values. It is often felt that we may have lost, in our modern world, all possibility of any general or cross-cultural basis for values. One natural result of this uncertainty and confusion is that there is an increasing concern about, interest in, and a searching for a sound or meaningful value approach which can hold its own in today's world.

I share this general concern. I have also experienced the more specific value issues which arise in my own field, psychotherapy. The client's feelings and convictions about values frequently change during therapy. How can he or we know whether they have changed in a sound direction? Or does he simply, as some claim, take over the value system of his therapist? Is psychotherapy simply a device whereby the unacknowledged and unexamined values of the therapist are unknowingly transmitted to an unsuspecting client? Or should this transmission of values be the therapist's openly held purpose? Should he become the modern priest, upholding and imparting a value system suitable for today? And what would such a value system be? There has been much discussion of such issues, ranging from thoughtful and empirically based presentations such as that of Glad,[1] to more polemic statements. As is so often true, the general problem faced by the culture is painfully and specifically evident in the cultural microcosm which is called the therapeutic relationship.

I should like to attempt a modest approach to this whole problem. I have observed changes in the approach to values as the individual grows from infancy to adulthood. I observe further changes when, if he is fortunate, he continues to grow toward true psychological maturity. Many of these observations grow out of my experience as a therapist, where I have had the rich opportunity of seeing the ways in which individuals move toward a richer life. From these observa-

[1] D. D. Glad, *Operational Values in Psychotherapy* (New York: Oxford University Press, 1959).

tions I believe I see some directional threads emerging which might offer a new concept of the valuing process, more tenable in the modern world. I have made a beginning by presenting some of these ideas partially in previous writings;[2] I would like now to voice them more clearly and more fully.

I would stress that my vantage point for making these observations is not that of the scholar or philosopher: I am speaking from my experience of the functioning human being, as I have lived with him in the intimate experience of therapy, and in other situations of growth, change, and development. To me these seem to express some core human values which a humanistic ethics can support with confidence.

SOME DEFINITIONS

Before I present some of these observations, perhaps I should try to clarify what I mean by values. There are many definitions which have been used, but I have found helpful some distinctions made by Charles Morris. He points out that value is a term we employ in different ways. We use it to refer to the tendency of any living beings to show preference, in their actions, for one kind of object or objective rather than another. This preferential behavior he calls "operative values." It need not involve any cognitive or conceptual thinking. It is simply the value choice which is indicated behaviorally when the organism selects one object, rejects another. When the earthworm, placed in a simple Y maze, chooses the smooth arm of the Y instead of the path which is paved with sandpaper, he is indicating an operative value.

A second use of the term might be called "conceived values." This is the preference of the individual for a symbolized object. Usually

[2] Cf. C. R. Rogers, *Client-Centered Therapy* (Boston: Houghton Mifflin Company, 1951), Chap. XI, esp. pp. 522–24; and "A Theory of Therapy, Personality and Interpersonal Relationships," in S. Koch, ed., *Psychology: A Study of a Science,* Vol. III: *Formulations of the Person and the Social Context* (New York: McGraw-Hill Book Company, 1959), pp. 185–256—esp. pp. 210–35.

in such a preference there is anticipation or foresight of the outcome of behavior directed toward such a symbolized object. A choice such as "Honesty is the best policy" is such a conceived value.

A final use of the term might be called "objective value." People use the word in this way when they wish to speak of what is objectively preferable, whether or not it is in fact sensed or conceived of as desirable. What I have to say involves this last definition scarcely at all. I will be concerned with operative values and conceptualized values.

THE INFANT'S WAY OF VALUING

Let me first speak about the infant. The living human being has, at the outset, a clear approach to values. He prefers some things and experiences, and rejects others. We can infer from studying his behavior that he prefers those experiences which maintain, enhance, or actualize his organism, and rejects those which do not serve this end. Watch him for a bit:

> Hunger is negatively valued. His expression of this often comes through loud and clear.
>
> Food is positively valued. But when he is satisfied, food is negatively valued, and the same milk he responded to so eagerly is now spit out, or the breast which seemed so satisfying is now rejected as he turns his head away from the nipple with an amusing facial expression of disgust and revulsion.
>
> He values security, and the holding and caressing which seem to communicate security.
>
> He values new experience for its own sake, and we observe this in his obvious pleasure in discovering his toes, in his searching movements, in his endless curiosity.
>
> He shows a clear negative valuing of pain, bitter tastes, sudden loud sounds.

All of this is commonplace, but let us look at these facts in terms of what they tell us about the infant's approach to values. It is first of all a flexible, changing, valuing *process*, not a fixed system. He likes food and dislikes the same food. He values security and rest, and rejects it for new experience. What is going on seems best described as an organismic valuing process, in which each element, each moment of what he is experiencing is somehow weighed, and selected or rejected, depending on whether, at that moment, it tends to actualize the organism or not. This complicated weighing of experience is clearly an organismic, not a conscious or symbolic function. These are operative, not conceived values. But this process can nonetheless deal with complex value problems. I would remind you of the experiment in which young infants had spread in front of them a score or more of dishes of natural (that is, unflavored) foods. Over a period of time they clearly tended to value the foods which enhanced their own survival, growth, and development. If for a time a child gorged himself on starches, this would soon be balanced by a protein "binge." If at times he chose a diet deficient in some vitamin, he would later seek out foods rich in this very vitamin. He was utilizing the wisdom of the body in his value choices, or perhaps more accurately, the physiological wisdom of his body guided his behavioral movements, resulting in what we might think of as objectively sound value choices.

Another aspect of the infant's approach to value is that the source or locus of the evaluating process is clearly within himself. Unlike many of us, he *knows* what he likes and dislikes, and the origin of these value choices lies strictly within himself. He is the center of the valuing process, the evidence for his choices being supplied by his own senses. He is not at this point influenced by what his parents think he should prefer, or by what the church says, or by the opinion of the latest "expert" in the field, or by the persuasive talents of an advertising firm. It is from within his own experiencing that his organism is saying in nonverbal terms—"This is good for me." "That is bad for me." "I like this." "I strongly dislike that." He would laugh at our concern over values, if he could understand it. How could anyone fail to know what he liked and disliked, what was good for him and what was not?

THE CHANGE IN THE VALUING PROCESS

What happens to this highly efficient, soundly based valuing process? By what sequence of events do we exchange it for the more rigid, uncertain, inefficient approach to values which characterizes most of us as adults? Let me try to state briefly one of the major ways in which I think this happens.

The infant needs love, wants it, tends to behave in ways which will bring a repetition of this wanted experience. But this brings complications. He pulls baby sister's hair, and finds it satisfying to hear her wails and protests. He then hears that he is "a naughty, bad boy," and this may be reinforced by a slap on the hand. He is cut off from affection. As this experience is repeated, and many, many others like it, he gradually learns that what "feels good" is often "bad" in the eyes of others. Then the next step occurs, in which he comes to take the same attitude toward himself which these others have taken. Now, as he pulls his sister's hair, he solemnly intones, "Bad, bad boy." He is introjecting the value judgment of another, taking it in as his own. To that degree he loses touch with his own organismic valuing process. He has deserted the wisdom of his organism, giving up the locus of evaluation, and is trying to behave in terms of values set by another, in order to hold love.

Or take another example at an older level. A boy senses, though perhaps not consciously, that he is more loved and prized by his parents when he thinks of being a doctor than when he thinks of being an artist. Gradually he introjects the values attached to being a doctor. He comes to want, above all, to be a doctor. Then in college he is baffled by the fact that he repeatedly fails in chemistry, which is absolutely necessary to becoming a physician, in spite of the fact that the guidance counselor assures him he has the ability to pass the course. Only in counseling interviews does he begin to realize how completely he has lost touch with his organismic reactions, how out of touch he is with his own valuing process.

Let me give another instance from a class of mine, a group of prospective teachers. I asked them at the beginning of the course, "Please list for me the two or three values which you would most wish to pass on to the children with whom you will work." They turned in many value goals, but I was surprised by some of the items. Several listed such things as "to speak correctly," "to use good English, not to use words like ain't." Others mentioned neatness—"to do things according to instructions"; one explained her hope that "When I tell them to write their names in the upper right-hand corner with the date under it, I want them to do it *that way,* not in some other form."

I confess I was somewhat appalled that for some of these girls the most important values to be passed on to pupils were to avoid bad grammar, or meticulously to follow teacher's instructions. I felt baffled. Certainly these behaviors had not been *experienced* as the most satisfying and meaningful elements in their own lives. The listing of such values could only be accounted for by the fact that these behaviors had gained approval—and thus had been introjected as deeply important.

Perhaps these several illustrations will indicate that in an attempt to gain or hold love, approval, esteem, the individual relinquishes the locus of evaluation which was his in infancy, and places it in others. He learns to have a basic *dis*trust for his own experiencing as a guide to his behavior. He learns from others a large number of conceived values, and adopts them as his own, even though they may be widely discrepant from what he is experiencing. Because these concepts are not based on his own valuing, they tend to be fixed and rigid, rather than fluid and changing.

SOME INTROJECTED PATTERNS

It is in this fashion, I believe, that most of us accumulate the introjected value patterns by which we live. In this fantastically complex culture of today, the patterns we introject as desirable or undesirable come from a variety of sources and are often highly contradictory in their meanings. Let me list a few of the introjections which are commonly held.

Sexual desires and behaviors are mostly bad. The sources of this construct are many—parents, church, teachers.

Disobedience is bad. Here parents and teachers combine with the military to emphasize this concept. To obey is good. To obey without question is even better.

Making money is the highest good. The sources of this conceived value are too numerous to mention.

Learning an accumulation of scholarly facts is highly desirable.

Browsing and aimless exploratory reading for fun is undesirable. The source of these last two concepts is apt to be the school, the educational system.

Abstract art is good. Here the people we regard as sophisticated are the originators of the value.

Communism is utterly bad. Here the government is a major source.

To love thy neighbor is the highest good. This concept comes from the church, perhaps from the parents.

Cooperation and teamwork are preferable to acting alone. Here companions are an important source.

Cheating is clever and desirable. The peer group again is the origin.

Coca-colas, chewing gum, electric refrigerators, and automobiles are all utterly desirable. This conception comes not only from advertisements, but is reinforced by people all over the world. From Jamaica to Japan, from Copenhagen to Kowloon, the "Coca-Cola culture" has come to be regarded as the acme of desirability.

This is a small and diversified sample of the myriads of conceived values which individuals often introject, and hold as their own, without ever having considered their inner organismic reactions to these patterns and objects.

COMMON CHARACTERISTICS OF ADULT VALUING

I believe it will be clear from the foregoing that the usual adult —I feel I am speaking for most of us—has an approach to values which has these characteristics:

The majority of his values are introjected from other individuals or groups significant to him, but are regarded by him as his own.

The source or locus of evaluation on most matters lies outside of himself.

The criterion by which his values are set is the degree to which they will cause him to be loved or accepted.

These conceived preferences are either not related at all, or not clearly related, to his own process of experiencing.

Often there is a wide and unrecognized discrepancy between the evidence supplied by his own experience and these conceived values.

Because these conceptions are not open to testing in experience, he must hold them in a rigid and unchanging fashion. The alternative would be a collapse of his values. Hence his values are "right"

—like the law of the Medes and the Persians, which changeth not.

Because they are untestable, there is no ready way of solving contradictions. If he has taken in from the community the conception that money is the *summum bonum* and from the church the conception that love of one's neighbor is the highest value, he has no way of discovering which has more value for *him*. Hence a common aspect of modern life is living with absolutely contradictory values. We calmly discuss the possibility of dropping a hydrogen bomb on Russia, but then find tears in our eyes when we see headlines about the suffering of one small child.

Because he has relinquished the locus of evaluation to others, and has lost touch with his own valuing process, he feels profoundly insecure and easily threatened in his values. If some of these conceptions were destroyed, what would take their place? This threatening possibility makes him hold his value conceptions more rigidly or more confusedly, or both.

THE FUNDAMENTAL DISCREPANCY

I believe that this picture of the individual, with values mostly introjected, held as fixed concepts, rarely examined or tested, is the picture of most of us. By taking over the conceptions of others as our own, we lose contact with the potential wisdom of our own functioning, and lose confidence in ourselves. Since these value constructs are often sharply at variance with what is going on in our own experiencing, we have in a very basic way divorced ourselves from ourselves, and this accounts for much of modern strain and insecurity. This fundamental discrepancy between the individual's concepts and what he is actually experiencing, between the intellectual structure of his values and the valuing process going on unrecognized within him—this is a part of the fundamental estrangement of modern man from himself. This is a major problem for the therapist.

RESTORING CONTACT WITH EXPERIENCE

Some individuals are fortunate in going beyond the picture I have just given, developing further in the direction of psychological maturity. We see this happen in psychotherapy where we endeavor to provide a climate favorable to the growth of the person. We also see it happen in life, whenever life provides a therapeutic climate for the individual. Let me concentrate on this further maturing of a value approach as I have seen it in therapy.

In the first place, let me say somewhat parenthetically that the therapeutic relationship is *not* devoid of values. Quite the contrary. When it is most effective, it seems to me, it is marked by one primary value; namely, that this person, this client, has worth. He as a person is valued in his separateness and uniqueness. It is when he senses and realizes that he is prized as a person that he can slowly begin to value the different aspects of himself. Most importantly, he can begin, with much difficulty at first, to sense and to feel what is going on within him, what he is feeling, what he is experiencing, how he is reacting. He uses his experiencing as a direct referent to which he can turn in forming accurate conceptualizations and as a guide to his behavior. Gendlin has elaborated the way in which this occurs.[3] As his experiencing becomes more and more open to him, as he is able to live more freely in the process of his feelings, then significant changes begin to occur in his approach to values. It begins to assume many of the characteristics it had in infancy.

INTROJECTED VALUES IN RELATION TO EXPERIENCING

Perhaps I can indicate this by reviewing a few of the brief examples of introjected values which I have given, and suggesting what happens to them as the individual comes closer to what is going on within him.

> The individual in therapy looks back and realizes, "But I *enjoyed* pulling my sister's hair—and that doesn't make me a bad person."
>
> The student failing chemistry realizes, as he gets close to his own experiencing—"I *don't* value being a doctor, even though my parents do; I don't like chemistry; I don't like taking steps toward

[3] E. T. Gendlin, *Experiencing and the Creation of Meaning* (New York: The Free Press of Glencoe, Inc., 1962); and "Experiencing: A Variable in the Process of Therapeutic Change," *American Journal of Psychotherapy,* XV (1961), 233–45.

being a doctor; and I am not a failure for having these feelings."

The adult recognizes that sexual desires and behavior may be richly satisfying and permanently enriching in their consequences, or shallow and temporary and less than satisfying. He goes by his own experiencing, which does not always coincide with the social norms.

He considers art from a new value approach. He says, "This picture moves me deeply, means a great deal to me. It also happens to be an abstraction, but that is not the basis for my valuing it."

He recognizes freely that this communist book or person has attitudes and goals which he shares as well as ideas and values which he does not share.

He realizes that at times he experiences cooperation as meaningful and valuable to him, and that at other times he wishes to be alone and act alone.

VALUING IN THE MATURE PERSON

The valuing process which seems to develop in this more mature person is in some ways very much like that in the infant, and in some ways quite different. It is fluid, flexible, based on this particular moment, and the degree to which this moment is experienced as enhancing and actualizing. Values are not held rigidly, but are continually changing. The painting which last year seemed meaningful now appears uninteresting, the way of working with individuals which was formerly experienced as good now seems inadequate, the belief which then seemed true is now experienced as only partly true, or perhaps false.

Another characteristic of the way this person values experience is that it is highly differentiated, or as the semanticists would say, extensional. As the members of my class of prospective teachers learned, general principles are not as useful as sensitively discriminating reactions. One says, "With this little boy, I just felt I should be very firm, and he seemed to welcome that, and I felt good that I had been. But I'm not that way at all with the other children most of the time." She was relying on her experiencing of the relationship with each child to guide her behavior. I have already indicated, in going through the examples, how much more differentiated are the individual's reactions to what were previously rather solid monolithic introjected values.

In another way the mature individual's approach is like that of the infant. The locus of evaluation is again established firmly within the person. It is his own experience which provides the value information or feedback. This does not mean that he is not open to all the evidence he can obtain from other sources. But it means that this is taken for what it is—outside evidence—and is not as significant as his own reactions. Thus he may be told by a friend that a new book is very disappointing. He reads two unfavorable reviews of the book. Thus his tentative hypothesis is that he will not value the book. Yet if he reads the book his valuing will be based upon the reactions it stirs in him, not on what he has been told by others.

There is also involved in this valuing process a letting oneself down into the immediacy of what one is experiencing, endeavoring to sense and to clarify all its complex meanings. I think of a client who, toward the close of therapy, when puzzled about an issue, would put his head in his hands and say, "Now what *is* it that I'm feeling? I want to get next to it. I want to learn what it is." Then he would wait, quietly and patiently, trying to listen to himself, until he could discern the exact flavor of the feelings he was experiencing. He, like others, was trying to get close to himself.

In getting close to what is going on within himself, the process is much more complex than it is in the infant. In the mature person it has much more scope and sweep, for there is involved in the present moment of experiencing the memory traces of all the relevant learnings from the past. This moment has not only its immediate sensory impact, but it has meaning growing out of similar experiences in the past.[4] It has both the new and the old in it. So when I experience a painting or a person, my experiencing contains within it the learnings I have accumulated from past meetings with paintings or persons, as well as the new impact of this particular encounter. Likewise the moment of experiencing contains, for the mature adult, hypotheses about consequences. "I feel now that I would enjoy a third drink, but past learnings indicate that I may regret it in the morning." "It is not pleasant to express forthrightly my negative

[4] Gendlin, *Experiencing and the Creation of Meaning.*

feelings to this person, but past experience indicates that in a continuing relationship it will be helpful in the long run." Past and future are both in this moment and enter into the valuing.

I find that in the person I am speaking of (and here again we see a similarity to the infant) the criterion of the valuing process is the degree to which the object of the experience actualizes the individual himself. Does it make him a richer, more complete, more fully developed person? This may sound as though it were a selfish or unsocial criterion, but it does not prove to be so, since deep and helpful relationships with others are experienced as actualizing.

Like the infant, too, the psychologically mature adult trusts and uses the wisdom of his organism, with the difference that he is able to do so knowingly. He realizes that if he can trust all of himself, his feelings and his intuitions may be wiser than his mind, that as a total person he can be more sensitive and accurate than his thoughts alone. Hence he is not afraid to say—"I feel that this experience (or this thing, or this direction) is good. Later I will probably know *why* I feel it is good." He trusts the totality of himself.

It should be evident from what I have been saying that this valuing process in the mature individual is not an easy or simple thing. The process is complex, the choices often very perplexing and difficult, and there is no guarantee that the choice which is made will in fact prove to be self-actualizing. But because whatever evidence exists is available to the individual, and because he is open to his experiencing, errors are correctable. If this chosen course of action is not self-enhancing this will be sensed and he can make an adjustment or revision. He thrives on a maximum feedback interchange, and thus, like the gyroscopic compass on a ship, can continually correct his course toward his true goal of self-fulfillment.

SOME PROPOSITIONS REGARDING THE VALUING PROCESS

Let me sharpen the meaning of what I have been saying by stating two propositions which contain the essential elements of this viewpoint. While it may not be possible to devise empirical tests of each proposition in its entirety, each is to some degree capable of being tested through the methods of science. I would also state that though the following propositions are stated firmly in order to give them clarity, I am actually advancing them as decidedly tentative hypotheses.

1. *There is an organismic base for an organized valuing process within the human individual.*

It is hypothesized that this base is something the human being shares with the rest of the animate world. It is part of the functioning life process of any healthy organism. It is the capacity for receiving feedback information which enables the organism continually to adjust its behavior and reactions so as to achieve the maximum possible self-enhancement.

2. *This valuing process in the human being is effective in achieving self-enhancement to the degree that the individual is open to the experiencing which is going on within himself.*

I have tried to give two examples of individuals who are close to their own experiencing: the tiny infant who has not yet learned to deny in his awareness the processes going on within; and the psychologically mature person who has relearned the advantages of this open state.

There is a corollary to this second proposition which might be put in the following terms. One way of assisting the individual to move toward openness to experience is through a relationship in which he is prized as a separate person, in which the experiencing going on within him is empathically understood and valued, and in which he is given the freedom to experience his own feelings and those of others without being threatened in doing so.

This corollary obviously grows out of therapeutic experience. It is a brief statement of the essential qualities in the therapeutic relationship. There are already some empirical studies, of which the one by Barrett-Lennard is a good example, which give support to such a statement.[5]

[5] G. T. Barrett-Lennard, "Dimensions of Therapist Response as Causal Factors in Therapeutic Change," *Psychological Monographs: General and Applied,* LXXVI, No. 43 (1962), 1–36.

PROPOSITIONS REGARDING THE OUTCOME OF THE VALUING PROCESS

I come now to the nub of any theory of values or valuing. What are its consequences? I should like to move into this new ground by stating bluntly two propositions as to the qualities of behavior which emerge from this valuing process. I shall then give some of the evidence from my own experience as a therapist in support of these propositions.

3. *In persons who are moving toward greater openness to their experiencing, there is an organismic commonality of value directions.*

4. *These common value directions are of such kinds as to enhance the development of the individual himself, of others in his community, and to make for the survival and evolution of his species.*

It has been a striking fact of my experience that in therapy, where individuals are valued, where there is greater freedom to feel and to be, certain value directions seem to emerge. These are not chaotic directions but instead have a surprising commonality. This commonality is not dependent on the personality of the therapist, for I have seen these trends emerge in the clients of therapists sharply different in personality. This commonality does not seem to be due to the influences of any one culture, for I have found evidence of these directions in cultures as divergent as those of the United States, Holland, France, and Japan. I like to think that this commonality of value directions is due to the fact that we all belong to the same species—that just as a human infant tends, individually, to select a diet similar to that selected by other human infants, so a client in therapy tends, individually, to choose value directions similar to those chosen by other clients. As a species there may be certain elements of experience which tend to make for inner development and which would be chosen by all individuals if they were genuinely free to choose.

Let me indicate a few of these value directions as I see them in my clients as they move in the direction of personal growth and maturity.

They tend to move away from façades. Pretense, defensiveness, putting up a front, tend to be negatively valued.

They tend to move away from "oughts." The compelling feeling of "I ought to do or be thus and so" is negatively valued. The client moves away from being what he "ought to be," no matter who has set that imperative.

They tend to move away from meeting the expectations of others. Pleasing others, as a goal in itself, is negatively valued.

Being real is positively valued. The client tends to move toward being himself, being his real feelings, being what he is. This seems to be a very deep preference.

Self-direction is positively valued. The client discovers an increasing pride and confidence in making his own choices, guiding his own life.

One's self, one's own feelings come to be positively valued. From a point where he looks upon himself with contempt and despair, the client comes to value himself and his reactions as being of worth.

Being a process is positively valued. From desiring some fixed goal, clients come to prefer the excitement of being a process of potentialities being born.

Perhaps more than all else, the client comes to value an openness to all of his inner and outer experience. To be open to and sensitive to his own *inner* reactions and feelings, the reactions and feelings of others, and the realities of the objective world—this is a direction which he clearly prefers. This openness becomes the client's most valued resource.

Sensitivity to others and acceptance of others is positively valued. The client comes to appreciate others for what they are, just as he has come to appreciate himself for what he is.

Finally, deep relationships are positively valued. To achieve a close, intimate, real, fully communicative relationship with another person seems to meet a deep need in every individual, and is very highly valued.

These then are some of the preferred directions which I have observed in individuals moving toward personality maturity. Though I am sure that the list I have given is inadequate and perhaps to some degree inaccurate, it holds for me exciting possibilities. Let me try to explain why.

I find it significant that when individuals are prized as persons, the values they select do not run the full gamut of possibilities. I do not find, in such a climate of freedom, that one person comes to value fraud and murder and thievery, while another values a life of self-sacrifice, and another values only money. Instead there seems to be a deep and underlying thread of commonality. I dare to believe that when the human being is inwardly free to choose whatever he deeply values, he tends to value those objects, experiences, and goals which make for his own survival, growth, and development, and for the survival and development of others. I hypothesize that it is characteristic of the human organism to prefer such actualizing and socialized goals when he is exposed to a growth-promoting climate.

A corollary of what I have been saying is that in *any* culture, given a climate of respect and freedom in which he is valued as a person, the mature individual would tend to choose and prefer these same value directions. This is a highly significant hypothesis which could be tested. It means that though the individual of whom I am speaking would not have a consistent or even a stable system of conceived values, the valuing process within him would lead to emerging value directions which would be constant across cultures and across time.

Another implication I see is that individuals who exhibit the fluid valuing process I have tried to describe, whose value directions are generally those I have listed, would be highly effective in the ongoing process of human evolution. If the human species is to survive at all on this globe, the human being must become more readily adaptive to new problems and situations, must be able to select that which is valuable for development and survival out of new and complex situations, must be accurate in his appreciation of reality if he is to make such selections. The psychologically mature person as I have described him has, I believe, the qualities which would cause him to value those experiences which would make for the survival and enhancement of the human race. He would be a worthy participant and guide in the process of human evolution.

Finally, it appears that we have returned to the issue of universality of values, but by a different route. Instead of universal values "out there," or a universal value system imposed by some group—philosophers, rulers, or priests—we have the possibility of universal human value directions emerging from the experiencing of the human organism. Evidence from therapy indicates that both personal and social values emerge as natural, and experienced, when the individual is close to his own organismic valuing process. The suggestion is that though modern man no longer trusts religion or science or philosophy nor any system of beliefs to *give* him his values, he may find an organismic valuing base within himself which, if he can learn again to be in touch with it, will prove to be an organized, adaptive and social approach to the perplexing value issues which face all of us.

SUMMARY

I have tried to present some observations, growing out of experience in psychotherapy, which are relevant to man's search for some satisfying basis for his approach to values.

I have described the human infant as he enters directly into an evaluating transaction with his world, appreciating or rejecting his experiences as they have meaning for his own actualization, utilizing all the wisdom of his tiny but complex organism.

I have said that we seem to lose this capacity for direct evaluation, and come to behave in those ways and to act in terms of those values which will bring us social approval, affection, esteem. To buy love we relinquish the valuing process. Because the center of our lives now lies in others, we are fearful and insecure, and must cling rigidly to the values we have introjected.

But if life or therapy gives us favorable conditions for continuing our psychological growth, we move on in something of a spiral, developing an approach to values which partakes of the infant's directness and fluidity but goes far beyond him in its richness. In our transactions with experience we are again the locus or source of valuing, we prefer those experiences which in the long run are enhancing, we utilize all the richness of our cognitive learning and functioning, but at the same time we trust the wisdom of our organism.

I have pointed out that these observations lead to certain basic statements. Man has within him an organismic basis for valuing. To the extent that he can be freely in touch with this valuing process in himself, he will behave in ways which are self-enhancing. We even know some of the conditions which enable him to be in touch with his own experiencing process.

In therapy, such openness to experience leads to emerging value directions which appear to be common across individuals and perhaps even across cultures. Stated in older terms, individuals who are thus in touch with their experiencing come to value such directions as sincerity, independence, self-direction, self-knowledge, social responsivity, social responsibility, and loving interpersonal relationships.

I have concluded that a new kind of emergent universality of value directions becomes possible when individuals move in the direction of psychological maturity, or more accurately, move in the direction of becoming open to their experiencing. Such a value base appears to make for the enhancement of self and others, and to promote a positive evolutionary process.

UTOPIA AND HUMAN BEHAVIOR*

B. F. Skinner

In *Walden Two*[1] I described an imaginary community of about a thousand people who were living a Good Life. They enjoyed a pleasant rural setting. They worked only a few hours a day—and without being compelled to do so. Their children were cared for and educated by specialists with due regard for the lives they were going to lead. Food was good and sanitation and medical care excellent. There was plenty of leisure and many ways of enjoying it. Art, music, and literature flourished, and scientific research was encouraged. And it seemed to me that life in Walden Two was not only good but feasible—within the reach of intelligent men of goodwill who would apply principles then emerging from the scientific study of human behavior. Some readers thought I was writing with tongue in cheek, but I was actually quite serious.

To my surprise, the book was violently attacked. *Life* magazine called it a "slander on some old notions of the 'good life.' . . . Such a triumph of mortmain, or the 'dead hand,' [as] has not been envisaged since the days of Sparta . . . a slur upon a name, a corrup-

* An earlier version of this article appeared in *The Humanist*, XXVII, No. 4 (1967), 120–22, 136–37. Reprinted by permission of *The Humanist*.

[1] B. F. Skinner, *Walden Two* (New York: The Macmillan Company, 1948).

tion of an impulse." In *The Quest for Utopia*[2] Negley and Patrick agreed that sooner or later "the principle of psychological conditioning would be made the basis of the serious construction of utopia . . . ," but found they were quite unprepared for "the shocking horror of the idea when positively presented. Of all the dictatorships espoused by utopists," they continued, "this is the most profound, and incipient dictators might well find in this utopia a guide book of political practice." And Joseph Wood Krutch soon devoted a substantial part of his *The Measure of Man* to an attack on what he called my "ignoble utopia." [3] The controversy has grown more violent and more puzzling as the years pass.

There are probably many reasons for the current revival of interest in utopian speculation. I doubt that the pattern is set when, as one psychoanalyst has suggested, "in need of and in despair for the absent breast, the infant hallucinates the fulfillment and thus postpones momentarily the overwhelming panic of prolonged frustration." It is possible that for many people a utopia serves as an alternative to the kind of political dream which is still suppressed by vestiges of McCarthyism. For some it may show dissatisfaction with our international stance; an experimental community is a sort of domestic Peace Corps. Whatever the explanation, there is no doubt of a strong tendency to scrutinize our way of life, to question its justification, and to consider alternatives.

But this is also an anti-utopian age. The modern classics—Aldous Huxley's *Brave New World* [4] and George Orwell's *Nineteen Eighty Four*[5]—describe ways of life we must be sure to avoid. George Kateb has analyzed the issue in *Utopia and Its Enemies*[6]—a title

[2] G. Negley and J. M. Patrick, *The Quest for Utopia* (New York: Schuman, 1952).

[3] J. W. Krutch, *The Measure of Man* (Indianapolis: The Bobbs-Merrill Co., Inc., 1953).

[4] A. Huxley, *Brave New World* (Garden City, N.Y.: Doubleday & Company, Inc., 1932).

[5] G. Orwell, *Nineteen Eighty Four* (London: Secker & Warburg, 1949).

[6] G. Kateb, *Utopia and Its Enemies* (New York: The Free Press of Glencoe, Inc., 1963).

obviously based on Karl Popper's *The Open Society and Its Enemies,*[7] which was itself an early skirmish in the war against utopia. The strange thing is the violence. One of Plato's characters calls his *Republic* "a city of pigs," but never before have dreams of a better world raised such a storm. Possibly one explanation is that now, for the first time, the dreams must be taken seriously. Utopias are science fiction, and we have learned that science fiction has a way of coming true.

UTOPIAN TECHNIQUES

We can take a step toward explaining why Utopia now seems within reach by looking at some classical examples. In his *Republic* and in parts of other dialogues, Plato portrayed a well-managed society patterned on the Greek city-state. He suggested features which would presumably contribute to its success, but he put his faith in a wise ruler—a philosopher-king who, as philosopher, would know what to do and, as king, would be able to do it. It is an old and a not very honorable strategy: when you do not know what should be done, assume that there is someone who does. The philosopher-king was to patch up a defective governmental design as the need might arise.

There are those—among them theologians—who argue that the next great utopian vision was the Christian heaven. St. Augustine developed the theme in his *City of God.* It was certainly a good life based on the highest authority, but important details were missing. Everyone who went to heaven was to be happy, but it was not clear just why. No one, in fact, has ever portrayed a very interesting heaven. St. Augustine's mundane version set the pattern for the monastic communities of early Christianity, but it would be hard to defend it as a good life. The monastery was a transitory state to which men turned with assurance that it was to be followed by a better life in a world to come.

Plato hoped to find the good life *sub homine,* and St. Augustine

[7] K. Popper, *The Open Society and Its Enemies* (London: Routledge & Kegan Paul Ltd., 1945).

sought it *sub deo.* It remained for Thomas More to propose that it might be found *sub lege.* More was a lawyer, and history had begun to show the importance of charters, constitutions, and other agreements which men might make among themselves in order to live peacefully together. The title of his book, *Utopia,* which gave the name to this kind of speculation, has an ambiguous etymology. The Greek root of Utopia denotes a place, but the prefix means either good or nonexistent—or possibly, and cynically, both. Within a century another lawyer, Francis Bacon, had extended More's appeal to reason in his fragmentary utopia, *The New Atlantis,* in which he also looked to government and law—although he suggested that scientists might be called on as advisers. (The scientific institution he described—Solomon's House—was in fact the model on which the Royal Society was soon founded.)

But was law and order the answer? Erasmus thought not. He supported More's utopian vision, but he had reservations. Reason might contribute to the good life, but it was a mistake to overlook other things. Erasmus was amused by the fact that More's name was the Latin root for "fool," and he whimsically defended his friend by writing *The Praise of Folly.* Government, he said, is all very well, but were it not for the folly of sex no one would be born, and were it not for the folly of appetite no one would survive, to be governed.

It was not long before further doubt was cast on the necessity or sufficiency of law and order. Round-the-world voyagers returning from the South Seas brought back stories of a good life which flourished without benefit of civilization on the European pattern. Men were peaceful and happy although completely ignorant of Western morals and with little or no visible government. Diderot developed the theme in his *Supplement to the Voyage of Bougainville*—for example, in the amusing scene in which a Catholic priest and a Tahitian chief discuss sexual morality. Jean-Jacques Rousseau took a stronger line: government was not only unnecessary, it was inimical to the good life. Natural man—the noble savage—was wise and good; government corrupted him. Here were the beginnings of a philosophy of anarchy which still finds a place in utopian speculation.

(The South Seas proved that natural man was not only good but self-sufficient. Governments made men dependent upon other men, but the shipwrecked sailor, aided by the abundant resources of a tropical isle, could be master of all he surveyed. A special kind of utopian writing began to take shape when Robinson Crusoe put the solitary good life to the test. Frontier America offered many opportunities to the individual *coureur de bois,* and the theme was still strong in the middle of the nineteenth century when Henry David Thoreau built his own tropical island on the shores of Walden Pond.)

Exaggerated reports of life in the South Seas led to a rash of idyllic utopias, many of them set in the tropics. And now, for the first time, such a world seemed feasible. It is true that the Greeks dreamed of Arcadia, which was a real place, and proposals to found a utopia were occasionally made (according to Gibbon, the Emperor Gallienus was on the point of offering the philosopher Plotinus a captured city so that he might try Plato's experiment when, perhaps fortunately for Plotinus, the emperor was called away on emergencies of state), but More and Bacon were not drawing blueprints; they were simply describing societies with which contemporary life might be compared. The South Seas, however, were real, and life on that pattern could therefore be taken seriously. Etienne Cabet's *Voyage en Icarie*[8] was one of the most popular of the idyllic utopias, and Cabet actually came to America in the 1850s planning to set up Icaria on the Red River in Texas. He died in St. Louis, Missouri, but a community on the Icarian principle survived for some time in the Middle West.

It was the idyllic type of utopia which Karl Marx attacked. To portray a good life was one thing, to bring it about quite another. In this sense Marx was anti-utopian, but he had his own vision, and it was not entirely unrelated to the South Sea idyll. It was possible that human happiness might be traced not so much to the absence of government as to an abundance of goods. Nature could not always be counted upon to supply what men needed to be happy in the style of the South Seas, but man would provide for himself if he were able. A Utopia hinged on economic principles.

The notion had been developing for a long time. Goods were

[8] E. Cabet, *Voyage en Icarie* (Paris: Bureau du Populaire, 1848).

essential to the good life, but where were they to be found? Bacon had argued that science was power, and the technology which he advocated and which began to emerge in the seventeenth century seemed a possible answer. If men were not producing the wealth they needed to be happy, it was because they did not know how. Science would come to the rescue. The great encyclopedia of Diderot and D'Alembert was to have this effect. Many recipes, formulae, and systems for the production of wealth were trade, guild, or family secrets. Publish them and men would go busily to work.

Marx thought he saw another reason why men were not producing the wealth they needed for happiness: the means of production were being sequestered by selfish people. The good life would follow when the tools of production were made available to everyone. This was the solution emphasized in nineteenth-century utopias, exemplified in England by William Morris's *News From Nowhere*[9] and in the United States by Edward Bellamy's *Looking Backward.*[10] The doctrine that the good life will follow when each has been supplied "according to his need" is scriptural: it is St. Augustine, not St. Karl. It has remained, of course, a strong utopian theme: technology is to solve all our problems by making everyone affluent. A few years ago Mr. Khrushchev announced that before long all food, clothing, and housing in Russia would be free. The good life was just round the corner.

An irritating problem survived. Given both the skills and the means, men may still not produce wealth. Nineteenth-century theorists found it necessary to appeal to a natural compulsion to work. William Morris describes a man looking for work, not to earn money but simply to express a need. When I once asked a Russian economist why men will work when all food, clothing, and housing are free, he replied with a confident smile, "For the common good," but that is by no means certain. "To each according to his need" must be balanced by "from each according to his ability"—an assignment which has so far proved to be beyond the reach of economics. And

[9] W. Morris, *News from Nowhere* (Boston: Roberts Brothers, 1890).
[10] E. Bellamy, *Looking Backward* (Boston: Ticknor and Company, 1888).

there are other kinds of goods which physical technology has not yet been able to supply. A more comprehensive behavioral science is needed.

BEHAVIORAL UTOPIAS

Rousseau knew that natural man would not solve all his problems, and Marx knew that economic principles would not suffice, and both took other characteristics of human behavior into account. A thoroughgoing behavioral utopia, however, was to wait for the twentieth century. The two leading figures of behavioral science in this century are Freud and Pavlov. Curiously enough, no utopian novel seems to have been written on Freudian principles. Pavlov was drawn into utopian speculation by accident. In 1917 the Russians needed the principle of the conditioned reflex to support their ideology, and they made Pavlov a national hero. If men were neither productive nor happy, it was the fault of their environments, and with the help of Pavlovian principles the Russian government would change the world and thus change men. But by the early 1930s the position had become embarrassing, as Bauer has noted.[11] The government had had its chance, and Russians were not yet conspicuously productive or happy. Pavlov went out of favor, and for twenty years Russian research on conditioned reflexes was confined to physiological processes not closely related to behavior. When the Second World War restored Russia's confidence, Pavlov returned as an intellectual hero, and the conditioned reflex was given another chance to build the good life.

Meanwhile, Aldous Huxley had explored the utopian implications of Pavlov's work in *Brave New World*. The book is, of course, a satire, heralding the threat rather than the promise of the conditioned reflex. There is nothing really new about conditioning, and Huxley seems to have known it. When Miranda in *The Tempest* exclaims, "Oh, brave new world that has such creatures in it," she is talking about creatures washed up on the shores of her utopian island who

[11] R. Bauer, *The New Man in Soviet Psychology* (Cambridge: Harvard University Press, 1952).

have come from the contemporary world.[12] For Huxley the conditioned reflex was a means of determining what the citizens of his brave new world should call good. It was important, for example, that certain kinds of workers should not be distracted by literature or nature, and babies who were destined to be workers of that sort were therefore appropriately conditioned. They were put on the floor of a laboratory near a few attractive books and bouquets. As they moved toward them and touched them, they were electrically shocked or frightened by loud noises. When they tried again, the treatment was repeated. Soon they were safe: they would never again take an interest in literature or nature. Pavlov had something to say about changing what is good about the good life because he had studied responses which have to do with what one feels. The good life which Huxley portrayed (with contempt, of course) *felt* good. It is no accident that it turned to an art form called the "feelies" and to drugs which produced or changed feelings.

The good things in life have other effects which need to be considered. One is the satisfaction of needs in the simple sense of the relief of distress. We sometimes eat to escape from the pangs of hunger and take pills to allay pain, and out of compassion we feed the hungry and heal the sick. For such purposes we design a culture which provides for each "according to his need." But satisfaction is a limited objective; we are not necessarily happy because we have everything we want. The word *sated* is related to the word *sad*. Simple abundance, whether in an affluent society, a benevolent climate, or a welfare state, is not enough. When people are supplied according to their needs, *regardless of what they are doing*, they remain inactive. The abundant life is a candy-mountain land or Cockaigne. It is the *Schlaraffenland*—the idler's land—of Hanns Sachs, and idleness is the goal only of those who have been com-

[12] The title of the French translation—*Le meilleur des mondes*—makes the same point. Pangloss assures Candide that it is *this* world, in spite of its diseases, earthquakes, and famines, which is the best of all possible worlds. Nor were Huxley's economics part of any world of the future; they were early Keynesian or Rooseveltian. His psychedelic drug "soma," though it anticipated other versions, was used in a manner not unlike that of alcohol on a lost weekend.

pulsively or anxiously busy. The important thing is what people are doing at the moment they receive the things which "satisfy their needs." The things called good strengthen any behavior which produces them.

The rewarding effects of goods have, of course, not gone unrecognized. The philosophy of hedonism asserts that men act to achieve pleasure and avoid pain, and utilitarianism applies the principle to economics, government, and religion. But philosophies are not enough. Wages, personal affection, and imprisonment are rewards and punishments, but predictions based on them frequently go awry. We may know how much a person is paid, but we cannot thereby predict how hard he will work. We may know that a child's parents are affectionate, but we still cannot tell whether the child will conform or rebel. We may know that a government is tyrannical or benevolent, but we cannot predict whether its people will submit or revolt. To explain our failures we invent other kinds of pleasures, pains, and needs—many of them quite fanciful.

The basic principle in hedonism or utilitarianism is not wrong, it is simply not precise. It is true that men work for money and affection and to avoid the whip, and that they pursue happiness and seek relief from pain. At a comparable level of analysis it is true that water boils when heated, freezes when chilled, runs down hill, and soaks into a sponge. Both sets of facts are useful and may be important in the early stages of a science, but neither remains important for very long in either an effective technology or a precise analysis.

A further step is to learn more about the kinds of consequences which serve as rewards or punishments and to create new kinds, possibly through Pavlovian conditioning. But the important thing is not the quantity or nature of pleasures and pains, or of their sources. What we need to know is exactly what a man is *doing* when he "maximizes pleasure" or "minimizes pain"—how, in other words, so-called rewards and punishments are contingent upon his behavior. This is the field of operant conditioning (not to be confused with the conditioned reflexes of Pavlov). An experimental analysis of contingencies of reinforcement has made it possible to predict and control behavior with surprising precision in a wide variety of circumstances. The facts and principles it has uncovered are obviously relevant to the design of social systems.

The curious thing is that contingencies of reinforcement have so long been overlooked. Yet this fact is perhaps only an example of the principle of operant conditioning itself. It may be that men go straight to the things which make life good simply because they are reinforced for doing so. Food, sex, security, the approval of one's fellow men, works of art, music, and literature—these are the things men want and act to get, and therefore the things they mention when they are asked to describe a world in which they would like to live. The significant fact is that *they seldom mention what they are to do to get them.* They specify a better world simply as they wish for it, dream of it, or pray for it, giving no thought to the manner of their getting it.

It may be argued that contingencies of reinforcement become less and less important as men do less and less to get the things they want. Food, shelter, and protection from predators and enemies were once secured only through long hours of exhausting and often dangerous labor. But the invention of clothing, housing, agriculture, and weapons has changed all that, and the acts of invention have been reinforced by the change. It may eventually be unnecessary to do more than push a button (an almost effortless electronic button at that) to solve such problems. That will be little more than wishing, and contingencies can then, indeed, be ignored. But that day is not yet here, nor are all contingencies so easily disposed of. Social reinforcers, for example, are particularly hard to analyze and arrange (in part just because they have been misused in solving the simpler problem; men have avoided hard or dangerous work by getting others to work for them, just as they got some of the good things in life by stealing them). And in any case, we still have to face the problem of what men will do, and enjoy doing, when it is not necessary to do anything. We are just beginning to appreciate the significance of the problem of leisure.

In throwing fresh light on the contingencies of reinforcement under which men live, the experimental analysis of operant behavior has led to a technology of behavioral management foreshadowed by the "behavioral engineering" and the "cultural engineering" of *Wal-*

den Two. At the time the book was written (1945) these technologies were largely fanciful, but they have now been successfully realized in a number of different kinds of "communities" such as institutions for psychotics, homes for retardates, and traing schools for juvenile delinquents, not to mention standard classrooms. It is true that these communities are not composed of representative samples of the population at large, but they are not too far from communities in the utopian sense.[13]

A community may be thought of as a pilot experiment, similar to the pilot plant in industry or the pilot experiment in science, where principles are tested on a small scale to avoid the risks of size. It is no accident that utopias have usually been isolated geographically, since border problems can then be neglected, or that they have usually implied a break with tradition (symbolized in religious communities, for example, by a ritual of rebirth), since problems raised by conflicting cultures are then minimized. A community also has a special advantage over the world at large because practices can be more easily initiated there and the effects more clearly observed. Given these helpful simplifications and the demonstrated power of a behavioral technology, a successful utopia is not too hard to imagine. Why is it feared?

LIKING A WAY OF LIFE

A common objection to Walden Two (and no doubt to other utopias) goes like this: "I shouldn't like to live there. I don't mind doing the things the author is at pains to save me from doing, I don't like to do some of the things I should be expected to do, and I like to do things I could not do. Granted that life there meets many traditional specifications of the Good Life and compares favorably with existing cultures, it is still a world designed to please the author, and he is bound by his own culture, not mine. He would like to live there, of course, but he must not expect me to join him."

We "like" a way of life to the extent that we are reinforced by

[13] Some experiments in behavioral management are reported in R. Ulrich, T. Stachnik, and J. Mabry, *Control of Human Behavior* (Glenview, Ill.: Scott, Foresman & Company, 1966).

it. We like a world in which both natural and social reinforcers are abundant and easily achieved and in which aversive stimuli are either rare or easily avoided. Unfortunately, however, it is a fact about man's genetic endowment and the world in which he lives that immediate rewards are often offset by deferred punishments, and that punishments must often be taken for the sake of deferred rewards. To maximize net gains we must do things we do not like to do and forgo things we like. A culture cannot change these facts, but it can induce us to deal with them effectively. Indeed, this is its most important function.

It is not too often successful. A common practice, for example, is to extract rules from the prevailing contingencies, natural or social, and to make positive and negative reinforcers contingent upon the behavior of following them. The rule-following contingencies are often unskillfully designed, and members of a culture seldom take net consequences into account. On the contrary, they resist control of this sort. They object to what they are asked to do and either drop out of the culture—as hermits, hobos, or hippies—or remain in it while challenging its principles.

Contingencies of reinforcement which maximize net gains need to be much more effectively designed. Conditioned reinforcers can be used to bridge the gap between behavior and its remoter consequences, and supplementary reinforcers can be arranged to serve until remote reinforcers can be brought into play. An important point is that effective contingencies need to be programmed. That is, they are effective only when a person has passed through a series of intermediate contingencies. Those who have reached the terminal contingencies will be productive, creative, and happy—in a word, maximally effective. The outsider confronted with the terminal contingencies for the first time may not like them or be able to imagine liking them.

The designer must take something else into account which is still more difficult to bring to bear on the individual member. Will the culture *work?* It is a question which is clarified by the concept of a community as an experiment. A community is a thing, having a life of its own. It will survive or perish, and the designer must keep that fact in mind. The problem is that survival is often furthered by behavior which is not only not reinforced but may have punishing (even lethal) consequences. Phylogenic contingencies of survival supply examples. When a member of a herd of grazing animals spots the approach of a predator and utters a warning cry, the group is more likely to escape and survive, but the member who emits the cry calls attention to himself and may perish. Ontogenic contingencies of reinforcement work in the same way: a culture induces a hero to die for his country or a martyr for his religion.

Contingencies which promote survival are also usually badly designed. Something seems to be gained if the culture can be identified with a race, nation, or religious group, but this leads to jingoistic excesses. Contrived sanctions, positive and negative, are often spurious. The result is a different kind of dropout, who objects to taking the survival of a culture as a "value." The protest sometimes takes this form: "Why should I care whether my way of life survives or contributes to the way of life of the future?" An honest answer would seem to be, "There is no good reason, but if your culture has not convinced you that there is, so much the worse for your culture." The thoughtful person may inquire further. Why should the *culture* care whether it survives? Survival for what? How do we know that a culture is evolving in the right direction? Questions of this sort show a misunderstanding of the nature of evolution, biological or cultural. The processes of mutation and selection do not require, and may not provide, any advance plan of the state toward which they lead.

A well-designed culture is a set of contingencies of reinforcement under which members behave in ways which maintain the culture, enable it to meet emergencies, and change it in such a way that it will do these things even more effectively in the future. Personal sacrifice may be a dramatic example of the conflict of interests between the group and its members, but it is the product of a bad design. Under better contingencies behavior which strengthens the culture may be highly reinforcing. A jingoistic nationalism may be an easy way of underlining the good of a group, but the survival of a culture regarded simply as a set of practices, quite apart from those who practice them, can also be made the basis for a design. (It is significant that current discussions of survival are likely to speak of competition between ways of life rather than between nations or religions.) Here again effective contingencies must be programmed, and the terminal contingencies will not necessarily be "liked" by those who confront them for the first time.

The problem, in short, is not to design a way of life which will be liked by men *as they now are* but a way of life which will be liked by those who live it. Whether those who are not part of a culture like it may have a bearing on whether they join and therefore on the promotion of a new culture and possibly on the design of early features intended to attract outsiders or prevent the defection of new members. It has no bearing on the ultimate goodness of the design. It is nevertheless in its effects on human nature—on the genetic endowment of the species—that any environment, physical or social, is to be evaluated.

The man who insists upon judging a culture in terms of whether or not he likes it is the true immoralist. Just as he refuses to follow rules designed to maximize his own net gain because they conflict with immediate gratification, so he rejects contingencies designed to strengthen the group because they conflict with his "rights as an individual." He sets himself up as a standard of human nature, implying or insisting that the culture which produced him is the only good or natural culture. He wants the world he wants and is unwilling to ask why he wants it. He is so completely the product of his own culture that he fears the influence of any other. He resists change, like the child who said: "I'm glad I don't like broccoli because if I liked it, I'd eat a lot of it, and I hate it."

OBJECTIONS TO A DESIGNED CULTURE

Many of those who like a given way of life may still object to it if it has been deliberately designed. Suppose one of the critics of *Walden Two* were to happen upon a small isolated community where—to repeat our first paragraph—people were working only a few hours a day and without compulsion, children were being cared for and educated by specialists with due regard for the lives they were going to lead, food was good and sanitation and medical care excellent, and art, music, literature, and science flourished.

Would he not exclaim, "Here is the good life!" But then let him discover that the community was the product of an explicit design, and the spectre of the designer would spoil it all. Why?

Design implies control, and there are many reasons why we fear it. The very techniques are often objectionable, for control passes first to those who have the power to treat others aversively. The state is still identified with the power to punish, some religious agencies still claim to mediate supernatural punishments, and schoolboys are still caned. This is "control through fear," and we naturally fear it. Nonaversive techniques are available to those who can use positive reinforcement—a wealthy government can reinforce the behavior it wants instead of punishing the behavior it does not want—but the end state may still show exploitation.

The archetype of a nonexploiting controller is the benevolent dictator. We suspect him because we cannot imagine why he should control benevolently. Yet in some of the special communities we have noted, the contingencies which control the designer do not conflict with those he uses in his design. In the design of a ward in a hospital for psychotics, for example, the fact that patients will make fewer demands on the staff and yet display as much dignity and happiness as their pathology permits is enough to explain the behavior of the designer. If in a home for retarded children, aversive control is minimal and happiness and dignity therefore maximal, and if some of the children can learn enough to be able to live effectively in the world at large, these effects will be among the important reinforcers of those who design such a community. If juvenile delinquents behave well in a training school and at the same time acquire skills which will permit them to lead nondelinquent lives after they leave it, the design of such a culture can be explained. In each of these communities a way of life is designed for the good of those who live it and for the good of the designer, and the two goods do not conflict. Nevertheless, technologies of this sort are often opposed just because control is being exerted.

Democracy is an effort to solve the problem by letting the people design the contingencies under which they are to live or—to put it another way—by insisting that the designer himself live under the contingencies he designs. It is reasonable to suppose that he will not use aversive techniques if he himself will be affected by them or positive techniques which lead to exploitation if he himself will be exploited. But specialization is almost inevitable (minorities readily understand how difficult it is to keep the controller and the controllee in the same skin), and specialization implies special contingencies which are still open to suspicion.

One safeguard against exploitation is to make sure that the designer never controls; he refuses to put his design into effect himself or is forbidden to do so or—better still—dies. In *Walden Two* the protagonist, Frazier, has simply abdicated. (As an additional assurance that he exerts no current control, he was given what might be called negative charisma.) But he may still be feared. A particularly subtle kind of exploitation survives. No matter how benevolent he may be, or how far from the exercise of power, the designer gets credit for the achievements of the community, and the credit is taken from those who live in it. A ruler who discovers a better way of inducing people to behave well gets credit for an orderly society, but at the expense of those who live in it, who would be more admired if they behaved well in a disorderly society. A man who designs a better way of teaching gets credit for the benefits of improved education, but at the expense of the students, who would be more admired if they learned when badly taught or not taught at all. The industrialist who designs a better way of producing goods gets credit for increased production, but at the expense of the workers, who would get more credit for being efficient and enterprising under another system. A utopia as a completely managed culture seems to work a wholesale despoliation of this sort. Its citizens are *automatically* good, wise, and productive, and we have no reason to admire them or give them credit. Some critics have gone so far as to say that they have been robbed of their very humanity. Mr. Krutch has accused me of dehumanizing men, and C. S. Lewis entitled a book on this theme *The Abolition of Man.*

We admire people and give them credit for what they do in order to induce them to behave in admirable ways. As I have shown elsewhere,[14] we are particularly likely to do so when no other kind of

[14] B. F. Skinner, "Man," *Proceedings of the American Philosophical Society,* CVIII, No. 6 (December 1964).

control is available. When alternative practices are invented, or when the world changes so that the behavior at issue is no longer necessary, the practice of admiration is dropped. (It is a temporary measure, the weakness of which is suggested by the fact that we do not admire those who are obviously behaving well simply because they have been admired for doing so.) Admiration often supplements aversive control (we admire those who meet their responsibilities and hence need not be punished), and it may indeed represent an early form of an alternative practice, but it must eventually yield to other alternatives. As we come to understand human behavior and its role in the evolution of cultures, and practically the contingencies which induce men to design cultures, we must dispense with the practice of giving personal credit. But that step is disturbing for other reasons.

MAN AND HIS DESTINY

The notion of personal credit is incompatible with the hypothesis that human behavior is wholly determined by genetic and environmental forces. The hypothesis is sometimes said to imply that man is a helpless victim, but we must not overlook the extent to which he controls the things which control him. Man is largely responsible for the environment in which he lives. He has changed the physical world to minimize aversive properties and maximize positive reinforcements, and he has constructed governmental, religious, educational, economic, and psychotherapeutic systems which promote satisfying personal contacts and make him more skillful, informed, productive, and happy. He is engaged in a gigantic exercise of self-control, as the result of which he has come to realize more and more of his genetic potential. He has reached a very special point in that story. He is the product of an evolutionary process in which essentially accidental changes in genetic endowment have been differentially selected by accidental features of the environment, but he has now reached the point at which he can examine that process and do something about it. He can change the course of his own evolution through selective breeding, and in the not too distant future he will quite possibly change it by changing his chromosomes. The "value judgments" which will then be demanded are beginning to attract attention.

The point is that *we have long since reached a comparable stage in the evolution of cultures.* We produce cultural "mutations" when we invent new social practices, and we change the conditions under which they are selected when we change the environments in which men live. To refuse to do either of these things is to leave further changes in our culture to accident. But accident is the tyrant really to be feared. Adventitious arrangements of both genetic and environmental variables have brought man to his present position, but we must remember that they are responsible for its faults as well as its virtues. The very misuse of personal control to which we object so violently is the product of accidents which have made the weak subject to the strong, the dull to the sharp, the well-intentioned to the selfish. We can do better than that. By accepting the fact that human behavior is controlled—by things if not by men—we take a big step forward, for we can then stop trying to avoid control and begin to look for the most effective kinds.

Whether we like it or not, survival is the value by which we shall be judged. The culture which takes its survival into account is most likely to survive. To recognize that fact is not, unfortunately, to resolve all our difficulties. It is hard to say what kinds of human behavior will prove most valuable in a future which cannot be clearly foreseen. Nor is it easy to identify the practices which will generate the kinds of behavior needed, but here at least we have made some progress. The design of behavior to specification is the very essence of a technology derived from an experimental analysis.

The authors of the classical utopian literature proposed to achieve the good life they described in ways which are now seen to be inadequate, but the value of utopian thinking must not be underestimated. In a curious way it has always taken cultural evolution into account. It has scrutinized the sources of social practices, examined their consequences, and proposed alternatives which would presumably have more desirable consequences—and all in an experimental spirit characteristic of science.

In the long run, of course, we must dispense with utopian simplifications, for the real test of a culture is the world at large. (The anti-utopians, of course, are talking about that world too; they would scarcely be so violent about a community of a few hundred people.) And the persistent question about that test is this: Is it to be *our* culture which survives and contributes most to the culture of the future? We can point to certain reassuring features. We enjoy the advantages which flow from the very practice of changing practice; until recently we have been perhaps unique in our disposition to try new ways of doing things. We give thought to consequences. Our practice of asking whether something works or whether something else would work better is often criticized as a crude pragmatism, but it may prove to have been an important cultural mutation. We readily change practices because we are not greatly restrained by revelation or immutable decrees, and for similar reasons we are free to pursue a science of behavior. Above all, we have recognized the need for the explicit design of a way of life.

But not all signs are propitious. The contingencies of reinforcement which shape and maintain the behavior of the cultural designer are not yet very clear. Obvious economic contingencies bring yearly improvements in automobiles, for example, but there are no comparable forces at work to improve governmental and ethical practices, education, housing, or psychotherapy. The survival of the culture has not yet been brought to bear in a very effective way on those who are engaged in government in the broadest sense.

Another danger signal is anti-utopianism itself (the clarification of which may be one of the most important contributions of utopian thinking). Anti-utopian arguments are the utopian arguments of an earlier era; that is why we call them reactionary. At one stage in the evolution of a culture, for example, aversive control may be effectively centralized in a despotic government. The appropriate philosophy or literature which supports it may outlive its usefulness without losing its power and will continue to support those who oppose any change—say, to democratic practices. Something of the same sort is now happening with respect to the doctrine of individual freedom. In undermining despotic control it is important to convince the individual that the power to govern derives from him, that he can free himself of restraining forces, that he can make a unique contribution, and so on. This is done by calling him free and responsible, admiring him for meeting his responsibilities, and punishing him for failing to do so. The supporting philosophy or literature has remained effective. It is responsible for the current anti-utopianism which insists that individual freedom is the chief goal of a culture.

A scientific analysis of human behavior and of genetic and cultural evolution leads to a different position, in which the individual is not regarded as an origin or source. He does not initiate anything. Nor, of course, is it he who survives. (The doctrine of survival after death is a source of personal reinforcers appropriate only to an earlier design.) What survives are the species (Homo sapiens) and the culture. They are "above the individual" in the sense that they are responsible for him and outlive him. Nevertheless, a species has no existence apart from its members or a culture apart from the people who engage in its practices. It is only through effects on individuals that practices are selected or designed. If by "man" we mean a member of the human species with its unique genetic endowment, its human nature, then man is still the measure of all things. But it is a measure we can use effectively only if we accept it for what it is, as this is revealed in a scientific analysis rather than in some earlier conception, no matter how convincing that conception may have been made or how effective it may have proved to be in an earlier stage of the culture.

It has been argued that it was the well-governed city-state which suggested to the Greeks that the universe itself might show law and order and that in their search for the laws which governed it they laid the foundations of modern science. The problems of government have grown more difficult, and no modern state is likely to be taken as the model of a lawful system. It is possible that science may now repay its debt and restore order to human affairs.

HUMAN EXCELLENCE

John P. Anton

1

A society of men that multiplies its problems faster than it can solve them cannot be a happy one, although it evidently will not be an idle one. If this society happens also to equate the good life with the materially abundant life, it is destined to work itself to death, and its members perhaps will never experience the satisfactions of consummatory pleasures. In either case, such a society will soon show visible signs of sickness, and even if we hesitate to call it sick its members will no less suffer from an increasing deficiency in self-esteem and humaneness. And even if all the imaginative utopian thinking in the world and all technology were placed at its disposal, the possibility of turning itself into a happy society would continue to depend on whether it chose to alter significantly its value framework. The sickness of any such society is commensurate to the unhappiness generated by an inability on the part of its members to remove the difficulties that cause them to mistreat themselves and inflict unnecessary pain upon their dependents. I do not mean to say that any human society can be irremediably or absolutely sick; rather, what I intend to say is that none of our social systems today can point to its achievements as unqualified embodiments of the good life or of humanistic excellence.

It would be sheer folly to depreciate the significant attainments of modern man in the natural and biological sciences, the discoveries in the fields of medicine and techniques for restoring health, the methodological advances in the social sciences, and the development of remarkable working models for solving problems in social hygiene; just as it would be historical provincialism to refuse to recognize the genuine gains that mark the rich record of the arts since the end of the middle ages and, in particular, during the last hundred years. The major breakthroughs in the sciences, the arts, the social techniques, the therapeutical endeavors, the space explorations, and the expanding horizons of material resources are spectacular achievements destined to give our era a special place in the history of mankind. However, it cannot be overlooked that the ethical background of this phantasmagoric setting is permeated with a preoccupation with suffering and a persistence of guilt in the face of social injustice. The political and social revolutions, cultural upheavals, and intellectual manifestoes that have challenged the institutionalized values, and the sweeping diagnoses of men like Locke, Rousseau, Kant, Marx, Freud, and Dewey have contributed substantially to the passion for reform and revolution.

All men of good will have aimed at the alleviation of suffering. But in the case of the development of certain values, our tendency to remove suffering has taken the ubiquity of evil for granted, and has become so engrossed with the effects it wanted to produce that it has left these very values unprotected from banality. Take, for instance, the resultant prolongation of life with the aid of medical technology. The modern concern for health, though quite normal as such, while explaining our unprecedented support for the medical sciences, gave the desire to secure longevity for all men an inordinate preeminence. The recent and anticipated successes in organ transplants are opening a legal and moral Pandora's box, the complex aspects of which can cause a veritable revolution. The point is that it takes an affluent society with an abundance of means, money, and trained manpower to promote and attain longevity. The advantages of the "haves" over the "have-nots" are too obvious to debate; they point to a different issue in international affairs and cultural survival and also touch on the matter of dominance.

The concern for longevity cannot be explained solely on the basis of a natural need, because life has built in us the desiring of death as the end of a long journey well-spent and enjoyed. As an intense preoccupation it might also point to a survival of a religious belief in a secularized Christianity, serving its holders if not as a substitute for the defunct notion of immortality, at least as a way to assume a basic role which the Christian God so mysteriously exercised. However, whether longevity can be viewed in the light of the concept of the good life, and what relevant matters must be introduced for the proper analysis of this entire problem, are still moot questions. In the meantime longevity remains one of the basic objectives in our affluent culture and perhaps one of its unexamined assumptions. The recent successes of medicine in transplanting organs is already inviting critical discussion that will no doubt enable us to see how to change the character of longevity from a quantitative value into an integral component of the full and happy life.

2

Western society has been dominated during the last few centuries by an attitude that places high value on power and acquisitiveness. There has been a steady display of an uncontrolled passion for innovation. We may not all agree on our diagnoses of the ultimate motives that brought the present mood to the foreground of our social and political life, but few can deny that there are at least three basic factors: (1) the persistent obsession of modern man with the many faces of evil and suffering; (2) the strong desire to detect "problems" behind every aspect of our diverse institutions and modes of social and individual lives, to the point where a situation relatively free of problems is often branded as itself a "problem"; and (3) the reluctance to come to terms with the task that matters most: a bold investigation of the concept of the good life and of the necessary means to attain human happiness. To state the issue in a more direct way: we continue to rationalize our reluctance to define and translate into public and personal conduct enduring ways of securing a positive, joyful, and fulfilling conception of the good life. What is absent in our society is not genius or labor but true concern for *excellence.*

To define the problem of excellence is one of the basic goals of ethics. But we cannot solve the problem of virtue unless we first define our concept of the *good man.* To succeed in this quest is to make a significant contribution to human wisdom. When men are pressed to give honest answers and to rank their inquiries in some order of importance, none stands higher than a response to the questions, "What is happiness?" or "What is the good life?" In order that we may discuss the *good life* we need first to know what are our human materials, resources, limitations, aspirations, and prejudices. Furthermore we must appraise what we have accomplished culturally with our materials, traditions, inherited values, opportunities, and available talents. It is as important to know what our accomplishments have been, as it is to be aware of how and with what parts of our natures we have achieved them. It is conceivable that such an analysis might reveal that our present attainments have been reached by only a partial utilization and a distortion of our human potentialities.

That we have really shown a proper regard and concern for the elucidation of the idea of the *good life* may be seriously questioned. Perhaps we may label the modern outlook—one which we have been aiming at for centuries—as an "affluent" and/or "efficient" life. There is no reason why we cannot speak of kinds of "excellences" that accompany and are in fact needed to sustain this sort of life. These are worked out in the basic structure of social habits and provide a kind of "mean" which enables us to achieve the ultimate end that the efficient-affluent life sets for itself. Modern conceptions of the efficient-affluent life have espoused ideals and virtues such as righteousness, loyalty, obedience, obligation, responsibility, duty, freedom, equality, industriousness, efficient teamwork, creativity, and the like, but received their operative meaning under conditions of organized competitiveness. The result is that the human individual has been sacrificed on the altar of so-called Progress.

The prevailing conception of the good life—and I am speaking here primarily of the one developed in the industrialized societies of man—has suffered from a futile effort to preserve a hopeless mixture of its own prescriptions with inherited yet powerful ethical strains: the Hebrew ethic of "commandment" and the Christian ethic of "salvation," with its preoccupation with "grace" and "redemption," and the fixation on the virtues of "faith," "hope," and "charity." We are thus burdened with a composite ethic of social progressivism and an underdeveloped if not crude philosophy of pleasure. How, one may ask, could Western man, being a Christian for so long and borrowing so heavily from Biblical legalism, ever have developed an adequate theory of pleasure? Here was a range of conduct-potential which his religion told him to dislike, but which he could not—which he felt compelled to suspect, yet pursued at the same time with a vengeance. Add to this the modern imperative that one ought to "express oneself," and here are the ingredients out of which were concocted the hodgepodge which we innocently identify as "contemporary man."

There was a time when the religious life had so broadened its scope as to reduce the idea of the good life to a minor though indispensable theme. Yet even in the life of devotion the theme of human happiness, absorbed as it was by the salvational concern, was never completely silenced. Its fulfillment was merely postponed until after death. Preference for the future life in heaven dimmed the vision of the religious man when he looked at the evanescing moments of transient joys or when he lamented the abundant presence of evil in situations of lasting pain. Real happiness allegedly awaited the pious soul after the body was firmly encased in its grave. The good life, therefore, for the Western religious man (and for many in the East) has been a matter of serious concern but realizable only in an afterlife. What is in question about this conception of the human *end* is not that it denies the possibility of happiness, but whether it affirms its attainability under conditions that include bodily existence, what we ordinarily call "this life," the here and now, the only one that satisfies empirical tests. What is in doubt is whether the religious outlook can offer a genuine answer to the search for the good life, one that does not compromise our intelligence or diminish our natural human resources.

Lest the reader infer that I am indulging in wholesale condemnation and ready to declare cultural bankruptcy and total decadence, I hasten to state with confidence that we are going through a period of resurgent humanism. The kingdom of man is expanding steadily to all the corners of the globe. We are now witnessing the development of a radical shift in value orientation of human thinking that took centuries to gain its present momentum and force. The sciences and the arts have contributed immensely to this transformation, while the migration of ideas by means of rapid communication has made the new enlightenment available to all the people of the world. Some critics of the rising humanism no doubt view it as the deification of man, while others see it as the inevitable phase of total secularization bringing in its wake a host of evils, from cultural nausea to social suicide. This is not the place to expose the shortcomings of such critical reactions to the new humanism. What is more pertinent to our theme is the quality of ethical standards and the conception of the good life that the new humanism was expected to place at the pinnacle of a system of values.

A close inspection of the intellectual contours its supporters have followed in their efforts to clarify their thinking for themselves and their expected adherents reveals an ideological weakness in the approach that has been hitherto used. The difficulty with the new humanism, particularly in the United States, lies in the negligence in developing a solid support for the humanistic outlook: the science of the good life. In the absence of such theoretical foundation, the conception of the good life which humanism was trying to promote did not have the credentials of careful planning. The reason is that the spokesmen for the new humanism have been reluctant to consider carefully the problem of human excellence and to treat it apart from the dominant ideological factors and pressures of affluence and efficiency. The result is that this side of substantive ethics is still controlled by traditional religious values sufficiently "humanized" to soothe the consciences of the converts to humanism. Perhaps what I am attempting to identify here is the surreptitious presence in humanistic outlooks of supernatural ethics and religious conceptions of excellence which are ultimately incompatible with the ends of a thoroughgoing humanistic and naturalistic philosophy of man.

3

The survival of traditional elements in novel and emerging value systems is unavoidable and difficult to control when the assimilation of the old into the new actually occurs. Hence, it would be unfair to attribute the absence of a carefully formulated theory of human excellence suitable to the cultural climate of contemporary man exclusively to the undetected religious background of the defenders of recent humanism. The reluctance to come to grips with the problems which the quest for excellence poses has its roots partly in the modern interpretations of the place of the scientific method in ethics, and partly in the current views about human nature. The former points to the demand to keep ethical generalizations as open and provisional in character as scientific hypotheses are, with the obvious merit of securing for ethics freedom from dogmatism and preserving in its conclusions the pluralistic and open-textured qualities of experience. The latter has permitted ethical theory to bypass thorny issues that attend the systematic effort to base substantive considerations and definite valuational prescriptions on a theory of man supported by rigorous scientific evidence. The consensus among behavioral scientists has been for quite some time that the nature of man is to have no nature. In the face of such formidable obstacles from the sciences of man, the science of the good life was never launched.

Given the widespread prevalence of this fluid conception of human nature, it is easy to see why efforts to formulate a system of humanistic excellences within the scope of substantive ethics have been by and large inhibited. It is common knowledge that professional philosophers have cautiously avoided even mentioning the existence of such an enterprise in their list of endeavors. The only course left open to the daring advocates of nonreligious substantive ethics was mainly one which led to a soft and scientifically inoffensive "open-textured" humanism of fulfillments. The philosophy on which the view rested was as derivative as the utilitarian and pragmatic features which constituted its basic appeal. What has been missing all along was the bold effort needed to give the new humanism the respectable objectivity that only a science of the good life could provide. But in the absence of a firm foundation the gospel of plural fulfillments is subject to the same treatment given to loud manifestos and protean promises. Its appeal is more to our sentimentality than to our critical faculties. One thing is clear: the new humanism has demonstrated its power to persuade. What the time calls for is more wisdom. It is precisely on this point that the humanism of classical Greece has demonstrated its relevance, but not every humanist is prepared to agree with me on this issue.

It might be instructive to cite a fellow humanist who not only expresses the spirit of humanistic optimism but asserts with assurance the superior outlook of modernity. Charles Frankel writes in his *The Case for Modern Man*:[1]

> No other age has gone so far in the belief that the spirit of modernity might be widely shared and that all men might participate in the goods and responsibilities of a modern civilization. The modern spirit of Athens was a brief and glimmering thing, arising in a society based on slavery. The modern spirit in fifteenth-century Italy was an aristocratic phenomenon, limited to an elite. But our own revolution of modernity has led to the unprecedented vision of a society in which the opportunity for personal achievement and social power would be generally diffused among men, and not limited to a selected group.
>
> (p. 200)

Frankel's social humanism of the visionary liberal democrat has a confident tone but suffers from the weakness of facile cures. What is left unmentioned is the presence of alienation, social estrangement, and the invisible forms of slavery—the new management, the technological elite, the hierarchies of power and decision-making groups, and above all, the threat of the machine. Without a redefinition of *excellence*, "personal achievement" often degenerates into self-promotion, and "social powers" into the will to control others. This, I take it, is hardly what humanism wants. It is hardly my intention to dampen the spirit of optimism or to undermine the foundations on which such expectations rest. My interests are primarily those of the difficult ally who is unwilling to accept favorable forecasts without some prior inspection of the quality of the

[1] New York: Harper & Row, Publishers, 1956.

relevant facts and some knowledge of the total landscape in which they fit.

Part of our present landscape is the random character which modernity was allowed to assume. It is one thing to praise our times for making opportunities for personal achievement and social power available to all groups and individuals, but it is quite another to leave the ends unspecified, and in certain cases even to undermine all basis for giving meaning to achievements. The criteria for identifying what powers and achievements are genuinely worth pursuing, and perhaps even dying for, have been left to fate, fortune, and force to work out. All this may have proved advantageous to maintaining the competitive mode of conduct, so vital to the preservation of an acquisitive society, and also to accentuating certain cherished aspects of individuality so central to the political pluralism of institutions in Western democracy. However, by refusing to embark on a sustained effort to formulate and deepen a reasonable conception of the criteria of achievement and excellence, we have permitted a cleavage between public conduct and personal quality that weakens the fabric of modern culture.

Perhaps the most astonishing deficiency of our time is the absence of an ethos of excellence. One cannot but wonder why it is that a society amazingly affluent and efficient in so many ways has been remiss in this vital area. What happened to the efficacy of our rational power? Why do personal opportunities so readily available to young men and women become a basis for psychic adventurism and abusive experiments in destructive groping? How is it that with so much ability to plan and control we have also succeeded in outsmarting our rational selves? If the salvational ideal of the religious man is open to criticism from the point of view advanced here, so is the technological conception of man and its concomitant idols of affluence and efficiency. Far be it from me to say that our modernity is so base that we should condemn it to the flames of hell. Actually, what I want to do here is to raise the question of how to identify certain deficiencies and how to effect the qualitative change that could lead to the needed educational reforms and cultural transformations to secure the good life. As for the uncritical admirers of the technological man who want to believe that we have all that is needed, we could confront him with the following questions: "Wherein lies the answer to the question of the good life?" and "Who is the good man in modern society and how would we recognize him if we saw him?" It is assumed, of course, that we would not seriously accept our glib uses of such adjectives as "excellent," "good," "perfect," and the like, as carrying with them the magic power of qualifying the subjects upon which they are generously bestowed. Just as an "excellent" businessman may not be an excellent man, so a "perfect" typist may not be a perfect woman.

It is important that we do not close our eyes to the failure of modernity to deal with the nature of human excellence. My impression is that we have not faced the issue for two basic reasons: The first is due to our faith in the efficacy of a modified Christian ethic to answer the "practical" side of virtue (to use an Aristotelian term). The second is due to our increasing dependence on the educational ideal of "scientific" enlightenment and its potency to inculcate appropriate rational habits capable of spontaneous application to the "passions" of the soul (to use a Platonic term). The potion was a product of cultural alchemy, not wisdom, and the effects were anything but health and happiness.

With all our enthusiasm for applying rational methods to everything that lies between business management and computerizing the humanities, and for all our faith in expensive training in higher education, we find it difficult to admit that a course in logic and scientific method no more makes us immune to irrational outbursts than training in the scientific laboratory satisfies the quest for self-knowledge. The dark forces of the soul are still enjoying a fine holiday. They have proved their potency in the ease with which they convert the noble search for erotic satisfactions into an abuse of sexuality; the need to associate with one's peers into tight group stratification by age brackets; the freeing of time from labor into gross inability to fill leisure with playfulness; the idealism of the quest for peace into pugnacious protests; the inventions to conquer distances into a game of speed and morbid traffic deaths; the tools of securing public safety into means of adaptation for organized crime; the need for significant enlargement of experience into a way of rebellion and excuse for thoughtless use of narcotics. One could give all this a light touch and turn it into a caricature. One could fill the canvas of modernity with disgruntled intellectuals, students in revolt, alienated artists, theologians writing gospels on the death of god, all joining hands in the dance of anxiety forming a faceless crowd drumming anti-rhythms on the brittle floor of existentialism. We may even call the spectacle a vision of super-anti-life. Our purpose is not to promote cute ways of castigating, but to offer appraisal and cultural critique. Hence if all the tendencies and practices which beset our gains in science and technology, especially the spread of drug use along with the cult of the eccentric and the frantic chase after the gimmick in the arts, are taken as indications of the quality of life we are fighting for, perhaps we should no longer call this "The Age of Anxiety." We may as well label it "The Age of Exhaustion."

4

The quest for the good life in its applied sense is the effort to realize in conduct the most desired possibilities of human nature. The effort to clarify what is meant by "most desired possibilities" and to express the outcomes of this endeavor as the distilled ideal of human excellence is the high mark and glory of classical Greek ethics. The lesson which the Greek experience has taught us provides an instructive point of contrast between the ancients and moderns. If we assume that it is the *artist*, the man who puts his creative intelligence and imagination to work in perfecting the possibilities of his medium, to whom we must turn for a revelation of what the good life means, then we have much to learn from ancient Greece. We must go to the sculptors and the poets, including Plato, and the other artists who gave us their vision of perfection as models for man to live by. If this is what *art* does for men, then when we turn to the arts of our own time in search for a set of statements and visions to *live by*, they may prove disappointing as *ideals and conceptions of human excellence*. Yet to the arts we must go, and I include here not just the *fine arts* and the *arts of fiction and poetry*, but all those enterprizes which do something with our natural and human resources: i.e., our industries, our political instrumentalities, and our social, economic, and cultural technologies. As arts of man they are also disclosures of what we really believe men ought to be doing when they are doing something with themselves. They tell us what skills are primary and what important ends they can serve. It is with these skills, promoted and perfected as indispensable parts of our industrial culture, that we can hope to understand what we really want to mean by the good life.

Despite its range and depth of wisdom—all the envisaged excellence expressed in its poetry and philosophy, drama and ethics—Greek culture slowly declined and succumbed to the dark forces from within and without. The admirable thing though about the Greeks is that even in the hour of decline they maintained their superb *autognosia,* self-consciousness. Every step of the way they recognized the impending doom creeping in and corroding the foundations of their cultural edifice. They looked the onrushing disintegration straight in the eye. They did not deceive themselves. Plato's obsession with cultural diagnosis is one of his outstanding features. He is at once honest and correct when he spots corruption, political exhaustion, or cheap rhetoric. When he wants to blame someone for what has happened to the city of Athens, he does not lash at the corrupt demagogues who come after Pericles, not even the sons of Pericles, for these are the symptoms and the effects. The responsible agents are Pericles himself, Themistocles, and Cimon, "who have filled the city with harbours and dockyards and walls and tributes instead of righteousness and temperance" (*Gorgias,* 519a). Strangely enough, twenty-five centuries later human beings are still emulating Pericles. Nowadays we call it "urban renewal." What we usually suppress in our story is our tacit tolerance of the forces that sustain the conditions which create the slums.

What was it in Greece that declined? This is an interesting question. What the Greek genius articulated as rational vision and as ethics of excellence was never literally lost. It has become the heritage of man, the kernel of our funded humanistic wisdom. The Greek failure, usually seen as a decline, was a gradual compromise of aspiration, an unwillingness to see virtue "steadily and whole," to promote its educational value within the community and demand its qualitative embodiment. "Failure of nerve," Gilbert Murray called it. What Plato insists actually happened is that cheaper ethical commodities replaced the ideal of excellence. The seductive power of Hellenistic softness was felt not only in the Agora, but also in the Academy.

Modern ethical humanism, in many ways continuous with that of the Greeks, has formulated the following principles:[2]

> 1. *Humanism is democratic.* It aims at the fullest possible development of every human being.
> 2. *Humanism seeks to use science creatively, not destructively.*
> 3. *Humanism is ethical.* It affirms the dignity of man and the right of the individual to the greatest possible freedom of development compatible with the rights of others.
> 4. *Humanism insists that personal liberty is an end that must be combined with social responsibility* in order that it shall not be sacrificed to the improvement of material conditions.
> 5. *Humanism is a way of life,* aiming at the maximum possible fulfillment, through the cultivation of ethical and creative living.
>
> The primary task of humanism today is to make men aware in the simplest terms of what it can mean to them and what it commits them to. By utilizing in this context, and for purposes of peace, the new power which science has given us, humanists have confidence that the present crisis can be surmounted. Liberated from fear, the energies of man will be available for a self-realization of which it is impossible to foresee the limit.

We may now return to the original quest: to what extent have we responded to the need to define *excellence* within the framework of the modern pursuits and understanding of human capabilities? One thing stands out quite clearly: it is a fact that our philosophers, sociologists, political scientists, and psychologists have not come anywhere close to producing for our time what Plato and Aristotle did for their age: a full-scale study of the range and kinds of excellences our cultural materials and *modus vivendi* afford. In other words, we have yet to see the modern *opus* that compares to Aristotle's *Nicomachean Ethics.* The reason why we have failed in our attempts, whenever such attempts were made, is that contemporary Western man finds it extremely difficult to admit that he has been

[2] From the Declaration of the Congress in Amsterdam on August 26, 1952.

a successful inquirer into everything except what matters most: his own self. To admit this publicly is most embarrassing, particularly to the Westerner, who as a Christian declares on the one hand that there are no barbarians on the earth and insists, on the other, on asserting his superior intellect and power on an earth inhabited by men, who in the major documents of Western political literature are said to have been "born equal." Pointing out this omission, *viz.*, how the fundamental problem of ethics has been neglected by Western man, makes him most uncomfortable. The longer the problem remains unanswered, the stronger the compulsion to postpone the solution. In the meantime, he will continue to make every effort to rationalize this deficiency by appealing to all sorts of ideological devices he can extract from the sciences of man. As a case in point, I have selected for illustration the enticing though fluid conception of human nature, allegedly supported by the findings of modern science, which Gardner Murphy belabors in his recent book *Human Potentialities.*[3] His conception of man supports, to be sure, a humanism, yet all it can do is to advocate an open-textured humanism of vague fulfillment and a freedom of choice full of spectacular displays of undelivered promises:

> . . . Far from believing, with the Aristotelian school of thought, that it is simply the business of man to realize his own nature, our thesis would be that there are many possible natures within him from which he must freely choose; there is no law of self-sufficient entelechy or self-fulfillment which could act in the manner of "hard-determinism." Rather, the potential self-fulfillments lie scattered there beyond the horizons and man, with all the wisdom which he can marshall, must strive to define them—and then to choose among them.
>
> (p. 301)

Now, we may ask, why is this panorama of invisible choices from among human natures desirable? It is evident to me that we have hardly been able to explore fully the possibilities of the familiar old-fashioned human nature. But we are ready, if attention is paid to Murphy's advice, to get on the bandwagon for a new safari into the jungle thickness of unperceived possibilities lurking behind

[3] New York: Basic Books, Inc., Publishers, 1958.

every tree trunk. It is Sartre who has said that the nature of man is that he has no nature! Small wonder that we have frustrated every effort to get at a science of the good life. Any effort to pursue this quest would amount to ingratitude to the unstable thing we call "human nature," and even worse it would mean that we are trying to restrict man's freedom for unlimited and infinite strivings. Yet the problem still remains that without a vision of the good life, a conception of excellences, of guiding idealities, we are at the mercy of change. Once this is done, we have really no choice but to turn this metaphysics of change into a boon and to worship change for its own sake. Hence, it is no mystery that all we have been able to produce in modern substantive ethics is a gospel of infinite fulfillments—that is, the preaching of a life of successes arranged *seriatim,* like a chain of highlights from an endless movie, where action follows action and scene follows scene, and where the rapidity of events keeps us so captivated that only exhaustion can defeat us, never boredom or rest.

We call this a concern for man. We think of it as a liberation of human nature from the restrictions of old-fashion essences. We even have a new semi-religious cult which consecrates cinematographic-like excitement of qualitative endlessness and change. Small wonder, again, that we can come to view our destiny as a life without destiny and a process which remains inconclusive, Protean, wishfully phantasmagoric. Our poetry and prose reflect this very notion: it is the literature of infinity in which men of all sizes have but one ambition: to be apostles of the Nietzschean mission to engage in the never-ending task of the transformation of all values.

5

I find it disturbing that we men of the twentieth century can speak of a genuine humanism and at the same time invite our fellow men to try to accomplish things that simply are not given to man to do. It is simply not within our power to perform the cosmic acrobatic acts of infinite exploratory tricks and unlimited choices. To try such superhuman things is to invite disaster and court endless frustration. We have worked out on the level of behavioral sciences a Madison Avenue technique which aims at selling a whole line of human goodies to greedy little people who are eager to get into the land of fantasy and who forget what their limitations are. Now this kind of humanism is not only false but dangerous. For it leads to a flagrant renunciation of rationality, despite its claiming of support from the sciences of man. The only thing that it does for man is to help him forget the awful situation into which he has fallen as a result of his imprisonment by the magnificent machines that he has created. Only the disparaged prisoner indulges in the escaping device of the dream of infinite freedom. The sober and unenslaved citizen needs no such subterfuges; he has the genuine thing: freedom within the context of determinate possibilities, or to put it differently, human nature and its limitations. He is the man who knows what he can and cannot do. He is the man whose reason does not fail him. He is the man of whom Euripides wrote, and who still embodies the spirit of the reasonable humanism, whether classical or contemporary:

> Happy is he who has knowledge
> That comes from enquiry. No evil stirs
> For his townsmen, nor gives himself
> To unjust doings,
> But surveys the unaging order
> Of deathless nature, of what is made,
> And whence, and how.
> In men of this kind the study
> Of base acts never finds a home.
>
> (Fragment 910 N)

The rationality Euripides speaks of is the sobriety of the wise man. It is the humaneness of reason which is sustained by self-respect: *aidōs*. One recalls at this point the strong sense of shame the Greeks could feel when caught in the snares of a contradiction. The *dramatis personae* in Plato's dialogues fear Socrates because of what he does to their arguments and to their dignity. Gorgias yields to young Polus when his own contradictory views have been exposed, and even the brash young Polus—the archetypal graduate student—must yield when caught in equivocations. Consistency is a mark of rational conduct. It is a fundamental fruit of character. Even Heraclitus had to give it a place in his world of flux. For

Aristotle it is synonymous with sanity. It is a persuasive principle of all scientific thinking and all significant discourse. Shame attends its denial. Truth without consistency is unthinkable, and so is excellence. And if the excellences are interrelated at all, as Plato believed, their mutual involvement cannot at any point of contact exhibit disharmony. Man is of a piece, his wholeness is a *sine qua non* for ethics. His wisdom depends upon it. This demanding basis of human personality somehow has failed to find its way in our conceptions and practice of human conduct.

We are practical and utilitarian. We are rational when we have to be, and irrational when convenient. Our multiple standards or lack of standards would have shocked the Greeks. The "self" of modern man as a set of roles is no doubt a more efficient tool, but it is as permissive as it is insidious. The primitive tribesman may have been barbarous and superstitious, but the modern man of multiple roles is as rapid as he is versatile and industrious. His multi-faced existence allows for every conceivable standard and can accommodate any combination of diverse elements, so that when one and the same person plays a number of incompatible roles we call it "adaptibility." Since the utility of this instrument is most rewarding in productive efforts, the question of "consistency of roles" recedes to the background. That judgments and decisions in one role of the same person run counter to what a man does and says in some other capacity is acceptable and raises no questions until such time as it no longer produces useful returns. Such is the *dominant* conception of personality, and one that accommodates the diverse needs of our age of technology. The other rival versions of human conduct are simply surviving in a parasitical fashion. The "individual" in a literal sense is lost. *The bearer of roles* is what has become of man, with the emphasis on *roles*. What, then, we ask, can we do to bring this fact within the framework of a new *humanism*? How can we formulate a set of excellences to suit the *role* conception of human personality? This, I take it, is the most dreadful problem that confronts man today: i.e., to humanize a conception of self that by way of efficient operations is committed to a mode of conduct that deindividualizes man. This, I take it, is the reason why we have turned ourselves into many-splintered things. And this is the reason why we cannot be "wise men," and, if you wish, why we are perhaps even unable to visualize and comprehend the meaning of the Euripidean fragment.

As long as modern man is more interested in abundance and efficiency for the sake of sustaining his mere technological existence, his values will be like himself: many-splintered things, collections of objects of disconnected desires. As long as this is the case, neither science, art, religion, nor political coercion can teach him what he needs most to learn. For even these activities suffer from the same ailment: they are institutionalized splinters of the fragmented self. Perhaps our times cannot promise wisdom. If a basic trait of wisdom is "the ability to see life steadily, and see it whole," then wisdom is not ours to attain. We have developed science and put new spirit into art and our other social institutions. But their cooperation is forced, like that of the commuters in a New York subway. If what I have said is not untrue, then we must admit that ours is a science without wisdom. The fact that we are still capable of some humaneness or that our hearts beat out of pity is something to be thankful for. Yet the motives of our technological science can as easily express themselves in the unabashed pursuits of military superiority as it can in the control of disease. Until we humanize our sciences, our arts, our religious and political codes, modern humanism is destined to remain lame. We will know it has come of age when it can shine forth with a bold vision of excellence. Only then we will be able to say that "The Age of Anxiety" has ended. If and when the new conception of human excellence comes, we may rest assured that it will not take the shape of a model of official conduct. Whatever else it be, it will assuredly carry with it the time-honored responsibility to subject its own credentials to the same critical examination as it has done in the case of the ideals men proposed in the past. Understood, even in this limited way, the quest for human excellence will remain an art, perhaps the highest art, as it was with the Greeks: an enlightened process to promote and sustain the attainment of what is best for men. In their efforts to succeed once again in this undertaking, men may discover how the artistic vision of the good life, mixed with wisdom, is still a basis for an adequate humanistic ethic. Whatever the road, there is at least one area in which our generation possesses unparalleled endowment and resourcefulness: how to secure abundance and excellence of means. The sole but formidable obstacle that remains to be conquered is how to overcome the lack of courage to meet the challenge of priorities of ends. Not until this is done will modern man be entitled to complete his claim to success in the tough business of ethics.

III

THE INDIVIDUAL: LAW, MORALITY, AND SOCIAL ORGANIZATION

THE ENFORCEMENT OF MORALS*

Ernest Nagel

1

An adequate account of the different ways in which moral principles enter into the development, the operation, and the evaluation of legal systems would require an examination of a broad spectrum of difficult issues. Such an account is certainly not a task to which a relatively short paper can do justice, and the present paper is not an attempt to do the impossible. I am therefore restricting myself in it almost entirely to but one issue that arises in considering the relation of law to morality—to the question whether there is a sharply delimited domain of human conduct that is by its very nature excluded from justifiable legal control, and in particular whether a society is ever warranted in using the law to enforce what are held to be widely accepted moral rules. The question has a long ancestry in discussions of moral and political theory, and is closely related to issues raised in historical doctrines of natural law and inalienable rights. However, the question can be examined without reference to natural law theory, and in any case it is not simply of antiquarian interest, but is of vital interest to humanist writers. It is also directly relevant to a number of

* This article appeared in *The Humanist*, XXVIII, No. 3 (1968), 20–27. Reprinted by permission of *The Humanist*.

currently debated social problems, among others to problems created by changing attitudes toward euthanasia, obscenity, and deviant sexual practices; and it received considerable attention in recent years from legislators, judges, sociologists, and psychologists, as well as from philosophers and writers on jurisprudence.

Many current philosophical and jurisprudential discussions of the question I want to consider take as their point of departure a challenging essay by Lord Patrick Devlin—a distinguished British judge, who was for many years a Justice of the High Court, Queen's Bench, and subsequently a Lord of Appeal in Ordinary. Devlin's essay, entitled "The Enforcement of Morals" and published in 1959, tried to show that a fundamental principle to which many moral theorists subscribe and which had been recently invoked in support of certain recommendations for amending the English criminal law, is untenable—for reasons I will presently mention. Devlin's views have found some defenders, but have also been the subject of much severe criticism. Since my paper is for the most part a commentary on the main points in dispute between Devlin and his critics—especially H. L. A. Hart in the latter's *Law, Liberty, and Morality* (1963)—I must describe briefly the problem to which Devlin's essay was addressed, and the context in which the debate over his views has its locus.

In 1954, in response to widespread criticism of the provisions of the English criminal law dealing with prostitution and homosexual practices, a committee was appointed, headed by Sir John Wolfenden, to look into the matter and to recommend needed changes in the law. The Report of the Committee was issued in 1957, and proposed a number of modifications in the existing law relating to various kinds of sexual offenses. The factual findings and the detailed proposals of the Committee are not pertinent here. What is of interest is that the Wolfenden Committee based its recommendations on the view that

> . . . the function of the criminal law . . . is to preserve public order and decency, to protect the citizen from what is offensive or injurious, and to provide sufficient safeguards against exploitation and corruption of others, particularly those who are specially vulnerable because they are young, weak in body or mind, inexperienced, or in a state of special physical, official or economic dependence.

> It is not the function of the law [the report went on] to intervene in the private lives of citizens, or to seek to enforce any pattern of behavior, further than is necessary to carry out the purposes we have outlined.

Moreover, in recommending that solicitation of the young should continue to be punishable by law, but that "homosexual behavior between consenting adults should no longer be a criminal offence," the Wolfenden Report offered what it called a "decisive" reason, namely:

> . . . the importance which society and the law ought to give to individual freedom of choice and action in matters of private morality. Unless a deliberate attempt is to be made by society, acting through the agency of the law, to equate the sphere of crime with that of sin, *there must remain a realm of private morality and immorality which is, in brief and crude terms, not the law's business.* To say this is not to condone or encourage private immorality.[1]

Some of the Report's proposals were eventually adopted by Parliament. However, it is not my aim to examine either the merits of these recommendations or the recent history of English legislation. The question I do want to discuss is the adequacy of the general principle underlying the specific proposals of the Wolfenden Committee—that there is a realm of conduct which, irrespective of its morality or immorality, is not the law's business and by its very nature falls outside the legitimate concerns of the law. It is this principle that Devlin challenged on grounds that I will presently describe, even though he eventually expressed himself as being in agreement with some of the Report's specific recommendations; and it is largely to a critique of Devlin's stand on this principle that Hart's own book previously mentioned is devoted.

However, as the Wolfenden Report explicitly notes, the principle is stated by it only in brief and crude terms, without any attempt to articulate it clearly or to give supporting reasons for it. But there is little doubt that in its statement of the principle the Report was invoking the far more inclusive political doctrine which John Stuart Mill expounded at some length in his classic essay *On Liberty* (1859), and was simply applying that doctrine to the particular

[1] Patrick Devlin, *The Enforcement of Morals* (New York: Oxford University Press, 1965), pp. 2–3 [my italics]. All references to Devlin are to this book.

problem of the legal regulation of sexual practices. Accordingly, since both Devlin and Hart make constant reference to Mill's views on individual liberty, and since I want to discuss the principle espoused by the Wolfenden Committee when it is stated in its most general and influential form, it is desirable to quote the passage in which Mill expressed the central idea of his political philosophy. Mill declared that

> . . . The sole end for which mankind is warranted, individually or collectively, in interfering with the liberty of action of any of their number is self-protection. That the only purpose for which power can be rightfully exercised over any member of a civilized community, against his will, is to prevent harm to others. His own good, whether physical or moral, is not a sufficient warrant. He cannot rightfully be compelled to do or forbear because it will be better for him to do so, because it will make him happier, because, in the opinion of others, to do so would be wise, or even right. These are good reasons for remonstrating with him, or reasoning with him or persuading him, or entreating him, but not for compelling him, or visiting him with any evil in case he do otherwise. To justify that, the conduct from which it is desired to deter him must be calculated to produce evil to someone else. The only part of the conduct of anyone, for which he is amenable to society, is that which concerns others. In the part which merely concerns himself, his independence is, of right, absolute.[2]

Mill thus advanced a comprehensive rule for determining the limits of warranted interference with men's conduct through the use of *any* agency of social control and compulsion—not only through the operation of the law, whether civil or criminal, but also through other institutions, such as religious organizations, economic associations, or more temporary groups that may be formed to achieve particular ends. But in any event, the rule appears to provide a firm support for the recommendations of the Wolfenden Report, for on the face of it the general principle Mill enunciates excludes the use of the machinery of the law to enforce what the Report calls "private morality."

Nevertheless, the principle is not as determinate as it is often

[2] J. S. Mill, *Utilitarianism, Liberty, and Representative Government* (New York: Dutton, 1950, Everyman's Library edition), p. 73.

alleged to be; and it is debatable whether, in view of the complications involved in attempts to apply it to concrete cases, it suffices to define categorically a realm of conduct that is inherently outside the scope of the law. I propose to enter into this debate, by reviewing some of the problems confronting a doctrine such as Mill's that seeks to circumscribe the area of conduct into which no measure of social control can be justifiably introduced. I am afraid that little if anything I have to say will be unfamiliar, for the problems have been repeatedly canvassed; nor do I have a neat resolution for the controversy over the legal enforcement of morals, for if I am right there can be no wholesale answer to the question. But I hope that by distinguishing several issues that are often confounded, I will succeed in placing the controversy in clearer light.

2

Mill offers two formulations—a broader and a narrower one—for his principle to distinguish between conduct that does and conduct that does not fall within the scope of permissible social control. *1.* According to the broad formulation, a person's actions are matters for legitimate social scrutiny only if they are of "concern" to others, but not if they "merely concern himself." On this criterion for deciding on the justifiability of social control, the relevant question to ask is not whether an action is performed in private (e.g., within the walls of a man's home) or in public, but whether it has *consequences* that in some way may affect other men. However, as has often been noted, there are few if any actions, even when done in private, which can be guaranteed to have no effects whatsoever on others than the actors themselves, so that on this formulation of the principle the domain of conduct that is reserved for the exercise of individual liberty is at best extremely narrow.

2. In point of fact, it is not upon this broad formulation of his principle that Mill relies, but on the narrower one according to which no adult member of a civilized community can be rightfully compelled to perform or to desist from performing an act, unless the action or the failure to perform it is likely to produce *harm* or

evil to others. But it takes little to see that even on this narrower injunction relatively few human actions are in principle excluded from social regulation. For example, a successful courtship may bring joy to a lover but acute anguish to his rival; the acclaim won by a musician or a scientist may produce self-destructive feelings of inferiority in those who do not achieve such distinction; and the vigorous expression of heterodox opinions may cause severe distress in those hearing them. Mill himself was fully aware of this, and qualified his principle by excluding from the class of actions he regarded as "harmful to others" (in the sense that they are subject to social control) many actions which, though they may affect others adversely by causing them physical or mental pain, he designated as merely "inconveniences"; and he maintained that society should tolerate such inconveniences, without attempting to control the actions that are their source, on the ground that this is the price men must be prepared to pay for the enjoyment of individual liberty.

However, the actions mentioned by Mill as productive of inconveniences only, rather than of serious evils that warrant social intervention, are in some instances highly idiosyncratic; but they frequently also reflect attitudes and standards of conduct that were held by many other men of Mill's time and station in life. Thus, he saw in the prohibition of the sale of alcoholic beverages an infringement of personal liberty, despite the social evils that excessive consumption of alcohol may produce; and he maintained that though a person attempting to cross an unsafe bridge should be warned of the risk he is incurring, no public official would be warranted in forcibly preventing the person from exposing himself to danger. But Mill also believed that society is justified in compelling parents to educate their young; that society is warranted in forbidding marriages between individuals who cannot prove that they have the means to support a family; and that contracts between persons should be prohibited, even if no one else is affected by the agreements, when the parties bind themselves to abide by some arrangement for an indefinite number of years, if not in perpetuity, without the power to revoke the agreement. On the other hand, though Mill had no doubt that society must tolerate fornication and gambling, he evaded answering the question whether a person should be free to be a pimp or a gambling-house keeper.

I do not believe it is possible to state a firm rule underlying Mill's selection of conduct for inclusion in the category of actions whose consequences for others are merely annoying inconveniences, rather than serious evils that justify the adoption of some form of social regulation. Indeed, it is obvious that his principle for demarcating a realm of behavior which is exempt from social control excludes virtually *nothing* from the scope of justifiable legal enactment—*unless* some agreement is first reached on what to count as "harm or evil to others." But two points are no less clear: (1) an explication of what is to be understood as harmful to others (in the sense of warranting some type of social control), cannot escape reference to some more or less explicit and comprehensive system of moral and social assumptions—more fully articulated than Mill's, whether or not the moral theory involved in the explication is one about which reasonable men may differ; and (2) even when agreement on general moral principles can be taken for granted, it may be difficult to decide whether a given type of conduct is indeed harmful to others, especially if the circumstances under which the actions take place may vary considerably, or if the number of individuals who engage in them should increase. Each point merits brief comment.

1. There are various categories of behavior whose harmful character (as distinct from its mere inconvenience to others) is in general not disputed in our society—for example, actions resulting in physical injury to others, or in depriving them of their possessions (as in theft); and no elaborate moral theory is usually invoked in justifying legal measures designed to prevent such actions. Nevertheless, the point needs stressing that though in a given society certain kinds of conduct seem unquestionably harmful, the classification of such conduct as harmful may, and frequently does, involve far-reaching assumptions about the public weal—assumptions which may be modified for a variety of reasons, and which may not be operative in other societies. This is evident when we reflect that even in our own society not all actions resulting in physical injury to others, or in depriving others of their possessions, are held to be harmful in the sense here relevant. Thus the infliction of physical injury on others in duels or feuds currently counts as action that is harmful, but the infliction of such injury is not so regarded when it occurs in boxing contests, in acts of self-defense, or in many though not in all surgical operations. Moral assumptions and considerations of social policy surely control this classification of such conduct; and there have been societies in which those actions have been classified differently.

Again, it is pertinent to ask in the case of alleged theft, whether the article taken from a person "really" belonged to him. But the question is not settled by ascertaining whether the article had been in the person's actual possession—even when we limit ourselves to those relatively simple cases in which it makes sense to suppose that the articles under consideration can literally be in someone's physical possession. For in the context in which the question is being asked, the relevant answer to it is that the article is (or is not) his *property*. However, as is now widely recognized, the notion of property is a *legal* category, whose meaning and content are defined by some system of laws, and generally vary with different societies. Thus, a piece of land or a painting is a man's property, and not simply something in his possession, if he acquired the item in ways prescribed by the laws of the land. Similarly, a song composed by a musician is his property, only if there are copyright laws which grant him certain rights in it; it is his property only during the period of the copyright, but not after it has run its course; and if the copyright laws are changed, the status of the song as property is also altered. Accordingly, whether an action is a case of theft, and hence liable to legal sanctions, depends on whether the article taken from a man or used without his consent is indeed his property. In consequence, to justify the use of any form of social duress for compelling a man to abstain from theft, one must in the end justify the social policy, and therefore the moral commitments, underlying the laws that determine what is to count as property.

Let me cite one further example. Suppose that one individual promises another to perform an action in return for some favor, and assume that if the promise is breached the person to whom it was given suffers a loss, but leaving it open whether or not anybody else does so. Is such a breach of promise a harmful action, or only an inconvenience? There are many promises whose breach is ignored by the laws of our society, even when the breach is the source of great inconvenience to others than the parties to the agreement—for example, in return for the use of a colleague's car, a promise to coach his son for an important examination. But there are also many promises whose breaking society does not ignore, and the legal institution of contract is a social technique for the enforcement of promissory agreements. On the other hand, complete freedom of contract is not an unmixed blessing, as Mill recognized; and there are a variety of contractual arrangements that are forbidden in many societies—for example, in our society no one is permitted to sell himself into slavery. Accordingly, society does not intervene into a large class of promises, even when their consequences affect others than those making them, but regulates other kinds of promises even when their results do not appear to impinge directly on those not party to them. Moreover, in placing restrictions on the freedom to contract, society seeks through the instrumentalities of the law to achieve what is assumed to be a greater social good, often in the form of establishing more equitable conditions for the exercise of individual liberty than could be achieved without the regulation of what at first blush seem to be purely "private transactions." As Morris R. Cohen observed, contract law has a function not entirely dissimilar from that of criminal law—for both seek to standardize conduct by penalizing departures from certain norms whose validation involves moral considerations.

In short, attempts such as Mill's to delimit *a priori* a realm of conduct that is exempt from social regulation presuppose a fairly detailed moral philosophy that articulates what actions are to count as harmful to others. But the discussion thus far has also suggested that unless individual freedom (as the maximum non-interference with individual conduct) is taken as an inalienable and *absolute* right, which must never be compromised or curtailed for the sake of satisfying other human needs (such as security from physical want or the development of human excellence), there appear to be no determinate and fixed limits to the scope of justifiable legal regulation of conduct.

2. I will return to this observation, but will now comment on the second point mentioned earlier. Given some explication of the notion of "harm (or evil) to others," the question whether a certain form of conduct is indeed harmful can be settled only by an empirical study of its consequences—it cannot be resolved by appeal to uncriticized custom or by considering that conduct in isolation from the enormously complex field of human relations in which it may actually be embedded. Now it may in principle be always possible to find reliable answers to such questions, and frequently such answers are undoubtedly available; but it is also the case that in a large number of instances adequate answers are difficult to obtain. Thus, to mention a trivial example, it appears quite certain in the light of current physical and biological knowledge that the kind of clothing a man wears, especially in the privacy of his home, has no "harmful" consequences for others—although in this connection some geneticists have raised (but as far I know not resolved) the question whether the kind of clothing men wear affects the mutation rate of genes, and therefore the character of the gene stock in inbreeding human populations. On the other hand, while there are reasons to believe that were artificial insemination practiced with the full consent of both parties to a marriage, no undesirable consequences would ensue either for those directly involved or for anyone else, no one can say today with any surety what effects the practice might have on the institution of the family or on current systems of property relations, if the practice were to become widespread. More generally, one should not ignore the truism that men's actions have unintended consequences; and Hegel was at least partly correct in his claim that the owl of Minerva spreads its wings only when the dusk begins to fall.

These comments must not be construed to mean that no deliberate changes in policies of social control in respect to some type of conduct should ever be made, until throughly competent knowledge becomes available concerning the likely consequences for others of the proposed policy change. For the desired knowledge can often be acquired only if the change is instituted; and refusal to make a change in the absence of fully adequate knowledge of its consequences is itself a policy decision, whose own likely effects may also be unknown to us. The conclusion that does emerge from these observations is that the distinction between conduct which is merely of concern to the actors (and hence, according to Mill, should be excluded from the scope of the law), and conduct that affects others adversely (and hence may be a proper subject for social regulation), cannot be drawn precisely or once for all, and may require repeated revision as conditions change and our funded knowledge grows.

3

In the light of these reflections, I want now to examine the grounds on which Lord Devlin defends the thesis that under certain conditions the enforcement of morals through the agency of criminal law is justifiable. Devlin bases his argument on the premise that a society is constituted not only by individuals with certain more or less concordant habits of behavior which they exhibit despite differences in personal aims, but also by a "community of ideas"—and in particular moral ideas "about the way its members *should* behave and govern their lives."[3] The shared convictions of a community concerning what is the "right" mode of conduct in such matters as marriage or the protection of life and property make up what he calls the "public morality" or the "moral structure" of a society. And according to him, every threat to the moral order of a society is a threat to the continued existence of the society itself. But since on this view "society has the right to make a judgment [on morals], and has it on the basis that a recognized morality is as necessary to society as . . . a recognized government," Devlin concludes that "society may use the law to preserve morality in the same way as it uses it to safeguard anything else that is essential to its existence" (p. 11). To be sure, he believes that "there must be toleration of the maximum individual freedom that is consistent with the integrity of society" (p. 16),

[3] Devlin, *op. cit.*, p. 9 [my italics].

and also recognizes that "the extent to which society will tolerate . . . departures from moral standards varies from generation to generation" (p. 18). He nevertheless maintains that if in the collective but deliberate judgment of society some practice, even though it is carried on in private, would be gravely injurious to the moral order were it to become widespread, then society may well be justified *as a matter of general principle* in outlawing that "immoral" conduct—just as it is justified in taking steps to preserve its government by enacting laws against treason (p. 13).

In my opinion, Devlin makes out a strong case for the impossibility of constructing a firm and enduring boundary between conduct that is a matter for individual conscience or private morality, and conduct that properly belongs to the domain of public concern. On the other hand, although I also think that his argument for the conclusion that under certain conditions the state may be justified in using the criminal law to enforce rules of public morality is *formally* sound, the conclusion rests on premises whose content is unclear and whose merits appear to me doubtful. Let me mention some of my difficulties.

1. In the first place, while Devlin seems to me to be on firm ground in claiming that every social system involves a community of certain ideas among its members, he does not explain what is to be understood by the "preservation" or "destruction" of a social order (as distinct from the persistence or collapse of its form of government), or just how one is to distinguish between the supposition that a social order has been *destroyed* and the supposition that there has been only a *change* in some pervasive pattern of institutionalized behavior. Much talk about societies continues to be based on the model which compares them to living organisms, and there is a point to the analogy. But the analogy is misleading if it leads us to assume that a society can die or flourish in the same sense that a biological organism does. Thus, an organism is usually defined to be a living one, if its so-called "vital functions"—such as respiration or assimilation of food—are being maintained, and to be dead when these processes no longer continue. In the case of societies, there are also processes (such as the maintenance of the food supply or the education of the young) that are sometimes compared with biological vital functions; and a society could therefore be said to have perished when these processes have ceased or, in the extreme instance, when its members have been permanently dispersed or have died without leaving any progeny. But with the possible exception of this extreme case, there appears to be no general agreement on the activities that *define* what it is for a society to be destroyed, rather than to be undergoing some alteration in its modes of organizing human conduct. It is therefore difficult to know what Devlin is asserting when he says that a given society fails or succeeds in preserving itself.

2. But secondly, Devlin does not establish his claim that any *specific tenet* of public morality—that is, any concrete moral conviction most members of a community ostensibly share about how men should behave and govern their lives in connection with some determinate activity, such as the conviction that marriages should be monogamous or that animals should not be mistreated—is *actually included* in the community of ideas whose maintenance he thinks is *indispensable* for the preservation of a social order. There is considerable evidence for believing that members of a given community do have in common a variety of more or less *general* ideas and attitudes as to what are the proper ways in which men should conduct themselves—for example, in many societies if not in all, most men expect others to have some regard for the sanctity of the lives of fellow members in their society, to comply with current laws or customs and the rules for changing them, or to make allowances for differences in the conduct of others because of differences in age and capacity. Moreover, it is quite plausible to hold that human societies would be impossible without the existence of a community of such general moral ideas. Indeed, given the biological makeup of men, their common desire to live and to procreate, and their dependence on the services rendered by others, it would be surprising if this were not so. But however this may be, and assuming that the notion of what it is for a society to be destroyed has been clarified, neither logic nor history appears to support the supposition that the violation of any *specific* moral standards prescribed by public morality may threaten the life of a social order.

An example may help to make the point clearer. Assume for the sake of the argument that no society can exist if it does not have *some* form of private property and if its members do not in the main believe that *some* ways of acquiring private property are morally justifiable. On this assumption, the preservation of a given society therefore requires the preservation of the conviction among its members that private ownership is morally warranted. But suppose further that in a particular society slavery is legal during a certain period, that during this period most of its members think it is entirely moral to own human beings as articles of private property, but that because of widespread protests against the institution of slavery the conviction that the institution is moral becomes seriously weakened. However, it does not follow from the basic premise of the argument that a weakening of *this* particular conviction is a threat to the social order—for on that premise, a necessary condition for the preservation of society is not the continued commitment to the morality of *human slavery,* but rather the continued commitment to the justifiability of *private property* in some form; and it is evident that this latter commitment is entirely compatible with the rejection of the former one.

Moreover, it is difficult to find in the historical record unquestionable instances in which a society collapsed because some one specific tenet of public morality had been extensively violated in actual practice, or because widely held beliefs in such a tenet had been seriously weakened. Human societies do not appear to be such fragile systems that they cannot survive a successful challenge to some established norm of conduct, nor are they such rigid structures that they are unable to accommodate their institutions to deviations from customary patterns of behavior and approved moral standards. Thus, since the end of the eighteenth century there have been radical transformations in the U.S. not only in commonly held ideas about the morality of numerous forms of private property but also in ideas about the morality of various kinds of individual conduct—including sexual practices, the treatment of children by parents, and personal attitudes toward members of minority groups. On the face of it, at any rate, the society (or societies) occupying the territory of the U.S. during this period has adjusted itself to these changes in public morality. Or ought one to say that because of these changes in what were at various times deeply felt moral beliefs, American society has failed to preserve itself? In the absence of an unambiguous characterization of what constitutes the American social order and what is essential for its continuing existence, the question can be answered to suit one's preference. But if this is so, Devlin's major premise is either unproven (so that it cannot serve as a reason for accepting his conclusion), or the premise is so indeterminate in its content that a conclusion different from the one he reaches can also be drawn from it. There is therefore only a farfetched analogy at best between violations of public morality and treasonable actions—for there is no clear sense in which a social order is alleged to be capable of destruction by the former, while the downfall of established political authority can sometimes be correctly attributed to the latter. Accordingly, to build a case for the enforcement of morals on this analogy, as Devlin in effect does, is to build it on insubstantial foundations.

3. There are two other related assumptions in Devlin's argument that require brief notice. (a) Although he recognizes that public morality is subject to change, he appears to have no doubt that there is a quite definite community of moral ideas among members of a society during a given period. Moreover, he believes that the content of this morality can be ascertained without inordinate difficulty; and he suggests that for the purposes of the law, immorality is what any so-called "right-minded person" or "man in the Clapham omnibus," any jury of twelve men or women selected at random, is presumed to consider to be immoral.

However, neither assumption seems to me plausible. There have been communities in the past, and there are still some in the present, which were exposed to but a single intellectual and moral tradition, and were unaccustomed to the exchange and criticism of ideas on diverse subjects; and for such communities, the notion of a public morality which directs the energies of men into definite channels makes good sense. But in large urban societies such as our own, in which divergent ideals of life (often based on new scientific discoveries) are widely discussed, and technological advances in medicine as well as industry create opportunities for developing novel patterns of behavior, men differ widely in what they take to be moral conduct, and are in some measure tolerant of moral ideals which they do not themselves espouse. It is by no means evident whether in such pluralistic societies the notion of a public morality as Devlin conceives it is strictly applicable. For example, he declares that "The Institution of marriage would be gravely threatened if individual judgments were permitted about the morality of adultery; on [this matter] there must be a public morality" (p. 10). But there is reason to believe that Devlin overestimates the extent of current agreement on the immorality of extramarital relations and, as recent discussions of proposed reforms of divorce laws suggest, it is by no means certain that there is a real consensus on the immorality of adultery upon which the persistence of the institution of marriage is alleged to be contingent. Moreover, the educative and transformation function of the law must not be ignored. For while the effectiveness of a legal system undoubtedly depends on the support it receives from the prevailing moral convictions of a community, the law does not simply *reflect* those convictions, but is in turn frequently an agency for *modifying* accepted moral standards. The supposition that even during a relatively brief period there is a determinate and clearly identifiable public morality is not a realistic picture of modern societies.

(b) Devlin's recommendation on how to ascertain the content of public morality is certainly simple. But is it also sound? If the moral convictions of members of contemporary societies are as diverse and divergent as I have suggested they are, what reason is there to suppose that the unanimous judgment of a dozen individuals drawn at random to serve on a jury is representative of the moral standards (for what may be to them an unfamiliar type of conduct) that are entertained throughout the society? Moreover, since on Devlin's view actions judged to be criminal because they are held to be immoral are actions which threaten the safety of the social order, why should we assume that twelve "right-minded persons" in a jury box—who presumably have no specialized training for evaluating the effects on others of some form of deviant behavior, nor the opportunity to undertake a careful study of what is already known about them—are more qualified to make competent judgments on what may be complex moral issues, than they are to pass on the significance of a scientific idea or on the merits of a surgical technique? To be sure, Devlin does not intend, as some commentators accuse him of doing, that the snap decisions of unreflective morality based on mere feelings of dislike and indignation are to be the ground on which a practice is to be made criminal. Thus he declares that "before a society can put a practice beyond the limits of tolerance [and hence make it a criminal offense], there must be a *deliberate* judgment that the practice is injurious to society" (p. 17, my italics). Nor does he maintain, as some critics have suggested, that "the arm of the law" should always be used to enforce society's judgment as to what is immoral—on the contrary, he presents a number of important prudential considerations which severely restrict the use of the criminal law to eradicate such immoral behavior. But except for the suggestion that a reliable symptom of practices that could destroy a social order is whether they generate in all members of a jury (and inferentially, in a majority of "right-minded persons" in the community) strong feelings of reprobation and intolerance (p. 17), he gives no reasons for supposing that the "deliberate judgments" he has emphasized as essential can be obtained by the procedure he recommends for ascertaining whether some conduct is detrimental to the social order; and he does not even discuss obvious alternatives to his proposal, such as the use of special commissions like the Wolfenden Committee itself to determine whether a practice does indeed have adverse consequences for society.

In short, while Mill's attempt to delimit a category of conduct which is permanently immune to legal as well as other forms of social control seems to me unsuccessful, I also think the difficulties I have been surveying make inconclusive Devlin's argument that the use of the criminal law to enforce moral standards for so-called "private conduct" is justifiable, if it is essential for preserving the integrity of society.

4

However, Devlin has been criticized by Professor Hart and others for disavowing Mill's doctrine on the justifiable limits of interference with an individual's freedom, and especially for dissenting from Mill's view that it is never warranted to compel a person to do or refrain from doing an action merely for the sake of his own welfare. I want therefore to examine briefly the main line of Hart's defense of Mill.

There are a variety of practices which are illegal in many countries, though on the face of it only the parties directly involved in their performance are affected by them. I have already noted that Mill himself approved a number of such laws; but despite the doubtful consistency of his doing so, he offered no clear rationale for them. On the other hand, Devlin maintains that the existence of such laws can be explained only on the assumption that they illustrate society's efforts "to enforce a moral principle and nothing else."[4] But Hart rejects this interpretation, and in his discussion of several examples of such laws, he proposes what he claims to be a different one. I will comment on his views as he presents them in the context of two examples.

1. Bigamy is a crime in many countries. Why should it be made a criminal offense, especially since in most jurisdictions a married man is doing nothing illegal if, while his legal spouse is alive, he lives with another woman and appears in public with her as husband and wife—*unless* he also goes through a marriage ceremony with her? Hart denies that the law is justified as an attempt "to enforce private morality as such"; and after expressing some sympathy for the view that the law might be "accepted as an attempt to protect religious feelings from offence by a public act desecrating the ceremony" of marriage, he declares that on this view "the bigamist is punished neither as irreligious nor as immoral but as a *nuisance*. For the law is then concerned with the *offensiveness to others* of his *public conduct,* not with the immorality of his private conduct."[5] However, as Devlin has been quick to note, a marriage ceremony can be performed in the privacy of some civil servant's office, with no one but the celebrants and their intimate friends any the wiser; and it is therefore difficult to make sense of Hart's suggestion that

[4] H. L. A. Hart, *Law, Liberty, and Morality* (Stanford, Cal.: Stanford University Press, 1963), p. 7.

[5] *Ibid.*, p. 41 [my italics].

the bigamist is being punished for the offense created by a public act, if there was no such offense because the bigamous marriage ceremony was in fact performed in private. But however this may be, there is a more fundamental point to be made. Hart is begging the question if he assumes that to judge an action to be a nuisance (or offensive) to others, is always independent of any judgment of its morality. If bigamous marriages and other kinds of public conduct are crimes in the U.S. because they are offensive to others in America, they are in fact not offensive to members of other cultures in which Puritanical conceptions of moral behavior are not widespread; and such examples make it difficult to deny that some conduct is regarded as a nuisance to others, just because those others regard the conduct as immoral. Accordingly, if bigamy is a crime because it is a nuisance to others, it does not follow without further argument that the bigamist is not punished because he is judged by society to be immoral, but for some other reason. This further argument Hart does not supply; but without it, he has not presented a clear alternative to the claim that in the case of bigamy at any rate the law is being used to enforce morals.

2. Hart's second example is as follows. With some exceptions such as rape, the criminal law does not permit, and has never permitted, the consent of the victim in a case involving physical injury to be used as an argument for the defense. But if one person makes a pact with a second to be beaten or even be killed, and the second one does as he promised, why should he be liable to punishment by society, if the parties to the agreement were of sane mind when they made it, both entered into it voluntarily, and no one else was injured by the transaction? (Incidentally, the example is not as grotesque as it may seem—it states the situation covered by current laws forbidding voluntary euthanasia.) To punish the defendant in this case is in direct conflict with Mill's explicit injunction that the law must never be used to interfere with an individual's freedom to make his "private" arrangements as he thinks best, even though as others see the matter his best interests are not served by his actions. Can this rule of law be justified? Devlin thinks it can, but only in one way; and he offers the justification that will by now be familiar, namely, that "there are certain standards of behavior

or moral principles which society requires to be observed; and the breach of them is an offence not merely against the person who is injured but against society as a whole." [6] On the other hand, Hart denies this claim. How then does he justify this rule of law? He maintains that "The rules excluding the victim's consent as a defence to charges of murder or assault may perfectly well be explained as a piece of *paternalism,* designed to protect individuals against themselves." [7] In consequence, he finds fault with Devlin for failing to distinguish between what Hart calls "legal moralism" (the doctrine he attributes to Devlin and which justifies the use of the law to enforce positive morality), and "legal paternalism" (the doctrine which justifies using the law to protect people against themselves). According to Hart, Mill's principle of liberty excludes legal moralism. But while in general he aligns himself with Mill's principle, he believes that if it is to accommodate such rules of law as the one under discussion, the principle must be amended; and although he does not present a formulation of the revised principle, he suggests that the amended form must be consonant with legal paternalism.

However, Hart does little to make clear just how legal moralism differs from legal paternalism, and that it is not a distinction without difference. He suggests that while a legal moralist justifies a law regulating actions that are allegedly not harmful to others, on the ground that its aim is to enforce morality "as such"—whatever the phrase "as such" may signify—a legal paternalist who endorses the law will justify it on the ground that it seeks to protect people against themselves. But is there a substantive difference here? Can there be a rule of law that is compatible with legal moralism, but which is necessarily excluded by legal paternalism? Could not any law that is said to be simply an attempt to enforce morality be also construed as an attempt to protect men against themselves? Thus, Hart argues that the English law making the sale of narcotics a criminal offense is not concerned with punishing the seller for his immorality, as legal moralists claim, but with protecting the would-

[6] Devlin, *op. cit.*, pp. 6–7.
[7] Hart, *op. cit.*, p. 31 [my italics].

be purchaser.[8] But could not a legal paternalist offer an analogous support for *any* law endorsed by a legal moralist? And conversely, in endorsing the narcotics law on the ground that it punishes the seller for his immorality, the legal moralist can maintain that the seller is immoral *because* he makes available to others an article that is harmful to its users.

Hart also defends the distinction between legal paternalism and legal moralism by claiming that the former is a sounder moral policy than the latter. For according to him, the conceptions of men's best interests that legal paternalism seeks to enforce are the products of what he calls "critical morality," while the conceptions legal moralism would enforce are the creatures of blind custom and unexamined tradition. If there is this difference, it is undoubtedly an important one. But even if there is, Hart's claim presupposes that the distinction between legal moralism and legal paternalism has already been established; and it assumes without argument that there is a unique system of critical morality which underlies the proposals of legal paternalism, and that this system is a sound one. It is plain, however, that many systems of critical morality have been developed, and that their conceptions of what is to men's best interests do not always agree. There is certainly no consensus even among deeply reflective men as to which system of critical morality is the most adequate one, so that legal paternalists are likely to differ among themselves as well as with legal moralists as to the rules that should guide men's conduct. It surely does not follow that because legal paternalism is based on a critical morality, its proposals for regulating men's actions are necessarily sounder than the proposals of legal moralists.

But however this may be, if legal paternalism is a justifiable policy in the law—as Hart appears to hold—its adoption as a principle of legislation destroys the possibility of establishing a permanent division between conduct that is only of private concern and conduct that is of legitimate public interest. Adoption of the policy certainly permits the introduction of legal controls at which Mill would have been aghast.

[8] *Ibid.*, p. 32.

5

I have taken much time to belabor the simple point that Mill's principle is not an adequate guide to legal and other forms of social control of men's behavior. My excuse for doing so is that the principle is still very much alive in current discussions of legal and social philosophy, as the controversy between Devlin and his critics makes evident. Moreover, though the limitations of Mill's views on liberty have been often noted, they stress an important component in a reasonable ideal of human life—a component that needs to be stressed, if it is not to be swept aside by more insistent demands directed to realizing other human aspirations. But while I think Mill overdid the stress, how the ideal of individual freedom can be adjusted to competing aspirations is to me a question of perennial interest.

Like Tocqueville, Mill feared some of the leveling tendencies in modern democracies, and was apprehensive of the intolerance that custom-bound and unenlightened majorities can exhibit toward new ideas, fresh sensibilities, and intellectual as well as artistic excellence. He prized these achievements above all else, and believed they are indissolubly linked with the possession of maximum individual freedom that is compatible with life in society as he knew it. He therefore sought to secure the continuance of these achievements; and his principle of liberty was not only an expression of his conception of the human good, but also a protective wall to safeguard its pursuit.

As in the case of other political philosophers who saw in the pursuit of a multiplicity of objectives a danger to the realization of what they prized highly, Mill thus made individual freedom an absolute good to which he formally subordinated all other objectives—though his actual evaluations of social practices and his recommendations of changes in them are not always consonant with his formal principle. However, the elevation of individual liberty to the rank of the supreme good is clearly arbitrary. Most men do not cherish personal freedom above all else, even after prolonged and careful reflection; and in any case, they prize other things as well—indeed, sometimes as indispensable to a satisfactory and well-ordered life—such as health, some measure of worldly success and security, friendship and family, achievement and recognition by one's peers, or influence in the affairs of men. Moreover, maximum personal freedom is in general neither a necessary condition for the realization of all other legitimate objectives, nor is it compatible with some of them.

Accordingly, since many different interests, some of which may be conflicting ones, must be recognized in dealing with social problems, and since no one interest dominates the others permanently and in all contexts, it does not seem possible to set fixed limits to justifiable legal control of men's conduct. On the other hand, though it is frequently claimed that a compromise must be effected between the interests involved in a given problem, how the compromise should be made and in conformity with what rules, are questions to which I know no satisfactory answer. To be sure, broad rules have been proposed for dealing with this issue—for example, that the domain of personal freedom should be diminished as little as possible, or that the compromise should be so made as to maximize the expected social utility. But the proposed rules are vague and do not carry us very far. For in the absence of effective techniques for assessing the relative importance (or the utilities) of the various interests involved in the problem, it is not clear how the rules are to be applied; and despite the development of modern decision theory, there is no prospect that the needed techniques will soon be available.

There is then no general answer to the question whether certain categories of actions should be legally controlled and whether certain standards of conduct should be legally enforced. The question can be resolved only case by case, and though the proposed answers cannot be guaranteed to be the best ones possible, they are often the best ones available. And I cannot do better by way of a conclusion to this reflection than to quote a brief passage from Learned Hand:

> We shall never get along in matters of large public interest, if we proceed by generalization, indeed, if you insist, by principles, put forward as applicable in all circumstances. . . . The only way that public affairs can be successfully managed is by treating each case

> by itself; even so, the trouble is far from ended. We must ask what a proposed measure will do in fact, how all the people whom it touches react and respond to it? . . . Then—and this the more difficult part—one must make a choice between the values that will be affected, for there are substantially always conflicts of group interest.[9]

[9] Learned Hand, *The Spirit of Liberty* (New York: Alfred A. Knopf, Inc., 1960), pp. 172–73.

SOCIAL PROTEST AND CIVIL DISOBEDIENCE*

Sidney Hook

In times of moral crisis what has been accepted as commonplace truth sometimes appears questionable and problematic. We have all been nurtured in the humanistic belief that in a democracy, citizens are free to disagree with a law but that so long as it remains in force, they have a *prima facie* obligation to obey it. The belief is justified on the ground that this procedure enables us to escape the twin evils of tyranny and anarchy. Tyranny is avoided by virtue of the freedom and power of dissent to win the uncoerced consent of the community. Anarchy is avoided by reliance on due process, the recognition that there is a right way to correct a wrong, and a wrong way to secure a right. To the extent that anything is demonstrable in human affairs, we have held that democracy as a political system is not viable if members systematically refused to obey laws whose wisdom or morality they dispute.

Nonetheless, during the past decade of tension and turmoil in American life there has developed a mass phenomenon of civil disobedience even among those who profess devotion to democratic ideals and institutions. This phenomenon has assumed a character

* This article was published originally as "Social Protest and Civil Obedience" in *The Humanist,* XXVII, Nos. 5–6 (1967), 157–59, 192–93. Reprinted by permission of *The Humanist.*

similar to a tidal wave which has not yet reached its crest. It has swept from the field of race relations to the campuses of some universities, subtly altering the connotation of the term "academic." It is being systematically developed as an instrument of influencing foreign policy. It is leaving its mark on popular culture. I am told it is not only a theme of comic books but that children in our more sophisticated families no longer resort to tantrums in defying parental discipline—they go limp!

More seriously, in the wake of civil disobedience there has occasionally developed *uncivil* disobedience, sometimes as a natural psychological development, and often because of the failure of law enforcement agencies especially in the South to respect and defend legitimate expressions of social protest. The line between civil and uncivil disobedience is not only an uncertain and wavering one in practice, it has become so in theory. A recent prophet of the philosophy of the absurd in recommending civil disobedience as a form of creative disorder in a democracy cited Shay's Rebellion as an illustration. This Rebellion was uncivil to the point of bloodshed. Indeed, some of the techniques of protesting American involvement in Vietnam have departed so far from traditional ways of civil disobedience as to make it likely that they are inspired by the same confusion between civil and uncivil disobedience.

All this has made focal the perennial problems of the nature and limits of the citizen's obligation to obey the law, of the relation between the authority of conscience and the authority of the state, of the rights and duties of a democratic moral man in an immoral democratic society. The classical writings on these questions have acquired a burning relevance to the political condition of man today. I propose briefly to clarify some of these problems.

To begin with I wish to stress the point that there is no problem concerning "social protest" as such in a democracy. Our Bill of Rights was adopted not only to make protest possible but to encourage it. The political logic, the very ethos of any democracy that professes to rest, no matter how indirectly, upon freely given consent *requires* that social protest be permitted—and not only permitted but *protected* from interference by those opposed to the protest, which means protected by agencies of law enforcement.

Not social protest but *illegal* social protest constitutes our problem. It raises the question: "When, if ever, is illegal protest justified in a democratic society?" It is of the first importance to bear in mind that we are raising the question as principled democrats and humanists in a democratic society. To urge that illegal social protests, motivated by exalted ideals are sanctified in a democratic society by precedents like the Boston Tea Party, is a lapse into political illiteracy. Such actions occurred in societies in which those affected by unjust laws had no power peacefully to change them.

Further, many actions dubbed civilly disobedient by local authorities, strictly speaking, are not such at all. An action launched in violation of a local law or ordinance, and undertaken to test it, on the ground that the law itself violates state or federal law, or launched in violation of a state law in the sincerely held belief that the state law outrages the Constitution, the supreme law of the land, is not civilly disobedient. In large measure the original sympathy with which the original sit-ins were received, especially the Freedom Rides, marches, and demonstrations that flouted local Southern laws, was due to the conviction that they were constitutionally justified, in accordance with the heritage of freedom, enshrined in the Amendments, and enjoyed in other regions of the country. Practically everything the marchers did was sanctioned by the phrase of the First Amendment which upholds "the right of the people peaceably to assemble and to petition the Government for a redress of grievances." Actions of this kind may be wise or unwise, timely or untimely, but they are not civilly disobedient.

They become civilly disobedient when they are in deliberate violation of laws that have been sustained by the highest legislative and judicial bodies of the nation, e.g., income tax laws, conscription laws, laws forbidding segregation in education, and discrimination in public accommodations and employment. Another class of examples consists of illegal social protest against local and state laws that clearly do not conflict with Federal Law.

Once we grasp the proper issue, the question is asked with deceptive clarity: "Are we under an obligation in a democratic community always to obey an unjust law?" To this question Abraham Lincoln is supposed to have made the classic answer in an eloquent address on "The Perpetuation of Our Political Institution," calling for absolute and religious obedience until the unjust law is repealed.

I said that this question is asked with deceptive clarity because Lincoln, judging by his other writings and the pragmatic cast of his basic philosophy, could never have subscribed to this absolutism or meant what he seemed literally to have said. Not only are we under no moral obligation *always* to obey unjust laws, we are under no moral obligation *always* to obey a just law. One can put it more strongly: sometimes it may be necessary in the interests of the greater good to violate a just or sensible law. A man who refused to violate a sensible traffic law if it were necessary to do so to avoid a probably fatal accident would be a moral idiot. There are other values in the world besides legality or even justice, and sometimes they may be of overriding concern and weight. Everyone can imagine some situation in which the violation of some existing law is the lesser moral evil, but this does not invalidate recognition of our obligation to obey just laws.

There is a difference between disobeying a law which one approves of in general but whose application in a specific case seems wrong, and disobeying a law in protest against the injustice of the law itself. In the latter case the disobedience is open and public; in the former, not. But if the grounds of disobedience in both cases are moral considerations, there is only a difference in degree between them. The rejection, therefore, of legal absolutism or the fetishism of legality—that one is never justified in violating any law in any circumstances—is a matter of common sense.

The implications drawn from this moral commonplace by some ritualistic liberals are clearly absurd. For they have substituted for the absolutism of law something very close to the absolutism of individual conscience. Properly rejecting the view that the law, no matter how unjust, must be obeyed in all circumstances, they have taken the view that the law is to be obeyed only when the individual deems it just or when it does not outrage his conscience. Fantastic comparisons are made between those who do not act on the dictates of their conscience and those who accepted and obeyed Hitler's laws. These comparisons completely disregard the systems of law involved, the presence of alternatives of action, the differences in the behavior commanded, in degrees of complicity of guilt, in the moral costs and personal consequences of compliance and other relevant matters.

It is commendable to recognize the primacy of morality to law but unless we recognize the centrality of intelligence to morality, we stumble with blind self-righteousness into moral disaster. Because, Kant to the contrary notwithstanding, it is not wrong sometimes to lie to save a human life; because it is not wrong sometimes to kill in defense to save many from being killed, it does not follow that the moral principles: "Do not lie!" "Do not kill!" are invalid. When more than one valid principle bears on a problem of moral experience, the very fact of their conflict means that not all of them can hold unqualifiedly. One of them must be denied. The point is that such negation or violation entails upon us the obligation of justifying it, and moral justification is a matter of reasons not of conscience. The burden of proof rests on the person violating the rules. Normally, we don't have to justify telling the truth. We do have to justify *not* telling the truth. Similarly, with respect to the moral obligation of a democrat who breaches his political obligation to obey the laws of a democratic community, the resort to conscience is not enough. There must always be reasonable justification.

This is all the more true because just as we can, if challenged, give powerful reasons for the moral principle of truth-telling, so we can offer logically coercive grounds for the obligation of a democrat to obey the laws of a democracy. The grounds are many and they can be amplified beyond the passing mention we give here. It is a matter of fairness, of social utility, of peace, or ordered progress, of redeeming an implicit commitment.

There is one point, however, which has a particular relevance to the claims of those who counterpose to legal absolutism the absolutism of conscience. There is the empirically observable tendency for public disobedience to law to spread from those who occupy high moral ground to those who dwell on low ground, with consequent growth of disorder and insecurity.

Conscience by itself is not the measure of high or low moral ground. This is the work of reason. Where it functions properly the democratic process permits this resort to reason. If the man of conscience loses in the court of reason, why should he assume that the decision or the law is mistaken rather than the deliverances of his conscience?

The voice of conscience may sound loud and clear. But it may conflict at times not only with the law but with another man's conscience. Every conscientious objector to a law knows that at least one man's conscience is wrong, *viz.*, the conscience of the man who asserts that *his* conscience tells him that he must not tolerate conscientious objectors. From this if he is reasonable he should conclude that when he hears the voice of conscience, he is hearing not the voice of God, but the voice of a finite, limited man in this time and in this place, and that conscience is neither a special nor an infallible organ of apprehending moral truth, that conscience without conscientiousness, conscience which does not cap the process of critical reflective morality, is likely to be prejudice masquerading as a First Principle or a Mandate from Heaven.

The mark of an enlightened democracy is, as far as is possible with its security, to respect the religious commitment of a citizen who believes, on grounds of conscience or any other ground, that his relation to God involves duties superior to those arising from any human relation. It, therefore, exempts him from his duty as a citizen to protect his country. However, the mark of the genuine conscientious objector in a democracy is to respect the democratic process. He does not use his exemption as a political weapon to coerce where he has failed to convince or persuade. Having failed to influence national policy by rational means within the law, in the political processes open to him in a free society, he cannot justifiably try to defeat that policy by resorting to obstructive techniques outside the law and still remain a democrat.

It is one thing on grounds of conscience or religion to plead exemption from the duty of serving one's country when drafted. It is quite another to adopt harassing techniques to prevent others from volunteering or responding to the call of duty. It is one thing to oppose American involvement in Vietnam by teach-ins, petitions, electoral activity. It is quite another to attempt to stop troop trains: to take possession of the premises of draft boards where policies are not made; to urge recruits to sabotage their assignments and feign illness to win discharge. The first class of actions fall within the sphere of legitimate social protest; the second class are implicitly insurrectionary since it is directed against the authority of a democratic government which it seeks to overthrow not by argument and discussion but by resistance—albeit passive resistance.

Nonetheless, since we have rejected legal absolutism we must face the possibility that in protest on ethical grounds individuals may refuse to obey some law which they regard as uncommonly immoral or uncommonly foolish. If they profess to be democrats, their behavior must scrupulously respect the following conditions:

First, it must be nonviolent—peaceful not only in form but in actuality. After all, the protesters are seeking to dramatize a great evil that the community allegedly has been unable to overcome because of complacency or moral weakness. Therefore, they must avoid the guilt of imposing hardship or harm on others who in the nature of the case can hardly be responsible for the situation under protest. Passive resistance should not be utilized merely as a safer or more effective strategy than active resistance of imposing their wills on others.

Secondly, resort to civil disobedience is never morally legitimate where other methods of remedying the evil complained of are available. Existing grievance procedures should be used. No grievance procedures were available to the southern Negroes. The Courts often shared the prejudices of the community and offered no relief, not even minimal protection. But such procedures *are* available in the areas of industry and education. For example, where charges against students are being heard such procedures may result in the dismissal of the charges not the students. Or the faculty on appeal may decide to suspend the rules rather than the students. To jump the gun to civil disobedience in bypassing these procedures is telltale evidence that those who are calling the shots are after other game than preserving the rights of students.

Thirdly, those who resort to civil disobedience are duty bound to accept the legal sanctions and punishments imposed by the laws. Attempts to evade and escape them not only involve a betrayal of the community, but erode the moral foundations of civil disobedience itself. Socrates' argument in the *Crito* is valid only on democratic premises. The rationale of the protesters is the hope that the pain and hurt and indignity they voluntarily accept will stir their fellow citizens to compassion, open their minds to second thoughts, and move them to undertake the necessary healing action. When, however, we observe the heroics of defiance being followed by the dialectics of legal evasion, we question the sincerity of the action.

Fourth, civil disobedience is unjustified if a major moral issue is not clearly at stake. Differences about negotiable details that can easily be settled with a little patience should not be fanned into a blaze of illegal opposition.

Fifth, where intelligent men of good will and character differ on large and complex moral issues, discussion and agitation are more appropriate than civilly disobedient action. Those who feel strongly about animal rights and regard the consumption of animal flesh as foods as morally evil would have a just cause for civil disobedience if *their* freedom to obtain other food was threatened. They would have no moral right to resort to similar action to prevent their fellow citizens from consuming meat. Similarly with fluoridation.

Sixth, where civil disobedience is undertaken, there must be some rhyme and reason in the time, place, and targets selected. If one is convinced, as I am not, that the Board of Education of New York City is remiss in its policy of desegregation, what is the point of dumping garbage on bridges to produce traffic jams that seriously discomfort commuters who have not the remotest connection with educational policies in New York. Such action can only obstruct the progress of desegregation in the communities of Long Island. Gandhi, who inspired the civil disobedience movement in the twentieth century, was a better tactician than many who invoke his name but ignore his teachings. When he organized his campaign of civil disobedience against the Salt Tax, he marched with his followers to the sea to make salt. He did not hold up food trains or tie up traffic.

Finally, there is such a thing as historical timing. Democrats who resort to civil disobedience must ask themselves whether the cumulative consequences of their action may in the existing climate of opinion undermine the peace and order on which the effective exercise of other human rights depend. This is a cost which one may be willing to pay but which must be taken into the reckoning.

These observations in the eyes of some defenders of the philosophy of civil disobedience are far from persuasive. They regard them as evading the political realities. The political realities, it is asserted, do not provide meaningful channels for the legitimate expression of dissent. The "Establishment" is too powerful or indifferent to be moved. Administrations are voted into office that are not bound by their election pledges. The right to form minority parties is hampered by unconstitutional voting laws. What does even "the right of the people to present petitions for the redress of grievances" amount to if it does not carry with it the right to have those petitions paid attention to, at least to have them read, if not acted upon?

No, the opposing argument runs on. Genuine progress does not come by enactment of laws, by appeals to the good will or conscience of one's fellow citizens, but only by obstructions which interfere with the functioning of the system itself, by actions whose nuisance value is so high that the Establishment finds it easier to be decent and yield to demands than to be obdurate and oppose them. The time comes, as one student leader of the civilly disobedient Berkeley students advised, "when it is necessary for you to throw your bodies upon the wheels and gears and levers and bring the machine to a grinding halt." When one objects that such obstruction, as a principle of political action, is almost sure to produce chaos, and that it is unnecessary and undesirable in a democracy, the retort is made: "Amen, if only this were a democracy, how glad we would be to stop!"

It is characteristic of those who argue this way to define the presence or absence of the democratic process by whether or not *they* get their political way, and not by the presence or absence of democratic institutional processes. The rules of the game exist to enable them to win and if they lose that's sufficient proof the game is rigged and dishonest. The sincerity with which the position is held is no evidence whatsoever of its coherence. The right to petition does not carry with it the right to be heard, if that means influence on those to whom it is addressed. What would they do if they received incompatible petitions from two different and hostile groups of petitioning citizens? The right of petition gives one a chance to persuade, and the persuasion must rest on the power of words, on the effective appeal to emotion, sympathy, reason, and logic. Petitions are weapons of criticism, and their failure does not justify appeal to other kinds of weapons.

It is quite true that some local election laws do hamper minority groups in the organization of political parties; but there is always the right of appeal to the Courts. Even if this fails there is a possibility of influencing other political parties. It is difficult but so long as one is free to publish and speak, it can be done. If a group is unsuccessful in moving a majority by the weapons of criticism, in a democracy it may resort to peaceful measures of obstruction, provided it is willing to accept punishment for its obstructionist behavior. But these objections are usually a preface to some form of elitism or moral snobbery which is incompatible with the very grounds given in defending the right of civil disobedience on the part of democrats in a democracy.

All of the seven considerations listed above are cautionary, not categorical. We have ruled out only two positions—blind obedience to any and all laws in a democracy, and unreflective violation of laws at the behest of individual consciences. Between these two obviously unacceptable extremes, there is a spectrum of views which shade into each other. Intelligent persons can differ on their application to specific situations. These differences will reflect different assessments of the historical mood of a culture, of the proper timing of protest and acquiescence, and of what the most desirable emphasis and direction of our teaching should be in order to extend "the blessing of liberty" as we preserve "domestic tranquility."

Without essaying the role of a prophet, here is my reading of the needs of the present. It seems to me that the Civil Rights Acts of 1964 and the Voting Acts of 1965 mark a watershed in the history of social and civil protest in the U.S. Upon their enforcement a great many things we hold dear depend, especially those causes in behalf of which in the last decade so many movements of social protest were launched. We must recall that it was the emasculation of the 15th Amendment in the South which kept the Southern Negro in a state of virtual peonage. The prospect of enforcement of the new civil rights legislation is a function of many factors—most notably the law-abiding behavior of the hitherto recalcitrant elements in the southern white communities. Their *uncivil,* violent disobedience has proved unavailing. We need not fear this so much as that they will adopt the strategies and techniques of the civil disobedience itself in their opposition to long-delayed and decent legislation to make the ideals of American democracy a greater reality.

On the other hand, I think the movement of civil disobedience, as distinct from legal protest, in regions of the country in which Negroes have made slow but substantial advances are not likely to make new gains commensurate with the risks. Those risks are that what is begun as civil disobedience will be perverted by extremists into uncivil disobedience, and alienate large numbers who have firmly supported the cause of freedom.

One of the unintended consequences of the two World Wars is that in many ways they strengthened the position of the Negroes and all other minorities in American political life. We do not need another, a third World War, to continue the process of liberation. We can do it in peace—without war and without civil war. The Civil Rights and Voting Acts of 1964 and 1965 are far in advance of the actual situation in the country where discrimination is so rife. Our present task is to bring home and reinforce popular consciousness of the fact that those who violate their provisions are violating the highest law of the land, and that their actions are outside the law. Therefore, our goal must *now* be to build up and strengthen a mood of respect for the law, for civil obedience to laws, even by those who deem them unwise or who opposed them in the past. Our hope is that those who abide by the law may learn not only to tolerate them but, in time, as their fruits develop, to accept them. To have the positive law on the side of right and justice is to have a powerful weapon that makes for voluntary compliance—but only if the *reasonableness* of the *prima facie* obligation to obey the law is recognized.

To one observer at least, that reasonableness is being more and more disregarded in this country. The current mood is one of growing indifference to and disregard of even the reasonable legalities. The headlines from New York to California tell the story. I am not referring to the crime rate which has made frightening strides, nor to the fact that some of our metropolitan centers have become dangerous jungles. I refer to a growing mood toward law generally, something comparable to the attitude toward the Volstead Act during the Prohibition era. The mood is more diffuse today. To be law-abiding in some circles is to be "a square."

In part, the community itself has been responsible for the emergence of this mood. This is especially true in those states which have failed to abolish the *unreasonable* legalities, particularly in the fields of marriage, divorce, birth control, sex behavior, therapeutic abortion, voluntary euthanasia, and other intrusions on the right of privacy. The failure to repeal foolish laws, which makes morally upright individuals legal offenders, tends to generate skepticism and indifference toward observing the reasonable legalities.

This mood must change if the promise of recent civil rights legislation is to be realized. Respect for law today can give momentum to the liberal upswing of the political and social pendulum in American life. In a democracy we cannot make an absolute of obedience to law or to anything else except "the moral obligation to be intelligent," but more than ever we must stress that dissent and opposition—the oxygen of free society—be combined with civic obedience, and that on moral grounds it express itself as legal dissent and legal opposition.

THE POLITICAL RESPONSIBILITY OF THE INTELLECTUAL*

Charles Frankel

During the days when I was Assistant Secretary of State, a colleague of mine who occupied a high position in another department of government, and who, like myself, was on leave of absence from an agreeable position on the faculty of a university, remarked to me: "Well, I've learned one thing from this experience anyway. Not that I'm not having a good time, but independence is more attractive than power."

The theme is an old one. In abstract thought you have alternatives that you do not have when you must make decisions here and now. To exercise power is to accept a narrowing of one's options. It is, in a sense, to be reduced in freedom. There are pleasures in the life of the mind that immersion in the life of action and the business of government does not give. There is, if not a conflict, at least a certain discordance between holding ideas and holding public office. It was Plato who first noticed that intellectuals like to talk about public affairs, and that they are generally scornful about the way things are mismanaged and unhappy because they themselves have so little power. But it was Plato who also observed

* This article was published originally as "Politics and the Intellectual" in *The Humanist*, XXVIII, No. 4 (1968), 14–20. Reprinted by permission of *The Humanist*.

that it would probably be necessary to conscript intellectuals against their will if a society wanted to count on a steady supply of them in active public service. Indeed, he ended by proposing a complete reconstruction of society in order to produce the elementary conditions required to make the rule of intellect possible.

For there is—or there appears to be—an inherent dilemma in the intellectual life. It requires freedom from the urgencies of the moment; it needs a sense of distance from events; it seeks and thrives on a quality of disengagement. Yet the intellectual life cannot be divorced from its animal and emotional base. It seeks fulfillment and completion in action. As a usual matter, its very preoccupation with ideas and ideals, with a heightened consciousness and self-consciousness, precludes philistinism or complacency.

Plato was right. For the intellectual, what exists is merely what exists. It is of interest only for the order that can be found in it or made out of it, only as the aftertaste of some remembered ideal or the foretaste of some perfection yet unachieved. Thought makes for restlessness. It is an invitation to science, to art, to industry, to action, and when the intellectual declines this invitation he cannot help but do so with regret and with the feeling that some possible good has died aborning. If he treasures his independence he cannot enjoy the powerlessness that goes with it.

Nor can he today be sure that he can keep his independence by remaining powerless. The right not simply to dissent but, if one pleases, to be indifferent; the right to be private; the right to be useless from every respectable point of view; the right to be irreverent about what is officially sanctified—when have these rights ever been safe from the crowd? When have they been safe even from other intellectuals? For intellectuals have been among those—they have often been the leaders—who have denied the right to be independent to other intellectuals. But today a fundamentally new factor has entered.

If the right of intellectual independence is to be safeguarded, what has become the principal home of the intellectual—the college and university—must be safeguarded. For most intellectuals today, or, at any event, most of the most influential and eminent, are also scholars. Not all intellectuals, to be sure, are scholars; and certainly not all scholars are intellectuals. But it would take us far afield to spell out the distinctions and the relationships between these two categories, and for the purposes of the present discussion such an exercise is not necessary. Let us simply proceed on the premise that the primary home today of the intellectual life, as of the scholarly life, is the college and university.

This means, strange though it may seem, that government has come forward as a decisive force in protecting intellectual independence. I do not mean only the judicial arm of government, which provides negative safeguards, indispensable as these are. I mean the positive, affirmative action of the legislature and the executive. Few colleges and universities today can maintain the conditions, physical or psychological, for first-rate teaching and scholarship without the financial support, in one form or another, of government. If government does not support intellectual independence, it will not be supported very well. If government does a bad job, or attaches a foolish price to the support it gives, intellectual independence has a bad future.

Government, to be sure, may remain a junior partner in the enterprise. But its role, nevertheless, is decisive. And this means that the relationship of scholarly independence to political power has changed. It may once have been possible for scholars to guard their independence by keeping their distance from power. It may be possible for individual scholars to do that still. But it is not possible for the scholarly community as such to maintain its independence by running away from government. For key decisions that affect scholarly independence will be made in any event. And if they are made without the participation of men and women who know something about the nature and necessary conditions of scholarly and intellectual life, they cannot be expected to be the right decisions.

Thus, the dilemma of the scholar and the intellectual—the choice between engagement and disengagement, the effort to bring the two together in some integrated way—is more demanding than ever. Participation in the political process is no longer only an abstract obligation of the scholar *qua* citizen. It is an obligation to himself and to the intellectual community and traditions that sustain him and that need to be preserved. It is, not to speak circuitously, a matter of self-interest.

The new political responsibilities of the scholar and the new difficulties he faces in maintaining his independence are the symptoms, indeed, of something deeply paradoxical in his present situation. The scholar's independence is threatened today not so much because he is powerless but because he is increasingly powerful and influential. It is said repeatedly that the walls between scholarship and government or scholarship and the economy are crumbling; these pronouncements are made, ordinarily, in doleful tones, and with the suggestion that scholarship is therefore being perverted to purposes not its own and fundamentally inappropriate to it. But the fact is that the walls are crumbling not merely because government and industry have penetrated the university, but because scholars and their work have penetrated government and industry, and have become indispensable to them, and have changed them radically.

This can, I suppose, be stated in a more disturbing way. It can be said that the remark I have just made is simply a bland and noncommittal way of confessing that scholarship and the university have been harnessed to the Establishment, and have been turned into pillars of the *status quo*. It is useful to use such language, because otherwise it may be forgotten that scholarship can indeed be piously prostituted, and that the phrase "service to society" is an equivocal one which does not really tell us whether the activity in question is good or bad. But polemical slogans like "the Establishment" and "preservation of the *status quo*," have their own inexactness and their own associations with unthinking pieties. If scholarship can be used to preserve certain aspects of the *status quo* that are good, that is what scholarship should be used to do. And if scholarship can be harnessed to "the Establishment," this might be a good and liberating thing for the Establishment. My own problem is to identify what that occult phrase stands for.

But the real problem cannot be defined so long as it is framed in terms which treat scholarship as a means or instrument in the service of ends set by government or the economy. Neither government nor the economy can function without extensive reliance on scholarly methods, on the fruits of scholarly inquiry, and on the graduates of colleges and universities. This is a basic desideratum for a modern, industrial, heavily populated society, whatever the label we choose to apply to its political or social system. And this extensive reliance on the methods and results of higher learning means in practice that the spirit and tone of modern societies are affected, and that their latent purposes and direction of change are influenced.

In brief, when the scholar and his work are regarded just as a means to other, predetermined ends, a dangerous mistake is made. It is a mistake to which many who talk about the current condition of the university and the moral and political responsibility of the contemporary scholar are susceptible, whether they are satisfied with what exists or profoundly troubled by it. For the means that are used by a society affect the ends that are achieved. When the instrumentalities of scholarship are widely used, and when they acquire practical prestige, the possibilities available to a society and the ends it seeks are also affected. Revolutions in human affairs are indeed made by people who pronounce new ideologies or have new moral visions. But they are also made, and made perhaps more irreversibly, by changes in the fundamental instrumentalities on which a society comes to depend in order to cope with its daily problems.

Moreover, the modern scholar and the modern intellectual have steadily been acquiring an immensely significant social role, whatever their specialized fields of competence. It is their opinions, increasingly, which form other people's opinions, if not today or tomorrow, then the day after tomorrow. This is particularly the case with regard to the opinions that people hold about the moral legitimacy of their society's arrangements and actions. It is not only the individual scholar as expert who has become important and practically influential beyond perhaps what he imagines. It is the scholar as teacher and critic, as moralist and citizen and generalized intellectual. His opinions may or may not be better than those of his fellows. Certainly they are not the only opinions that are taken into account or that should be. But the prestige of scholarly and intellectual life is such that the scholar's or the intellectual's authority, the willingness of people to listen to him attentively, spills over into fields in which he may have no special competence or expertise. His word carries more weight than the shoemaker's. It is even beginning to catch up with the banker's. And this is true despite the anti-intellectualism that also exists. Indeed, it may be one reason for the resurgence of anti-intellectualism in the present century.

It is against this background that it may be illuminating to consider the moral rightness and intellectual soundness of attitudes toward government, politics, and power that are now burgeoning in intellectual circles. The war in Vietnam provoked a venomous quarrel between the Johnson Administration and the overwhelming proportion of the articulate members of the university and intellectual community. The venom has done no one any good, and we may hope that it will now subside a bit. But the situation would be even more disturbing if such a quarrel had not occurred. It was and is a necessary quarrel. We would have cause for complete despair about the sensibilities and courage of our academic community and about the utility of our political system if the quarrel had not taken place. The important issue is not that there has been a quarrel. It is what inferences should be drawn from the fact that it exists; it is what its limits should be, and what the rules or guidelines, if any, are by which it should be conducted. And it is whether there is anything else in the relationship of the intellectual to public affairs but an unavoidable quarrel.

One inference that has been drawn, and it has been drawn by people who have given thought to the subject, is that intellectuals make a mistake to imagine that they can play a practical part in public affairs. Their proper attitude, it is suggested, should be one, at best, of guarded and suspicious neutrality; more usually, indeed, scorn and hostility will be justified. This position is often put forward not simply as the recommendation of a specific attitude toward a specific national administration; it is recommended as the advisable attitude toward politics, government, and public affairs as such.

But what is it that is really being recommended? It is, I think, good advice to give to intellectuals that they should be careful about serving inside a government because they may do it harm and it may do them harm. Most intellectuals probably are unfit to perform the jobs which they might be interested in taking in government.

There is nothing special about them in this respect. Most doctors, businessmen, lawyers, and journalists would also be unfit to do the jobs in government that might interest them. For this is only to say that government work, like almost any other kind of work, requires certain special traits and talents which most people do not have. And this is not at all incompatible with the proposition, which I also believe to be true, that not enough ordinary citizens who really are qualified for government service, including intellectuals, take the chance of going to work for the government.

Perhaps, however, what is being recommended is that intellectuals should stay away from government because, no matter how useful they might be, government will be harmful to them. I take it that something more is meant by this kind of statement than that government work will take them away from their professions and, in time, cause their specialized intellectual skills to rust. Obviously, this is a matter of the nature of the work, and the length of time given to it; and it may well be counterbalanced by the unusual stimulation that an observing mind can receive from experience in the government arena.

The deeper fear is that government service will somehow undermine the intellectual's objectivity and integrity. It will make him a partisan; it will entangle him in a web of confidences that limits his ability to speak the truth as he sees it; it will make him think, write, and teach, even when he is not in government, with one eye out for the impact of what he is saying on his old governmental friends. I think that this kind of concern is both serious and legitimate. Individuals will vary in their susceptibility to the deformations mentioned. No scholar who thinks himself very susceptible should go into government unless he is prepared to make government his new career.

But undoubtedly everybody is susceptible to some extent. The question therefore arises whether anybody should risk his scholarly soul in the cause of government service. To this it seems to me that the answer is a guarded Yes. One should do so, that is to say, if one knows what one is doing, and has one's guard up. It is possible for the same man alternately to play a government official's role with complete devotion to that role, and to play a scholar's role with complete devotion to that. It isn't automatic or easy, but it is possible.

The counsel that no individual intellectual or scholar should ever risk his purity of intellect in government service is bad counsel, I think, for at least two reasons. In the first place, it is a counsel of perfection, and like all such counsels it falsifies the world. Intellectuals and scholars do not live in a setting in which people pay no attention to the partisan conflicts between schools of thought, or to webs of mutual confidence and loyalty, or to the vanities and feelings of those in power. These attitudes contaminate scholarly objectivity and integrity within the university. Seclusion from the quite similar temptations of public life, far from guaranteeing scholarly purity, may merely encourage scholarly insularity and self-righteousness. Indeed, the man who knows that the intellectuals' universe is only one among many may very well be able to transcend the pettinesses of intellectual life in a way that his insulated colleague cannot.

The second consideration follows from the first. As much as anything else I can think of, service in government by men who prize their independence and objectivity is what government needs. The contributions that the outside intellectual can make inside a government stem essentially from the fact that he is able to say at any time that he thinks he ought to go home. This freedom is no small matter. As a day-to-day affair, the presence of people with such freedom inside a government is what gives the ordinary citizen leverage in the committee rooms.

A wholesale case against participation by the individual intellectual in government, therefore, is not one that can be sustained. Or rather, it can be sustained, but only on the basis of an external political judgment that the particular government in question is a bad one, and that service to it is irretrievably service in an evil cause. There are some broad guidelines, however, which can be helpful, I believe, to most individuals when they put the question of participating in government in these terms. A government that does not itself permit a free and independent intellectual life in the society it governs is not a government that an intellectual can enter without obviously compromising his integrity. Further, one that is committed on principle to the denial of fundamental human rights is hardly a promising working environment, even apart from the morals of the issue.

Beyond these basic considerations, it is reasonable, further, to ask what it is that the particular man will be expected to do. Few governments, like few universities, are all of a piece. They do good things and bad; and among the bad things some are excusable errors and some are inexcusable. The individual has to ask where his assignment fits on this spectrum.

Moreover, once he has determined the "rights" and "wrongs" of his participation, he has also to ask about the relative utilities. Assuming he can join the government consistently with his principles, he must still ask whether he is doing more good that way. Individual answers will differ; but one thing, I think, is plain. Neither participation nor non-participation can be decided by abstract rule.

In short, the operative moral question is not whether the intellectual community should or should not consent to be "practical." It is not whether it should stay out of the social arena or go in, keep its purity by being useless or sell its soul by participating in unholy causes. Taken as a group, scholars as experts and scholars as critics have too large an influence and authority to be free from their share of responsibility for what takes place in the world. The operative question is what they will do. It is what departments of scholarship will be employed in the discussion of public questions. It is what intellectual and moral standards will guide scholars in their public roles. It is whether scholars and intellectuals will do the painful and hard things that need to be done to ensure that reliable knowledge, reasoned opinion, and conscious choice will have a part in determining the ends to which modern knowledge shall be applied, and not only in expanding our powers to achieve all ends, good or bad. And these questions apply whether a man is in a government or is a citizen outside it.

Obviously, if there is no formula that applies to all cases, what the individual should do depends, first of all, on what his special knowledge or special capacities are. And what he should do depends, too, on what he thinks is right. The social and political philosophies of individual intellectuals and scholars differ, and no man can lay down a complete formula for political responsibility that is binding on everyone unless he assumes that there is only one political philosophy that has any claim to the truth.

Nevertheless, there are, I would suggest, a few general guidelines which would seem to me to be broadly applicable. For there are at least some common truths on which objectively-minded men might be expected to agree.

The first of these is that the scholar has an obligation to guard the integrity and independence of his own discipline. He has this obligation to guard his discipline not only against those who may attack or suborn it from the outside, but against his own passions and prejudices. It is not an easy obligation to fulfill. Scholarly objectivity quite often ends where one's own interests or untouchable beliefs begin. But the principle remains valid even though none of us is entitled to boast about our own adherence to it. The scholar has a primary obligation, in this sense, to seek disengagement—which is the same thing as to say that he must seek engagement in and mastery of his discipline. And in doing this he fulfills a prime political obligation. He preserves and strengthens standards of reasoned inquiry, and extends their command over human thought and action. If he does not do this, the very conception of liberal civilization is dissipated.

Closely connected to this primary obligation is a second one. This is the obligation to maintain, within the limits of the possible, an objective attitude with regard to matters outside the scholar's own special province. One interpretation of this mandate which is frequently given is that the scholar should hesitate to express his opinions about public issues that lie beyond his ken. It is suggested that he takes unfair advantage of his fellows when he passes judgment on matters with regard to which his judgment is no better informed than that of the people who defer to him because he is a scholar.

I do not agree with this view. Objectivity does not entail intellectual celibacy. It is a strange definition of scholarly responsibility that requires scholars to be silent on matters on which, as citizens along with other citizens, they have a right to think and speak. The enforcement of such a definition would simply mean that the community was deprived of hearing the views of some of its most articulate and thoughtful members. Scholarly objectivity, in the sense in which it applies to matters outside an individual's special field, means a rule not of silence but of disciplined judgment.

The first element in disciplined judgment, as I understand it, involves the capacity to recognize when one is speaking without special knowledge and the willingness to say so. If the scholar has no special competence with regard to a given issue, he ought not to borrow from the authority of his discipline to lend prestige to his views, and he ought to take reasonable steps to discourage his audience from doing so. This sort of intellectual sophistication is what we expect of an educated man; to develop such sophistication is the central object, I believe, of what we know as liberal education. And a man with this capacity will know when to suspend belief and when to withhold opinion—which does not mean that he should be silent, for when there are dogmatists who talk without knowing what they are talking about, he can at least recognize that and say so. To know when we do not know is itself a very important kind of knowledge, and even the inexpert scholar can make a major contribution to public rationality if he is prepared to call the bluff of the dogmatists, the fanatics, and the purveyors of the conventional wisdom. The fact that he may find a certain number of scholars among these groups should not deter him.

But this, in turn, requires a second element in disciplined judgment. I mean the capacity and the readiness to recognize when special knowledge is decisive in separating the truths and falsehoods, the rights and wrongs, of a given issue and when it is not. We have the right to expect from a scholar the capacity to recognize his own incapacity in certain fields. He should have the ability to distinguish between the kinds and amount of evidence appropriate for one kind of argument and the kinds and amount of evidence appropriate for another kind. Thus, disciplined judgment has a more positive side to it too. While it calls for suspension of opinion when the individual does not have the special knowledge he ought to have to make a judgment, it also calls for the capacity to recognize what aspects of a question under consideration do not require any special knowledge at all. There are a great many public issues of this sort. Many of the most important are of this sort. They escape any particular specialty's single set of categories. They require specialized knowledge from many domains, but, beyond this, they require a kind of knowledge and good sense that is potentially every man's. The belief that important public issues are generally of this sort is, indeed, a fundamental premise of the democratic process.

This does not mean that where public questions are concerned one man's opinions are as good as any other man's. Individuals differ in their capacity for clear definition of issues, in their ability to reason logically, in their ability to recognize the variety of values that may be involved. They differ, too, in their ability to credit other people with some share in the human portion of reason. All these affect the worth of a man's judgment. And disciplined judgment is, among other things, precisely the active recognition of these factors, and of their importance in coming to sensible conclusions. The scholar has a special obligation to exercise this disciplined judgment.

Finally, the objectivity which we have a right to expect of the intellectual in his role as a generalized commentator and critic seems to me to include a deliberate, self-conscious, and sustained fidelity to those conditions which make for reasoned discussion and decision in the political arena. Given the special gift of words possessed by many intellectuals, it is too much to expect that they will cease to contribute their fair share of acid to the political scene. Certainly the world's literature would be poorer if this were to happen. But I think it is reasonable to expect that scholars will not indulge in personal venom and *ad hominem* remarks for their own agreeable sake alone. And it is also reasonable to expect that scholars will be more mindful than others that the measured and qualified opinion, while not invariably true, is usually more likely to be true.

Indeed, this takes us to a larger condition of reasoned political discussion. It is a condition that arises out of the very character of disciplined scholarly inquiry itself. Inquiry is always selective and limited, and what we know is always partial. We do not have to eliminate all errors before we can make any progress in knowledge, and we do not have to have a single system that encompasses everything before we go to work to find out what we can. The same principle applies, I believe, to political life; and recognition of this principle is a condition of a reasonably nonviolent political process. However much we may be moved by messianic utterances, however much we may be tempted to give to politics the excitement and the exaltation that comes from total belief and total opposition to those who disagree, this is not the way to preserve rational discussion. Whatever else the scholar may or may not do in political life, he has the obligation to remain in character or to admit that he has given up his calling. Skepticism, tolerance, a willingness to agree that a man may be right on some things even if he is wrong on others, and contempt only for the blowhard and the liar but not for the man who is honestly wrong—these are ingredients of intellectual etiquette, and they should be ingredients of the intellectual's political morality.

Beyond this, when he moves into political action, he has the responsibilities simply of any democratic citizen. The only special requirement upon him is that he take no action inconsistent with the orderly pursuit of scholarly activities, whether his own or those of his colleagues and students.

Within this framework, we come to the special case of the scholar who finds himself in public life. There is what might be called the "neutralist" view that the scholar has the obligation to serve as a consultant or as an official whenever a national administration asks him. I cannot accept this view, which seems to me to offer a formula that absolves the scholar from asking of himself the ordinary professional and personal questions that any conscientious man should ask. There is no wholesale formula that releases the individual from responsibility for his decisions. And this applies to the decision to serve government as well, since the duty to serve one's government is not invariably a higher duty than any other duty an individual may have.

In determining whether and to what extent he will enter public service, the scholar must balance the answers to a number of questions. What is it that he is being asked to do? Is he competent to do it? Is he in accord with the purposes for which his advice or his services are being sought? What is likely to happen, not to him personally, but to the things for which he cares if he refuses to take part? Finally, does he think that he is really willing to play the game? This does not mean to play a dirty or corrupt game or to relinquish principles. But it means to play a game with people who may have different principles from yours, to live with them and work with them, and to be prepared to accept an outcome which declares no one to be the complete victor. But what does not seem to me to be legitimate is the attitude that the scholar is merely an expert or a professional man, and that he owes his services to any bidder just as a doctor must tend any patient. Even when the bidder is one's country's government, this point of view does not seem to me to be justified. It is to decapitate the idea of scholarship and, indeed, of free citizenship, to take the position that people must do what they are asked without passing their own judgment on what they are asked to do.

This "neutralist" doctrine is in fact the brother under the skin of the doctrine we have already discussed which holds that there is a thick line between scholarship and practical public service which should never be crossed. Both deal with the moral issues that are present by denying their existence: the neutralist says that the morals of the case are not the individual's to judge; the other doctrine says that the morals of the case are always the same.

Of course, it is true that government service can be contaminating. Public life is certainly not for everybody. But this wholesale view rests more on *a priori* definitions of the nature of scholarship and politics than it does on empirical fact. Government service is obviously not necessarily contaminating. Like religion, the arts, or the female sex, its effects on individuals differ. And if there is a danger to objectivity and scholarly purity that derives from participation in public life, there is also a danger to objectivity and to scholarly relevance that derives from a flight from involvement.

Scholarly and intellectual purity are bought at a heavy price if they require that scholars and intellectuals regularly stand outside the arena where the battles are fought, and restrict themselves to condemning the wickedness of the world. There is a place, an important place, for the scholar and intellectual who remains wholly and always a critic. No society can keep its head unless it possesses a group of people who will not accept its working premises, and who do not want to accomplish anything except to make their fellows take thought about what their society is and what it is up to. But some of this detachment and disengagement are also necessary inside the arena of action.

What the scholar or intellectual who goes temporarily into public life should try to bring to it is precisely this capacity for disengagement. The fresh look, the willingness to question encrusted assumptions, the daily reminder that government is the public's business which the citizen who comes from the outside, and has his own independent base and career, can give his colleagues—these are the things that scholars and thinkers can bring government. Without them government is always in danger of carrying on through mere inertia.

Moreover, a national government is not like a university or a corporation or a club. Where the decisive public business is concerned, it is the only company we have. The scholar does not have an unconditional obligation to answer its call when he receives it. Other things being equal, however, he has the obligation of any other citizen to help conduct the public business. And he has a special obligation as a man of thought. Nor should we speak only of obligation. The opportunity for public service was for the Greeks the very essence of free citizenship. It is an exciting opportunity. And its existence is the breath of life in democratic politics, which can never be permitted to become entirely the business of professionals.

Of course, there are those who adopt the doctrine of nonparticipation not because they regard any government and any political process as inherently evil, but because they envisage a grand alternative to what exists—a kind of government and political process that unerringly serves wholly enlightened and rational ends, and serves them in an enlightened and rational way. It is in these terms, tacit or explicit, that they criticize the existing system and the scholars and intellectuals who do business with that system. But unless it is taken with a large grain of salt, this style of thought is, I think, dangerous and disabling.

Man's capacity to imagine wholly different worlds is a condition for his personal emancipation and for any emancipated civilization. But we also live from day to day, we must make decisions here and now, and if we can improve matters even a little bit it will make our wait for salvation a little more comfortable. No man can work in politics who takes all the evils in the world as his responsibility to cure. A global sense of responsibility, indeed, is the opposite of genuine moral responsibility. The man who would do something must be prepared to accept a limited conception of his powers and responsibilities; he must be prepared to go to work in the ramshackle structures that we have. There is no question that they could be lots better than they are. They will not be better if all we do is to condemn them, while saving ourselves for a wholly new day—which, if it comes, will have ramshackle structures of its own.

THE INDIVIDUAL, THE ORGANIZATION, AND PARTICIPATORY DEMOCRACY

Paul Kurtz

1 THE INDIVIDUAL AND THE ORGANIZALITY

Historically, a key ethical question concerns the relationship of the individual to the state or to the larger society of which he is a part. Why obey the state? What is the extent of my obligation and responsibility? Many humanists have been liberal democrats, and they have agreed with John Locke that limits should be placed upon the power of the state and that there are certain rights of the individual which should not be relinquished to the state. The liberal humanist has been committed to democracy on ethical grounds, and this has involved a commitment to a political system based upon rule by the majority, the right of opposition, a free market of ideas, constitutional safeguards, and equality before the law. Where governments exceed their authority and where there is no possibility for redress of grievances, liberals have held that individuals may engage in passive civil disobedience (Thoreau) or active revolution (Jefferson). In recent decades liberal democrats have recognized that political democracy without some measure of economic democracy is impossible to achieve. Hence, they have called for guarantees against economic hardship and deprivation, for equality of opportunity, and for the satisfaction of basic human needs, economic and cultural, as necessary conditions of a full democratic society. Liberals have written at length of the evils of totalitarian society, the tyranny of the majority, the oppressive church, and economic injustice, which all lead to the suppression of the individual. Yet liberal and democratic humanism is today faced with a similar problem, equally as pressing: how to liberate the individual from the pressures of an organizational society? How to provide some measure of participatory democracy for individuals within organizations? These questions are basic for any humanistic ethics that claim to be responsive to human needs.

The problem that I am raising may be restated as that of the individual within the "*organiz-ality*." I have introduced the term, "organizality," to combine the concepts of organization and personality. I can find no adequate term in ordinary language to get across what I wish to say: that organizations have become independent entities with "personalities" of their own. Not that these organizations are real entities—that is a fiction—but only that they are so regarded by those who come into contact with them and that they are endowed with special characteristics over and beyond the individuals who compose them. "Organization" is another name for institution, social group, or corporation; and the suffix "ality" is appended to designate the emergence of "organizality" in the eyes of those who deal with it as a distinct body with a history and identity, prerogatives and rights.

We have been aware of this serious development for some time. Berle and Means pointed out in the thirties the growth of the economic corporation, the concentration of economic power in a limited number of hands, the divorce between ownership and control. But we have since become aware that it is not simply the growth of our economic corporations that is the sole characteristic of our society (or of other complex industrial societies), but the growth of organizations in general—even though other organizations have been influenced by the corporate model. There are now a great number of such organizations: labor unions, farmers groups, cooperatives, political parties, government bureaus, colleges and universities, hospitals, prisons, churches, television networks, newspaper chains, publishing houses, associations and clubs of all sorts. The trend toward growth and concentration is very real in economic organization; but it likewise applies to other organizations. The organizational growth trend is not necessarily toward monopoly, but oligopoly—i.e., a limited number of large organizations tend to dominate a field.

The result of this concentration is that we are faced with a new creature and a new dilemma which did not exist for liberal humanists in the nineteenth century, or even in the early part of the twentieth century: the displacement of personality by organizality and the surrender of the individual to the organization. Let us be clear, it is not simply the mass man that I am talking about, the uprooted exurbanite, the status seekers, or white collar worker. I am dealing with a more basic and specific problem, and I am concerned with it in its ethical sense. I am interested primarily in large-scale organizations, but also in middle-sized and smaller groups which are beginning to take on the corporate model.

What is clear is that our theories of ethical duty, obligation, and responsibility have failed properly to diagnose the actual condition of contemporary man or to provide a set of proposals for its solution. Indeed, one of the reasons why the individual today frequently feels powerless and unable to affect decision-making processes in his society is that decisions emanate from organizations, not individuals; it is organizations which contend for power, not individuals. The individual entrepreneur of Adam Smith's day, and the individual writer or free thinker of John Stuart Mill's day are rapidly being replaced by the corporate organization, the publishing firm, or the multiversity. If we analyze the term "responsibility," we find that if viewed in individual terms it has lost much of its meaning, for to say that someone ought to do something implies that he can or that he has the power to act and to effect change. But the point is that individuals by themselves have been shorn of power. Moral choices are largely within the context of an organizational structure. Hence responsibility is organizational insofar as power and capacity are organizational.

We have always had organizations: the Roman Empire was an

organization, and so is the Catholic Church. Yes, but with the vast increase of population and the economic development of society, the tendency toward organization—vast and impersonal—has increased. In a sense organization is one of the basic keys to human progress. It is founded on the profound discovery that specialization and the division of labor is the key to productivity and efficiency. The organized factory system and mass production made possible rapid industrialization. Organizations have also made possible the creation of large systems of distribution and communication, mass education, the organization of teams for scientific research, the creation of efficient armies in times of war, and the fulfillment of many other social purposes. The point is that the organizational revolution seems to be an essential part of the technological revolution.

2 THE ORGANIZALITY SYNDROME

It would be useful to describe certain general characteristics which present-day organizations manifest. The first two characteristics are the defining properties of organizations.

1. Organizations have a primary purpose or set of purposes which they attempt to fulfill (profits, education, salvation, etc.), though these goals may change through time.

2. Organizations develop administrative structures. There are hierarchical systems of power by means of which decisions are made and resources are allocated. Concomitant with the different roles and functions within the structure, different duties and responsibilities develop.

3. Oligarchical rule tends to prevail in most of our organizations. The principle of succession is frequently by co-option; that is, leaders are designated by an organizational elite and leadership generally is rewarded to those who appeal to the inner circle. Increasingly, there is a rise of the managers and administrators and a decline of the professionals. "Legitimacy" of rule is based upon acceptance, which is very often defined by loyalty to the organization, rather than by skill or knowledge.

4. Organizalities, at least in advanced technological societies, rate highly two key norms: (a) "rationality" in structure, i.e., a so-called logically designed administrative organization, and (b) "efficiency" in operation, i.e., the most productive use of personnel and resources in order to achieve its purpose(s). Whether they achieve these norms is another matter.

5. Organizalities also develop subtle sets of latent functions over and beyond their primary manifest functions. They have become concerned with the total welfare of their employees (pensions, insurance, health, etc.). They also may become concerned with the extra-vocational private lives of their employees and their families, whose outside "moral conduct," for example, is often expected to be exemplary and not reflect ill upon the corporation. The organizality becomes a kind of miniature feudal kingdom, and the price that the individual may have to pay is conformity to the organizality.

6. There develops within the organizality a psychological climate, a set of values, and a normative code. There is a displacement of values away from the intrinsic qualities of work to its by-products of income, security, prestige, and leisure. There is a competition for status symbols with a resultant status panic in which status-anxiety is widespread. The organizality demands loyalty to its main purpose(s) and adherence to its rules and regulations. But insofar as the individual is swallowed up by the impersonal bureaucracy, there is a decline in his personal responsibility and a subtle corrosion of his integrity. The bureaucratic situation demands compliance with policy directives and freedom from conflict. Law and order, peace and harmony are essential conditions of a smoothly functioning organization. The "logic" of the organization is essentially conservative. Thus there is a standardization and consistency of behavior. Increasingly there is a tendency for individual responsibility to give way to corporate responsibility, and the individual denies he is responsible for what the corporation does.

If we examine people within organizalities in modern industrial society, we find that various types appear:

First, there are those who may be labeled "success-oriented achievers." These individuals rate status and success highly. They identify strongly with the organizality. Their lives are taken up with its decisions. They are generally "rational," "efficient," and self-disciplined conformists, in the sense that the organizality has their devotion and loyalty. This does not deny that these people may be daring and can innovate. I only wish to emphasize that the "good" of the organization becomes for them an internalized article of faith. They develop organizational virtues: striving, punctuality, the suppression of non-organizational emotions and motives. The profit rate of the Corporation, the development of the College, the authority of the Church, the victory of the Party are taken seriously as life goals. Although conspicuous consumers like the rest, these men find great satisfaction on the job, and theirs is a labor of love.

Second, the vast mass of people within organizations are "security oriented." These "personnel" (as Paul Goodman calls them) accommodate to the organization by doing their specific job as it is demanded; they rarely see the whole operation or the final product, or participate in the decision-making process. They are alienated from their occupation, and their labor becomes work or drudgery, not joy. Instead there is a displacement of energy, and their main interest often is with off-the-job satisfaction and entertainment. They become consumers first and foremost; their prime goal seems to be security, and their chief defense is an attitude of withdrawal.

Third, there is another group of people, "nonconforming ambivalents," perhaps only a minority, who may also be attracted by the lure of power, recognition, and success. Yet their behavior is ambivalent, for they cannot accommodate to the system or play the role required of them. Unable to accept the status system or the organizality's goals, such individuals rebel against it and may be eventually forced to leave. Nonconformists may be anomic or highly idealistic in motivation. The idealist within the organizality constantly harbors guilt feelings and suffers the disparity between the ideal and the actual. Unable to fit into the organization, he may flee to the academy, the church, or to the arts. Though here he may soon discover, much to his consternation, that big organizality is again present attempting to organize his talents, and that compromise with some organization is the fact of his existence. If he is to write, he needs a publisher; if he is to preach, a pulpit; if he is to teach, a school. Alas, the individual can scarcely survive outside of an organization without becoming entirely helpless and ineffectual; yet within it he is often smothered.

It is the dilemma of the nonconforming ambivalent within our organizations that especially interests me, the man within the organizality who is sensitive to its contradictions, the individual who sees that the "rationality" and "efficiency" of the organization does not necessarily mean the happiness of its members, that power in decision-making does not always fall into the hands of the competent, that competition between the ranks for status is more often than not an empty goal, that the requirements for discipline do not harmonize with the demands for individual autonomy, and that there is a need to balance organizational goals with human needs. The requirements of organizations and the needs of its personnel may at times coalesce. But at times they may diverge, and the organizality may enforce the priority of its needs by the use of sanctions and rewards. All organizational men learn that if they are to move ahead on the organizational ladder in security and status, they must be sensitive to the opinion of their administrative superiors.

Many nonconformists, independent in their political convictions, pacifists in regard to war, liberal in racial matters, tolerant in questions of sexual morality, are nevertheless reactionary in regard to their role within the organization. All too few have the honesty or courage to stand up against their own organizality when they think that it is wrong.

3 AN ORGANIZATIONAL MANIFESTO: PARTICIPATORY DEMOCRACY

Space does not permit a more detailed analysis of the organizality syndrome. There is extensive literature on this subject. I would like to suggest some methods for reform of organizations and especially to focus upon the extension of the democratic ethos to participatory democracy. Perhaps the credo of this "Organizational Manifesto" should be: "Organizality personnel of the world unite, you have nothing to lose but your statuses"! I submit that we need an organizality bill of rights, an emancipation proclamation by means of which we can build a plurality of democratic organizations. What should be done is always relative to a specific organization. Nonetheless there are some general observations that can be made.

What are the remedies to which a nonconformist, interested in preserving human values, can subscribe? One can, for example, advocate the position of the anarchist and demand that all organizations be abolished: "man is born free but is everywhere in organizations." Hence to liberate human beings we must destroy organizations. But it is patently clear that this proposal is sheer utopianism; for the whole fabric of modern life is so complex that without some organizational structures there would be a drastic breakdown of civilized life. There are too many vital services and functions to be performed which only the efficient ordering of human energies and labor can accomplish. It is conceivable that with a vast increase of automation the necessity for organizations may be lessened; but the total withering away of organizations at this stage of human development is hardly feasible.

Or again there is the recommendation which many do take seriously, that all organizations, particularly economic corporations, be placed under the control of the state. This proposal has had an allure for many twentieth-century liberals who look to the government as a kind of countervailing power, in a position to restrict and control the power of large monopoly formations. Regretfully, and much to our collective dismay, there is no guarantee that the creation of still another superbureaucracy will sufficiently correct the defects of an organizational society, or that it will not bring in its wake the still more terrible effects of a monolithic or totalitarian society. The Soviet Union is an organizational society, but that it has solved the problem of the suppressed individual is questionable. Indeed, a plurality of organizations may guarantee a higher measure of freedom for many individuals than that which is lost in a monolithic organization. Thus the panacea of central government planning of all organizational life has been seriously questioned in liberal democratic and socialistic societies, though this does not preclude, and indeed one can argue for, continuing government regulation of organizations and indeed governmental ownership of a limited number (a mixed economy). The SEC, FCC, NLRB congressional investigations of the drug industry, for example, illustrate the therapeutic role that government can play by regulating rather than by outright control. And partial nationalization of the railroads in Europe, or the TVA in the United States, show the important stimulus that this can have on vital sectors of the economy.

If we are thoroughly committed to the democratic process, then there are other avenues of reform of our institutions beyond complete nationalization. The legal system and the courts can be enlisted up to a point to guarantee due process within institutions. Moreover, there is within a democracy the power of public opinion and of moral suasion. Our organizalities must submit to the scrutiny of public discussion: business, labor, education, the churches, and private associations must be constantly examined and appraised by public opinion. For many or most of these large organizations have become quasi-legal and in some sense public (if not governmental) properties. Thus, there is a method of control, however ineffective it sometimes is, that can be exerted by the constituencies and clientele of the corporate organizations: consumers can protest by refusing to buy the products of industry, spectators can complain to sponsors of the mass media, voters can make known their objection to their congressmen, students protest bad teaching and bad administration, and parishioners refuse to attend churches. It is the responsibility of the organization to fulfill its service functions, and where it adulterates, distorts, or perverts the process the users have a right to insist that it cease and desist, and to demand quality of performance. But much has been said and written about this power, we have our consumer unions and our student cooperatives. There are also professional associations and groups which can set proper standards for organizations (American Association of University Professors, American Bar Association, etc.), and we can create new organizations to combat nondemocratic organizations. I do not believe, however, that these modes of reform by themselves are entirely sufficient. Moreover, they do not fully appreciate the centrality of the humanistic ethical principle which finds individuality a positive good and which seeks as a basic aim to rescue the individual from the forces that seek to negate him.

In the light of this ethical principle, I submit, that what we need to do is to reform and transform organizations by the men of the organizations themselves. It is here that our true frontier lies—within the organization, not without—and it is here that the crisis of responsibility is so keen. The most crucial problem that we as an organizational society face is the need to democratize our organizations by widespread participation in its workings at various levels. It is an unfortunate fact that all too few of our modern-day organizations and corporations are democratically controlled by the people within them.

There are various types of governments within organization. There is (1) rule by an hereditary family monarch, (2) the tyranny of an autocrat or czar, (3) rule by a closed oligarchical elite (the dominant mode in our corporate and financial trusts), or (4) rule by democracy. It is the democratic process within the organization that I would defend. For if democracy has ethical meaning in regard to our political life, then why not in our social, economic, educational, and religious life?

There are those who reject the democratic claim and insist that an organization requires an administrative structure if it is to be efficient, and that democracy will not work. It is clear that organizations need leaders and cannot avoid some hierarchical structures. An "elite" is bound to develop to some extent. But the same thing is true in our political democracy. What is at issue is not whether there are leaders, but the procedures that are employed in selecting them, in changing elites, and in making hierarchies sensitive to criticism. In other words, the democrat can consistently argue that representative government is essential even in organizations (which are too complex for town hall meeting governments), that the leaders in some sense should represent the whole organization, that organization "personnel" have some stake in their selection, and that rule should not be imposed from above but should come from below.

It is indeed unfortunate that the directors of our large corporations often represent self-perpetuating oligarchies, that they are very rarely elected by the stockholders, nor by the workers and foremen in the offices and plants. It is regrettable that many officials of labor unions can establish closed dynasties which are very difficult to break or that ecclesiastical hierarchies still dominate most of our churches. Surely, there have been attempts at organizational democracy, but these I should argue have not gone far enough. For example, many of our educational institutions have introduced some measure of democratic control by faculties and students. But it is clear that the real power of most of our institutions of higher learning still lies not with the faculties or students, but with absentee Board of Trustees (in many cases self-appointed), and that the administrative officials whom they elect to carry out their policies are more often responsive to them than to the people within their organizations.

What I am suggesting is that we need to respect participation at all levels in the decision-making process. We need decentralization of our organizational structures so that decisions are also made at the lower rungs of the scale. Above all, what we need is the principle of *freedom of dissent* and the *right of opposition* within the organization itself. At times this may even mean the right of *corporate disobedience*. If there are no legal mechanisms for a change in policies or for the redress of grievances, one has a right to disobey—within the limits of prudence and balance and in accordance with but not in violation of civil laws. Our corporate organizations all too rarely tolerate or respect disagreements. They all too rarely admit honest differences of opinion (outside of the elite). Instead they impose sanctions and penalties for those who resist the organizational system and who dissent from its policies. There may be harsh penalties for disagreement: failure to receive increments and promotions, salary cuts, or the ultimate penalty of being fired or expelled. Workers do have counter methods: the picket line, the slowdown, the strike, or his ultimate weapon of resigning and of accepting another position—mobility has a strong cutting edge. The point is, a man has a right to continue to be a part of a meaningfully organized social group to which he has devoted the major portion of his time and energy even if he dissents from or disobeys its policy directives.

What I am saying is this: aside from the uses of coercion and sanctions on either side, the spirit of individual creativity, innovation, uniqueness, and diversity should be respected by the organization in the name of democracy.

Contemporary American society is often said to be quasi-competitive, though real competition is more between organizations than individuals. To compete, we are told, an organization must be efficient; hence the argument for administrative coercion. But the fear of coercion is not the sole determinant of employee motivation and there are other subtle factors. One factor is confidence in the administration and belief that what one is doing is worthwhile. What better way to develop the spirit of loyal allegiance than by a system which fosters intelligent commitment and does not simply rely on fear or reward? Give a worker, a teacher, a student a real stake in his organization, and his feelings of alienation, impotence, and quiet desperation may be turned into that of a sense of belonging and of cooperative and devoted commitment. Corporations need truly to incorporate their employees in creating wholesome social communities rather than to treat them merely as means for the achievement of the ends of the administration. Thus involvement at all levels is an important prerequisite of an efficient organization.

What we need to develop is a pluralistic set of democracies where our organizations develop responsible individuals possessed of the courage to speak out against malpractices and the conviction to defend what they hold to be worthwhile without fear of reprisals. What we need is a new set of normative ideals that will inspire and utilize the virtues of individuality within our social organizations.

This sense of moral responsibility that I speak of applies not only to individuals separately but to organizations collectively. What is an organization but the individuals who comprise it, and what better guarantee of corporate responsibility toward its own inner structure and toward the broader society of which it is a part than the responsible individual? Perhaps, in the last analysis in the modern world, it is only within and by means of organizations that we can make our purposes and ends effective. To do this, our organizations must develop, along with their power, a sense of responsibility and a respect for freedom. Here are guidelines for the organizational man: the need to create a climate of opinion in which corporate dissent is tolerated and respected as a fundamental value of the democratic society. There is a sense of justice writ large in the State or Society (according to Plato); but there is a need today to create a model of justice writ large within the organizations in which we live, breathe, make our livelihood, and function.

4 COMPETENCE AND THE LIMITS OF PARTICIPATION

One may ask what is the epistemological status of participatory democracy as an ethical principle? I should reply that it has some basis in our social experience insofar as we are committed to a democratic ethic; it possesses for us some emotive force and dynamic attraction; and if it were implemented it would have consequences that we find would be worthwhile, in that it would enable us to realize other values—individual fulfillment and social justice—that we cherish. Yet merely to enunciate the general principle is not enough, the real test comes when we attempt to apply it to specific circumstances. All ethical principles share the same fate—being general they are often too formal and empty to tell us what to do in particular situations; yet to be meaningful a moral principle must be applicable to concrete contexts and be workable in detailed cases. One must guard against general ethical principles being transformed into mere slogans with quasi-mystical or religious force, or becoming ideological symbols used to defend extreme courses of action. Moreover, there no doubt are many ethical principles to which we are devoted, and each must be balanced and appraised in comparison with the others. General principles are rules which guide or direct policy and action; they are tested by their empirical consequences and in pragmatic terms; they are not to be taken as final or absolute principles.

Thus participatory democracy, though a general principle, must be applied in concrete contexts if it is to take on meaning and force. But there are numerous complexities which emerge when one attempts to do so. In other words, the levels of participation of individuals and the roles that they play in their organizations must be viewed in differential and prudential terms, always related to the functions and purposes of the particular organization. For example, participatory democracy in an army has its limitations. If a nation wishes to be victorious in war, then a certain degree of discipline must be enforced and military orders, rules, and regulations obeyed, else chaos may result, and an army become a mob. A chain of command appears essential in combat. The German General Staff created in the Wehrmacht an army of unquestioning obedience to orders. One may argue on the contrary and in defense of some form of participatory democracy that if an army's loyalty were based upon intelligent commitment and participation rather than fear, this would be a contributing factor to morale and efficiency; an obedient mass is no substitute for individual initiative, intelligence, and skill. Moreover, the stupidities and mistakes of an "infallible" officer class frequently can be unmasked by the practical wisdom of noncommissioned officers and enlisted men; and a citizens' militia is to be preferred in a democracy to sole dependence upon a professional army cadre. The democratization of the ranks thus to some extent may be functional for the performance of the chief end of the military organization. Yet, in spite of this, all should recognize that some limitation on democracy is necessary as long as national states and armies exist and as long as demands are made upon them for efficiency in operation. One cannot debate whether to go into battle when the opposing army menaces. Similarly a prison or penal institution can be democratized, but only up to a point. A prison in which the inmates can participate to some degree in the decisions affecting their welfare, and in which individuality is not destroyed by constraining force but in which prisoners are able to develop themselves, is perhaps better able to rehabilitate and reform human beings than one based upon brute compulsion and command. Yet insofar as prisoners are incarcerated, participatory democracy has its limitations, and order must supersede involvement. It is thus clear that not all institutions can be democratized in the same way: a labor union, an association, a corporation, or an educational institution differ in the methods of implementation.

A special problem arises in those institutions where talent and competence are held essential to the life of the organization. For example, one might argue that in hospitals patients should be consulted concerning treatment and care, food and fees; yet doctors and nurses are better able on the basis of knowledge and skill than patients to evaluate the wisdom of a course of medical treatment; no one would expect patients to diagnose symptoms or prescribe cures.

Perhaps the most frequent case of confusion concerning the relationship of participatory democracy to consideration of competence can be seen in the university. It is within the university recently that student movements have been most attracted to the ideal of participatory democracy. Universities in a sense are hierarchical organizations made up of three estates: administration, faculty, and students. From the one side comes the demand that faculty participate in the important policy decisions of the university and wrest power from powerful administrations. The imposition by Boards of Regents and Trustees of administrative officials, often success-achievers, upon faculty, and the view that professors are "employees" primarily passive and security-oriented is an archaic view. As a result faculty often become ambivalent toward their universities. But what is a top-flight university if not the faculty who make it up? And who should run the university, if not the faculty? The overemphasis upon organizality bureaucracy in American institutions of higher learning to be deplored; the same degree of centralization does not persist in European institutions. Administrators, in any case, where necessary, should be elected by the faculty, serve as their representatives, and with powers only insofar as they are delegated by the faculty. The argument from competence or special qualifications does not apply here. Indeed, one can argue that administrators are no more competent than the faculty, and probably less so.

From still another quarter comes the demand that students should participate in all decisions and policies concerning the university and the claim that they should share power equally with the faculty and the administration. The student often finds the multiversity unresponsive to his needs and remote from his interests; the academic organizality is hierarchical, conservative, and bureaucratic in style and thought. Specialization, isolation, and abstraction characterize its outlook. The faculty often represents from the student's point of view an elite whose first commitment is narrow specialization. The student is considered, if at all, an unimportant and passive element within the knowledge factory. No wonder that in such a situation students increasingly feel alienated, like chrome-plated and plastic-wrapped consumer products, standardized, automated, replaceable, largely irrelevant. The archaic university or college stands in the same position to its students as that of a parent, *in loco parentis* (in lieu of parents), i.e., it can therefore control their conduct to the same extent as parents can. In many universities the student is an outsider whose chief virtue is obedience and submission to authority. Students must knuckle under and accommodate themselves to the rules and regulations; those who are "difficult" may be disciplined by suspension or expulsion.

Participatory democracy would seek to correct these injustices. The arguments in favor of granting some measure of participatory democracy to students are numerous. An excellent university should not be organized along corporate authoritarian lines, but rather should seek to activate the creative potential of both students and faculty. The two estates should share in the common enterprise of learning and research and thus become a community of scholars in the full sense. What better way for students to learn if not by active involvement and identification with the process of education? What better way to stimulate and arouse motivation for goals than by helping to participate in creating them? Students should join together with professors in the noble effort of developing the university. They are entitled to certain elementary considerations; due process should always apply to them. Students should not be treated as children, but as adults and individuals.

Yet, after all of this has been said, the university *is* still a rather peculiar kind of organization; it *is* by its very nature hierarchical in structure, though this (in theory at least) is not based upon birth, class, or wealth, but upon scholarly attainment. In other words, a faculty is defined by its capacity, ability, knowledge, and competence. In most universities of quality there is a careful process of selection and standards of tenure, such that to be appointed a member of a faculty, to be promoted and receive the emoluments required, certain qualifications based upon education, training, and experience must be demonstrated. Tenure is an essential component in all great universities, and it serves a double function: (a) it protects the academic freedom of the professor, *Lehrfreiheit*, the freedom to teach and do research without fear of censorship or reprisal, and (b) it is a method for assuring the retention and promotion of faculty of the highest standards of excellence. Tenure has its limitations: there is always the danger that an entrenched oligarchy of senior professors will attempt to keep out new ideas and fresh blood.

Junior faculty need safeguards against prejudicial treatment, they need guaranteed due process, a method for redress of grievances against unjust tenured decisions.

Yet academic freedom and tenure are the essential principles upon which a university committed to the free pursuit of knowledge is based. *Lernfreiheit*, or the freedom to learn, is the essential prerequisite governing students—and all impediments to learning should be abolished. Yet if the student's right to learn cannot be questioned, this does not qualify students for the rights and privileges which members of the faculty, based upon demonstrated competence, possess: to teach and further research.

Democracy in the university means that students shall be given the opportunity to participate at appropriate levels within the university, not that they shall decisively control its academic policies. Participatory democracy in the university cannot mean that all students shall participate in all the decisions of the university. Students, for example, are not qualified to teach higher mathematics or philosophy, nor can they be responsible for the content of the medical school or engineering curriculum. They cannot make up or grade examinations, they cannot set the standards for the granting of degrees. They are not competent to judge the quality of a professor's research (though they may judge his teaching to some extent). If the chief tasks of the university are learning, teaching, and research, then teaching and research are the primary responsibilities of the faculty, and learning the primary responsibility of the students, and the two functions should not be confused (even though faculty research should enhance teaching and students in learning should be aroused by the passion for research). Over and beyond competence in a field of specialization, there are certain professional standards which faculty members possess, much the same as doctors or lawyers. It would be absurd to expect medical students to fully qualify as doctors before they have graduated from medical school or law students to qualify for the legal profession before they have passed the bar—though they should be given every opportunity to train on the job, to learn by doing, and to contribute to the educational process. Similarly it would be absurd to consider students, insofar as they are students, to qualify as professional educators, equal in competence and ability to decide on all matters concerning educational policy. The policy of allowing each vote—students and faculty—to count for one is made even more untenable considering the fact that most students are more apt to be transient members of an educational institution, whereas educators have a lifetime commitment to education.

There are other dangers that one must guard against. Many devotees of an ethical principle may be so carried away by the power of the principle—in this case participatory democracy—that they may fail to make important distinctions and may destroy other meaningful principles and values. What does participation mean? It does not mean politicizing the university. It does not mean that the primary purpose of the university—learning, teaching, research—can be dominated by political pressure groups. It does not mean that strong and vocal minorities, or *a fortiori* suppressive majorities, within the university can intimidate the community of scholarship. It does not mean that undemocratic means, force, and obstruction can be used to coerce faculties. It does mean that a university is a place for reason and moderation and for responsible and measured criticism; and that as well as being committed to the university as a place for a free market of ideas, it is committed to the widespread involvement of students, faculty, and administrators in the educational process of the university.

However, the crucial question that is often asked is, if students and faculty should share to some extent in the common task of education, which decisions are to be made by students and which by faculty? It is clear that students should be primarily concerned with those standards and rules which concern their own private behavior and moral choices. *In loco parentis* is no longer justifiable. The private lives and social activities of students are their own business, including what they do off and on campuses (within the bounds of the civil law).

Moreover, following the right to learn, students should have the freedom to invite outside speakers to campus, to organize clubs and groups, to publish and disseminate newspapers and magazines. They should have the full protection of those freedoms which are accorded other citizens in a democracy, including political freedoms, freedom of speech and assembly. This includes the right to recruit for organizations and causes and to be recruited for them—an idea consistent with the notion of an open campus. In addition, students should be permitted to grade their professors as a contribution to the improvement of university teaching; they should assist in selecting a number of scholars in residence or visiting professors (within the limits of the budget); and also should be permitted to suggest new courses and programs. They should be consulted about university facilities, the library, bookstore, cafeterias, transportation, fees, and tuition—that is, they should be involved in discussion of all of those matters which concern their welfare directly. They should be involved in discussions helping to formulate general educational goals and the role of the university in society.

There are certain decisions that should be left to the faculty and not relinquished to students: for example, standards for admission and graduation, matters concerning the grading of student performance, the final decisions about curricular content and subject matter of courses, and the educational goals of the university, the nature and character of faculty or university-sponsored research, the control of faculty appointments, promotions, and tenure, the free and uninhibited expression of ideas by faculty. These prerogatives appropriately belong to the faculty, follow from their professional competence, and are consistent with the right to *Lehrfreiheit*.

Clearly there are many decisions which concern *both* students and faculty. Students and faculty should always maintain continuous dialogue on a number of issues: concerning facilities (which the faculty also use) such as the library, bookstore, and cafeterias, but also the university calendar, the initiation and discussion of new programs, the extension of new services and opportunities, the long-range goals of the university and its place within society, and so on. And there are many creative methods by which cooperative ventures can be discussed and enacted: there should be a university-wide senate in which the faculty is predominant, but which should contain some student representation; there should be student membership and participation on some university committees—perhaps not all, only on those which concern student affairs and policy directly, not on those which pertain to the faculty's professional competence. There should be viable mechanisms for the open discussion of issues by faculty and students—in the classroom, in university sponsored forums and debates, in university publications, and so on. The life blood of a vital university is one in which there is a free give and take on all sides.

It should be apparent that the principle of participatory democracy in those institutions where competence and knowledge are basic does not entail either unbridled liberty or egalitarianism. Rather, to paraphrase Aristotle, it involves a form of proportional equality, or *proportional participation*, relative to the levels of competence of the participants. One has to be careful that this qualification on participatory democracy is not indiscriminately applied. There are dangers that organizations may claim specialized competence as a basis for excluding their "personnel" from the decision-making process. Such exclusions would be fraudulent in many or most cases; they are meaningful in the university up to a point, as we have seen, only insofar as it enables the university to achieve its chief aim, the furtherance of learning and knowledge.

Participatory democracy does not necessarily imply the drying up of incentive and initiative for those who are highly motivated, nor the denial of competence for those who have demonstrated ability and attainment. On the contrary, if fully operative, it should allow true initiative and competence to emerge; for it provides the best opportunities and conditions for motivating intelligent involvement and commitment and tapping potential talents. Participatory democracy does not deny the role of leadership, but it seeks to make it representative of and responsive to human persons. The basic premise of the democratic value system is that "he who wears the shoe best knows where it pinches." The most reliable way of directing the affairs of an organization within a democratic society is to give the people within it a chance to contribute to its maximum functioning. Organizations exist for their service to human beings, human beings do not exist for the sake of their organizalities.

In conclusion, we have seen that our society has presented us with a new and complex phenomenon: large-scale organizalities ready to suffocate the individual and to stifle him. We need to reawaken the sense of democratic community and an appreciation for democratic rights within organizations. There are dimensions of human freedom and responsibility that can only be expressed by the private individual within his own sphere and in terms of his own unique desires, needs, hopes, and ideals, and which cannot be relinquished to any organization. Thus our humanist concern is based at the same time upon a concern for individual freedom and for social justice.

ETHICAL THEORY, HUMAN NEEDS, AND INDIVIDUAL RESPONSIBILITY*

Rollo Handy

1 WHAT IS HUMANISM?

"Humanism" is a label that obviously has been used for a great many purposes in philosophic inquiry and elsewhere. In this paper, that version of humanism which is opposed to supernaturalism is emphasized. A humanist in the present sense may believe there is sufficient evidence to indicate the nonexistence of a supernatural realm, or he may prefer to remain technically agnostic on that point and hold instead that there is no need to use supernaturalistic categories, entities, and processes to describe and explain what goes on in this world. In either case, the kind of humanism I am discussing tries to describe and explain all that goes on (including the objects of inquiry of the physical, biological, and behavioral sciences) in terms of so-called natural processes. Human behavior is understood as including thinking, feeling, believing, etc., as well as more overt behavior.

Such a view is still extremely broad and can encompass many different approaches. For example, it is compatible with both highly

* A shorter version of this article appeared in *The Humanist*, XXVII, No. 1 (1967), 11–14. Reprinted by permission of *The Humanist*.

optimistic and highly pessimistic views of the potential of human beings, and is compatible with many views about the appropriate emphasis to be placed on the human part of the cosmos as contrasted to the rest of the cosmos. Such differences can be illustrated by quotations from Corliss Lamont and the early Bertrand Russell.

Lamont says:

> To define twentieth-century Humanism in the briefest possible manner, I would say that it is a philosophy of joyous service for the greater good of all humanity in this natural world and according to the methods of reason and democracy.

Russell says:

> Brief and powerless is Man's life; on him and all his race the slow, sure doom falls pitiless and dark. Blind to good and evil, reckless of destruction, omnipotent matter rolls on its relentless way . . .[1]

Although I take a more optimistic view of the potentialities of humanity than many people do, I also believe that too often humanists have become overly sentimental about man and that they sometimes project many of the traditional attributes of a supernatural God upon humanity in general.

The kind of humanism I espouse rejects (to use traditional labels) both supernaturalism and idealism, in favor of a thoroughgoing naturalism. At the same time, it is a more "hardheaded" attitude than that held by some humanists, and avoids any tendency to deify man and thus reinstate some of the supernaturalistic tendencies supposedly eliminated at the outset.

2 WHAT IS HUMANISTIC ETHICS?

Within the broad type of humanism just sketched, there is room for many types of ethical theory. This is not an appropriate place to list and to analyze critically the major types of humanistic ethical theory. What I shall do instead is to discuss some of the general ideas that would be acceptable to many, but not all, humanists,

[1] Lamont, *The Philosophy of Humanism* (New York: Philosophical Library, 1957), p. 9. Russell, "A Free Man's Worship," reprinted in Robert E. Egner and Lester E. Denonn, eds., *The Basic Writings of Bertrand Russell* (New York: Simon and Schuster, Inc., 1961), p. 72.

and then move on to those aspects of my view which would *not* be widely accepted by other humanists.

1. In general, naturalistic humanists think that all human values are grounded in this-worldly events, relationships, experiences, etc. Such an approach opposes the view of many Anglo-American philosophers that value terms designate "non-natural" properties or that the uses of value terms cannot be elucidated in terms of "natural" events. Obviously supernatural properties are likewise not appealed to by naturalistic humanists. Putting the matter another way, whatever goods are to be achieved by humans are this-worldly goods. Naturalistic ethics, in this sense, is likely to emphasize categories such as the satisfaction of interests, of needs, of desires, etc.

Without necessarily being identified with utilitarianism, the kind of humanistic ethics now being discussed is likely to put considerable emphasis on the consequences of human behavior. This is not, of course, to say that human motives and intentions are unimportant in ethical theory, but obviously the impact of one's actions on others and on one's own future is highly important. To be done an injustice through the good intentions of another may be more acceptable than being done the same kind of injustice through the bad intentions of another, but presumably our main interest is in eliminating the injustice.

The kind of humanism now being discussed is likely to emphasize morality as a social phenomenon, rather than as a purely, or primarily, private or individualistic matter. Both the good and the bad things we do and suffer are almost inextricably bound up with other people, with the social system in which we live, and with culturally determined patterns of behavior and response. The task, as many humanists see it, is not somehow to reform the spirit, but rather to socialize human drives.

Moral systems, then, are seen as forms of human behavior, to be inquired into by using scientific methods. The sanction for any particular moral rule is to be found in the natural world (not in some supernatural or non-natural area); and the matrix of morality is social.

2. Now I move to a more specific account of one possible approach to a humanistic ethics. Although I have no way of assessing

the degree of sympathy that would be found among humanists for what I have to say in this section, certainly many humanists will disagree with my view.

In the history of ethics there have been many disputes about how selfish man is, and the extent to which selfishness is socially and culturally conditioned. Many writers have urged that the most fundamental of drives is that of self-preservation, and hence at bottom any adequate ethical theory must be based on selfishness. Other writers, with a considerable show of evidence, have emphasized the malleability of "human nature," and have maintained that what seems so fundamental about selfishness is true only of certain types of social organization. Obviously, this kind of issue is not easily settled. For one thing, the terms central in such discussions—"selfishness," "egoism," "egotism," etc.—are given many diverse interpretations, and much confusion ensues.

However, if we adopt a relatively broad notion of self-preservation and bypass the issue of trying to specify precisely how strong the drive for self-preservation is compared to other drives, it seems plausible to say that the individual's drive for self-preservation is extremely strong, and an ethical theory ought to give considerable weight to that. In my opinion, the aim is not to attempt to make people less interested than they now are in their own self-preservation, but rather to try to structure our social organizations so that one's own betterment is dependent upon the betterment of others. In other words, we should try to organize human institutions so that, rather than one person's success being dependent on the failure of others, everyone's success should be dependent upon the success of others. This obviously is no easy matter, and in many cases the resources to be allocated are in fact fixed and one must divide up the pie unequally. But there are other instances in which the size of the pie is expansible, and to give someone a large piece does not necessarily mean that others go hungry.

Naturally, all this becomes extremely complex, especially when we deal with rewards such as prestige and reputation. In one sense, of course, prestige becomes meaningless as a reward unless it is distributed unequally. But prestige may be allocated by the group to those who are most successful in "doing in" their fellows, or to those who are most successful in helping their fellows. The latter alternative is the one I advocate.

What I have said so far may seem hopelessly naïve in some respects, so let me emphasize that I do not believe that my wishes, or anyone else's, are easily made fact. How economic rewards, prestige rewards, or self-satisfaction rewards are allocated is obviously dependent on a multitude of factors, including the basic mode of socio-economic organization under which people live. But I think cultural anthropologists have amassed enough evidence to show how amazingly variable so-called "human nature" is. The question is not whether humans biologically are flexible enough so that the drive for self-preservation can be channeled in socially desirable ways, but whether we can so arrange our social institutions that rewards are allocated in a way satisfactory to a humanistic ethics.

Before going further, some attention needs to be paid to the area of "meta-ethics," which has been central in recent Anglo-American treatises. Meta-ethics concerns not what is good or bad, and right or wrong, but the "meaning" of ethical terms, the way in which ethical judgments are confirmed or supported, and similar issues. In recent years, an enormous amount of energy has gone into an analysis of "common usage" or "ordinary language" in ethics. The entire topic is one of considerable complexity, and much of what has been written is highly subtle. The point of immediate relevance, however, is that many writers on meta-ethics believe the crucial test for any suggested specification of an ethical term is whether or not it is in agreement with the way we actually do use that term. For example, the attempt of hedonists to define "good" as "pleasant" would be rejected on the ground that ordinarily we do not use those terms interchangeably. In the same spirit, some rejections of determinism hinge on the fact that we ordinarily talk about free actions, and therefore a view which would make such talk mistaken must be wrong.

The belief of many contemporary philosophers that the various distinctions embedded in ordinary language have enormous significance is in marked contrast to the view of some social scientists. George Lundberg, for example, says:

> Man has always stood in awe of his verbalizations, especially when they are in written form and are traceable to ancient sources. No feeling is more widespread than that the structure of our language, that most fundamental repository of our culture, *must* represent, and closely correspond to, the structure and nature of reality. When, therefore, we find deeply engrained in our language different types of sentence structure, we are sure that the phenomena, the events, or the processes these sentences purport to describe are fundamentally of a different order.[2]

Without attempting to probe deeply into the relevant issues, a great many attempts to develop a naturalistic ethics would be rejected by many recent writers on ethics on the ground that the naturalistic suggestions about the way value terms should be used are not in accord with the way we ordinarily use those terms.

Such meta-ethical views, in my opinion, tend to assume that there already is an acceptable morality, or an acceptable language of morality, and the philosophic task is to discern the "meaning" of ethical terms, the "logic" of moral discourse, etc. This is precisely what is rejected by the type of humanistic ethics I am discussing. Traditional morality is composed of many things. On the positive side, it is the repository of many rules found useful in a wide variety of human contexts and human practices. But also it is deeply affected by the history of our culture, and is infused with supernatural and mentalistic notions. If we are to develop an ethical theory that can make full use of the scientific information we now possess, as well as what we hope to gain in the future, it is pointless to object to suggested specifications of value terms on the ground that they are not in accord with "what we mean" or with "how we use" ethical terms.

At the same time, we want specifications for value terms that bear some resemblance to the way we ordinarily use such terms; at least such an approach seems sensible to me. I think the general attitude to adopt is roughly the one current in scientific inquiry; terms are specified in ways that lead to ever-increasing powers of prediction

[2] George Lundberg, "Semantics and the Value Problem," *Social Forces*, XXVII (1948), 114.

and description. There is nothing sacrosanct about older attempts to say what is meant by this or that term, and the best specifications available today may be modified or rejected tomorrow. In other words, what I advocate is an experimental approach to the specification of ethical terms.

Going back a bit, many approaches labeled naturalistic seem to fit in this category. "Good" has been defined in terms of "pleasure," "interest," "preference," "satisfaction of drives," etc. All of these would call for a revision of some of the ethical language common in our culture, and yet would provide for some recognizable link with that language. In my opinion, then, the task becomes that of ascertaining which of the possible ways makes most sense in terms of what we expect from an ethical theory.

The answers are not easy, and doubtless much disagreement will ensue. A detailed consideration of the possible advantages and disadvantages of various naturalistic approaches would occupy much space. So here I will only sketch a view that seems to me to offer considerable promise, and mention a few of the advantages such an approach offers.

My suggestion is that value terms be directly linked to human needs. "Value" is specified as follows: "X is a value" = "X satisfies a human need." Obviously, then, a major point is how needs are construed. Here we must rely on the results of the sciences bearing on human behavior. Quite probably the most adequate present specification of "need," whatever it may be, will change in the future, as more scientific evidence becomes available. In the same way, the lists of needs that scientific inquiry may disclose will also change as inquiry proceeds. But for just those reasons, ethical theory and ethical practice would then be closely connected to the best available information about human behavior. This, in my opinion, is the major virtue of the theory.

Let us consider a few consequences. The need theory would make the determination of values "objective" rather than "subjective," in the sense that something's being a value would be a fact, even if the people involved did not realize it. What satisfies a need would be a value, even if it were not so recognized. The need theory thus rejects the emotivist contention that ethical language only or primarily expresses or evinces attitudes. Since "needs" are regarded in a scientific way, intuitionist or supernaturalistic approaches are also rejected.

Although the present view makes ethical judgments objective in the sense that whether or not something satisfies a need is not dependent on an individual's opinion, the theory is in one sense relativistic, since human needs have presumably changed in the course of evolution and presumably will continue to change. Also, differing social contexts will generate differing needs. In short, there is no assumption here that there is any one set of absolute needs that will apply to all humans, past, present, or future, under all circumstances.

An obvious question concerns what needs humans in fact have, and how the term "need" is specified. On the present proposal, both questions are regarded as scientific questions. "Need" is taken here to be roughly "an event or condition that aids the human to function adequately." What constitutes adequate functioning is of course an important question. To repeat, the suggestion of this paper is that those scientists who have investigated human behavior in its many ramifications are best equipped both to say what needs humans have and to specify what adequate functioning is.

One can hardly overemphasize the importance, for the present view, of rejecting any approach searching for "the meaning" of "good," "value," etc. Should the best available specifications of "need" turn out to have undesirable consequences for a humanistic ethical theory, then the whole project of specifying "value" in terms of "need" would be rejected. An experimental attitude is what is advocated here; I believe using needs as the key to an ethical system presently looks promising, but in no respect urge that the approach be followed if scientific inquiry indicates the hopes I have for the need theory are unwarranted.

Under the present proposal, "satisfies a human need" refers to any need for any human. If a qualified physician finds that Mr. Y needs morphine, then morphine is good for Y in that situation. At any given time, needs may exist for some person, or persons, or everyone, which are not recognized, and anything satisfying those needs would be a value (even though we are not aware of it). And something not recognized as being able to satisfy a need, but actually so capable of doing, would also be a value. In regard to objects, then, a fuller way of expressing the present proposal is: "X is good for Y in situation Z" = "X satisfies Y's need in situation Z." In regard to human actions, an action that results in the satisfaction of a need is valuable, and a contemplated but unperformed deed could be judged valuable if it would satisfy a need when performed. Finally, it is not intended that temporary states of satiety for X would result in X's ceasing to be valuable. Food is valuable, even if a given man at a given time is not hungry.

Those familiar with recent meta-ethical discussion will realize not only how controversial, but how sketchy, the above proposal is. The aim here is not to work out a detailed and relatively complete theory, but only to indicate the main thrust of the proposal within the context of humanism.[3] However, one of the obvious objections to the present proposal should be discussed.

The critic will probably ask how the present approach would handle "bad" needs, and how a conflict among needs would be resolved. The first point has been discussed indirectly. If scientific inquiry shows that there are genuine needs which a humanistic ethics regards as in some sense bad, there are several possibilities. If the incompatibility between the results of the inquiry and humanistic ethics is great enough, as mentioned earlier, the only thing to do may be to reject the need theory. If the incompatibility is judged as a minor one, and the theory otherwise seems to be more useful than alternative theories, then the judgment that the need is "bad" might give way. However, a basic assumption of this paper is that the adequate functioning of humans is a desideratum which is basic to a humanistic approach, and hence the incompatibility referred to above is not likely to arise.

Conflicts among needs are almost certain to arise, and a complete ethical theory needs to have some way of resolving such conflicts. Probably this can be handled by adopting a rule that, on the level

[3] Those concerned about a fuller and more technical treatment may be interested in R. Handy, *Value Theory and the Behavioral Sciences* (Springfield, Ill.: Charles C. Thomas, 1969).

of individuals, the greatest possible satisfaction of needs should govern, and that on the level of groups, the greatest possible satisfaction of needs for the group should govern. In the case of conflict among groups, the greatest possible satisfaction of needs for all mankind should govern. Obviously various elitist views would reject those rules, but some such rules seem implied by a humanistic approach to ethics.

To conclude this section, then, the intent has been to link scientific inquiry into human behavior closely to ethics, through the device of specifying "value" in terms of "needs." The proposal is a tentative one, and subject to future modification or rejection as scientific inquiry proceeds. No attempt has been made to develop a complete theory.

3 INDIVIDUAL RESPONSIBILITY

Many interesting and significant issues could be raised here, but space permits only a few matters to be discussed. For example, the important issue of individual responsibility viewed from the point of view of a social group—under what circumstances is it sensible for the group to hold the individual responsible for his behavior—will not be taken up here.[4] The focus, rather, will be on individual responsibility from the point of view of the person who finds himself in disagreement with the views of some larger group. We all have to learn how to live with people who are wrong, or whom we believe to be wrong.

What follows is linked to the earlier sections of this paper, but not in a tight fashion. One could hold something like the theory sketched earlier and reject the view of responsibility developed here, or accept something like that view of responsibility but reject the present approach to ethical theory.

Those who support unpopular or unconventional views frequently find themselves in a difficult situation in the group within which

[4] I have discussed this issue in "Determinism, Responsibility, and the Social Setting," *Philosophy and Phenomenological Research*, XX (1960).

they function. To cite only one type of example, a college teacher may oppose strongly the admissions policy of his college, or the degree to which student life is controlled, or the promotion policy of the college, or the curricular emphasis of his department. The kind of situation I have in mind encompasses issues of many degrees of importance, and groups of all types, including social, economic, civic, political, academic, etc. I am thinking not only of cases of the type such as the integrationist in the deep South, but also the professor who objects to the playing of Christmas carols on campus. What is such a nonconformist to do?

On the one extreme, he may take a purist approach, seizing every opportunity to denounce existing practices with which he disagrees, avoiding compromise, and fighting the good fight. On occasion such reformers achieve notable success, but they often become functionally isolated from the larger group, and thus have no effect on decisions, and sometimes they are fired. Whether they are separated from the group either in the sense of being ousted or in the sense of being isolated, they have lost the opportunity of reforming, from within the group, the practices to which they object.

On the other extreme, we have those who are so worried about having an influence on decisions that they almost always hide their views, go along with the majority, and think of themselves as consolidating their position within the group so that one fine day they can strike a blow for what they hold dear. The difficulty is that the fine day never arrives, for the person never sees himself as having enough strength to do what he wants.

The "purist" and the "opportunist" as just described are of course caricatures, yet examples approximating both types of behavior are not difficult to find. From the point of view of the reformer who wants to make changes, neither extreme works. How then does the responsible individual behave, so that there can be progress, desirable change, and humanization of deplorable conditions?

My view is that there is no simple answer in the sense of a maxim or group of maxims providing a magic key. In order to support this view, I want to look more closely at the situation within which the individual who is dissenting must operate.

In this connection, I think a great disservice is done by those who romantically pose the problem in terms of the individual opposed totally to the group. We are all so molded by our culture and by our relations to others that the starting point must be man as a bio-social organism, not the individual somehow separated or abstracted from his social connections. Almost everything we want to do is in many ways dependent on others. The most deviant among us still accept a great many socio-cultural norms, and their very deviation is expressed in terms of what is culturally available. Protesting youth chooses clothing, hair styles, etc., that are culturally regarded as appropriate to the opposite sex, for example. Or if neatness is a dominant socio-cultural norm, sloppiness may become a symbol of dissent. To take more significant examples, reformers and radicals of all shades of opinion primarily oppose neither the whole culture nor the whole of a smaller group to which they belong, but only segments of the larger organizations.

Many humans in many walks of life are convinced that it is relatively easy for man to control various aspects of his civilization. Those who hold optimistic views on such matters should read "Man's Control Over Civilization: An Anthropocentric Illusion," by the anthropologist Leslie A. White.[5] He says:

> During the last century we have witnessed attempts to control tiny and relatively insignificant segments of our culture, such as spelling, the calendar, the system of weights and measures, to name but a few. There have been repeated and heroic attempts to simplify spelling and make it more rational, to devise a more rational calendar, and to adopt an ordered system of weights and measures instead of the cumbersome, illogical agglomeration of folk measurements we now use. But what successes can we point to? Reform in spelling has been negligible. We have succeeded to a considerable extent but not wholly in eliminating the *u* from such words as *honor*. But to do away with silent letters, such as the *b* in *lamb*, is too big a mountain for us to move. And such spellings-and-pronunciations as *rough, cough, dough,* and *through* are much too strong to yield to our puny efforts. It usually takes a great political and social upheaval to effect a significant change in spelling or a calendrical system as the French and Bolshevik revolutions have

[5] This essay is Chapter XII of his *The Science of Culture* (New York: Grove Press, 1949). The quotations from White that follow are from pp. 332–33 and 353.

> made clear. And as for the metric system, it has found a place among the little band of esoterics in science, but yards, ounces, rods, pints, and furlongs still serve—awkwardly and inefficiently—the layman.
>
> We begin to wonder. If we are not able to perform such tiny and insignificant feats as eliminating the *b* from *lamb*, or modifying our calendar system, how can we hope to construct a new social order on a worldwide scale?

White does not hold that human effort lacks efficacy. He denies that "it is futile to try because what one does counts for nought," but goes on to say:

> . . . what one does, how he does it, and the end and purpose for which it is done is culturally determined. . . . More than that, what a person or group desires is determined or at least defined by the culture, not by them. What constitutes the "good life" for any people is always culturally defined.

In short, in my opinion, the situation is *not* Promethean man against the group, but rather the dissenter who, on the basis of his identification with and support for some aspects of his socio-cultural milieu, opposes other aspects of that milieu. A person who truly rejected all of his culture literally could not live.

So far, what has been said may possibly be interpreted as a glorification of the larger group and support for always conforming. This is not so. After all, the martyr or the purist may succeed in making changes. But more importantly for the purposes of the present analysis, the same kind of problem I have been discussing occurs within dissenting groups. For example, the person rejecting some entrenched cultural belief, such as that of a supernatural god, has to resolve problems generated in working with others who share his rejection of that belief. If he is to further his cause, he must work with others, but then almost certainly will be involved in differences of opinion. How militant an approach is justified at a given time? On what occasions may it be best to affect a compromise of some kind? How hard, at a given time and place, should one push for the elimination of school prayers?

In short, to get anything done, some cooperation is necessary.

Whenever several people try to cooperate there will almost certainly be differences of opinion—about principles, priorities, strategy, and tactics. The typical situation, then, is striking a balance between having things exactly as one wishes and compromising enough to get support from others.

What then is advocated, and how is this related to the earlier sections of this paper? As emphasized previously, there is no magic key. But in general, the more fundamental the human needs involved, the more careful one needs to be that the compromise does not lead either to doing nothing or to "selling out." For example, within one small community there may exist both public financial support for religious displays at Christmas time and gross economic exploitation of some ethnic group. One can't fight all battles at the same time, and it would seem unreasonable not to focus most attention on the economic exploitation. But if the evidence indicated that it was literally impossible to change the system of exploitation significantly, at a *given* time, and the evidence also indicated that there was a good chance of furthering the separation of church and state, temporarily most reformist energies might appropriately flow into the latter effort. One danger, of course, is that it is always tempting to say that the difficult is impossible; the dangers of rationalization in such matters are grave. One of the easiest ways of being irresponsible is to hold that no matter what efforts are brought to bear in a given situation, that situation cannot be changed. On the other hand, clearly there are times when desired change must either be extremely slow or cannot occur at all. On many occasions in world history, no matter how intelligently and effectively men of good will worked, there was no genuine possibility of eliminating chattel slavery. Those who insist on all-or-nothing in a purist way can be irresponsible, since the result may not only be "nothing," but may also be a genuine setback for the principles involved.

Such general situations can be difficult to judge, for there are some occasions when a compromise also may be worse than "nothing," in the sense that the compromise may blunt matters enough so that no further improvement occurs for a long time. What I am suggesting, then, is that one important type of irresponsibility is the failure to weigh evidence carefully and intelligently in an attempt to increase the satisfaction of human needs to the greatest extent possible in a given situation.

In short, too often discussions revolve around an abstract consideration of high principle with no attention paid to the problem of how much change is possible given a specific setting. The findings of social science can be especially helpful here. If the logical weight of the evidence were the only, or the main, factor leading to change, many present atrocities would have long since ceased to exist. In addition to great attention to the logical weight of the evidence, then, we also need to pay the closest attention to the whole question of how certain social phenomena become so entrenched, how they might be changed, etc. For example, we need to learn about the needs which traditional supernaturalism helps to satisfy, even if we believe we have adequate evidence that those same needs could be better satisfied in some other way. We should also learn what socio-economic circumstances bolster traditional supernaturalism, and how effectively to produce changes in that area. We need to realize, more clearly than reformers often do, that anti-human social structures which serve powerful vested interests will not disappear simply when their anti-human characteristics are clearly described and understood.

What I have tried to say is that in my view the responsible individual cannot be content simply to enunciate his principles, avoid temptation, and trust to his purity. He must make difficult, but important, judgments as to how those principles can be put into effect, how others can be persuaded to accept them, and how to generate a socio-cultural milieu in which the principles can be successfully applied.

IV

JUSTICE AND SOCIETY

HUMANIST ETHICS AND THE MEANING OF HUMAN DIGNITY

Abraham Edel

1 HUMANISMS AMONG THE "ISMS"

The concept of a humanist philosophy has both advantages and disadvantages. Its advantages stem from its orientation—it is frankly and avowedly man-centered. This has an important aspect in regard to its theory of knowledge. For a humanist philosophy sees human knowledge as a human construction; men's ideas are man-made instruments, used to interpret the world and to further human purposes. Like Jamesian pragmatism or Deweyan instrumentalism, humanism finds in men's pictures of the world the pervasive penetration of human purpose. Its view of man's place in nature attempts to be scientific, and, like naturalism, it looks for the continuities of man with the rest of the natural world. It turns away from impassable dualisms—whether Cartesian chasms between mind and matter, phenomenological contrasts of consciousness and natural reality, or theological chasms between the natural and the supernatural. Methodologically, humanism can incorporate the basic empiricism that has emerged in the modern world with the advances of the scientific outlook; and it has no reason to fear that the scientific study of man's psychology, his social and communal behavior, and his historical career, would involve a reduction of man's "essence."

On the other hand, there is a narrowness in humanism's basic strength. So persistent is its man-centered orientation that it sometimes forgets that man himself is a very special and very limited phenomenon in the history of the cosmos. There was a universe long before man existed and there will be a universe long after he is gone. Here humanism often lacks the strength of materialism or the dogged vision of realism that there is an independent reality to be faced—whether it favors or is hostile to man's purposes—that limits or even determines man's constructions. But sometimes humanism has the courage to incorporate such lessons.

Yet what, after all, is the point of talking of a humanist philosophy? If it is naturalistic in metaphysics, pragmatic in outlook, empirical in method, and allows the incorporation of the lessons of materialism and realism, why attempt at this late philosophical date to fashion it as a distinctive concept? Perhaps this is a criticism of all "ism" construction. It is at least as pertinent to humanism as a latecomer on the scene, as it is to the even more recent existentialism. Perhaps their "essence" is historically negative, to be found in different contexts of what they are *against* in the well-established philosophical "isms," rather than in positive systematic formulations. A humanist philosophy is nine-tenths in the great tradition of materialism and naturalism, but it resents their outcome for the conception of man. It fears that man will emerge as "merely" a material being, "merely" a natural being. But of course criticisms of such reductive views are found in the schools of materialism and naturalism themselves: a historical materialism gives man socio-historical depth and scope, and American naturalism criticizes the British-European naturalism which carries a flavor of biologism in its view of man.

If we forgo the attempt to speak of a humanist philosophy and concentrate instead on a *humanist ethics,* some of these difficulties would disappear. For it is precisely in this context that its special stresses are relevant. Its man-centeredness states the truth that ethics is a *human* creation, not in the superficial sense of arbitrary fashion or caprice, but in the deep and abiding sense in which language, kinship, political structure, and religion are human creations —forms of practice, expressing and servicing men's needs as they are understood at a given time. The fact that they are man-made carries with it the possibilities of improvement, revision, and reorganization. But more than man-centeredness is involved. There is also a basic this-worldliness, at least in the sense that every otherworldly move is interpreted as a symbolic representation of this world and its problems.

Both materialism and naturalism are man-centered in ethics, and they are certainly this-worldly in outlook. Both view morality as basically directed to human purpose, and in their more sophisticated forms both analyze the rich framework of ethical concepts as issues in the strategy of striving, geared to a growing knowledge of man and his world. Both materialism and naturalism in their more mature forms seek to combine a deterministic explanation of human morality, purpose, and thought with a theory of rational evaluation as a human process within a natural world. What then is left for a distinctive concept of humanist ethics?

Perhaps the answer again lies in negative terms—the itemizing of what is being rejected. If man had not so persistently believed he was more than human, or so persistently described himself in terms that made him less than a man (and what is worse, acted that way), there would have been no need for a distinctive humanist concept. (Similarly, if man had not so persistently run away from his responsibilities, or so fervently constructed rationalizing "systems," there might have been no base for an existentialist ethic.) In contemporary jargon, I feel tempted to describe humanist ethics as *the theory of the de-alienation of man!*

Even so, it does not yield a uniform concept. When religious thinkers begin to talk of, say, a Christian humanism, they are steering their religion to a deeper conscious concern with human relevance as the center of worth. (When it is asserted that God is dead, it is only to focus more sharply on the human relevance of Jesus.) In general, contemporary Christianity with its affirmation of the dignity of man does not always recognize how far it has traveled the humanist path. One has to turn back to St. Augustine to see how derivative human dignity was regarded—derivative from a proper alignment with God—and how categorical the condemnation of human goods sought for human purposes. For example, Augustine scrupulously condemns the very music of prayer or the very eloquence of it, if the sound with its aesthetic beauty in any way captures the spirit.

When Marxists turn to humanism and seek to fashion a Marxian humanism, as in contemporary Poland or Yugoslavia, a different type of rejection occurs. It is an attempted liberalization which will recognize the role of individual decision and individual creativity in an outlook that has stressed the determinisms of historical trends and the subordination of individual to collective decree. Practically, it is a rejection of dictatorial dogmatism.

When liberals in traditionally liberal contexts—the United States or England—form humanist schools, they are usually seeking to preserve the middle-class liberal individualism of the eighteenth and nineteenth centuries in the face of growing mass movements and increasing standardization and dehumanization.

If there is no positive "essence" to the concept of a humanist ethics, there may be a common endeavor. Perhaps this is what distinguishes it from the whole materialist-naturalist tradition in ethics, of which it is a part. This endeavor is to probe and awaken the powers of man in which he is regarded and regards himself as creative and responsible. Let me then conclude my response to the question, "What is humanist ethics?" by recapitulating that it seems theoretically unprofitable to construct a systematic humanist ethical theory, that most of it will turn out to be indistinguishable from a naturalist ethics or much of a materialist ethics. It is more illuminating to study the contexts of distinctive emphasis in the rise of humanist movements. These may prove to be contexts in which the responsibility and creativity of human beings are insufficiently recognized or appreciated and in which either theoretical trends or practical life give them insufficient scope. The concept of a humanist ethics may thus be regarded as a *corrective endeavor* within a naturalist ethics under the specific distortions that produce a neglect of creativity and responsibility.

2 THE MEANING OF HUMAN DIGNITY

The second task of this essay is to select some important phase of humanist ethics or to consider some important application of it. I have undertaken to examine the concept of human dignity. It is a concept increasingly invoked, especially as a protest when men are abused, herded in concentration camps, and in general treated in mass. Sometimes it is spoken of, in the context of interpersonal relations, as "respect for a person." An individual is said to "have dignity" and so to "deserve respect." Because dignity oftentimes is coupled with other concepts (e.g., freedom and dignity, justice and dignity), it is important to see what distinctive content it has, if any. Moreover, the problem of its analysis is complicated by the fact that it is often built into another concept, such as "person" or "man," so that "to be a person" immediately connotes "to have dignity" and "to treat him as a man" connotes "to treat him with respect."

Such complexities compel a methodological aside. There are various ways in which different analytic approaches would attempt to clarify the concept. At one extreme is the classical method which holds up the concept by itself and seeks a Platonic type of essence. It seems to assume that "dignity" is a quality-term and that the mind can grasp the quality by a comparison of instances. Modern philosophers inclining toward such a method are prone to look for a phenomenological quality in the situation in which one "observes" dignity. At the other extreme are the linguistic analysts who would refuse to discuss the term directly or by itself, claiming that it has meaning only in contexts of use, and even perhaps that each contextual use could be explicated separately without yielding an "essence" common to all contexts. For example, if you treat a man as having dignity in a conversation, you listen seriously to what he has to say, not just let your mind wander till you can break in; if legal officers treat a prisoner with dignity there is no torture or bullying, no forced confessions, and so on.

I should like to try out something in between these extremes—the kind of approach well developed in dealing with concepts in the philosophy of science, rather than metaphysics or ordinary life. It is more contextual than the first method, more systematic than the second. A term so complicated as "dignity" is more likely to be a *construct* than a simple quality-term, more likely to be a *theoretical term* than an observational one. Compare it to a term like "intelligence." One does not think "intelligently" in the same sense as one thinks "quickly," nor does the former submit to so simple a mode of measurement as the latter. If we wish to clarify the term and do not have an articulated meaning or an explicit criterion for its application, we have first to locate phenomena in connection with which it is used, even though we may not be able as yet to trace the precise connection. Just as we point to an intelligent performance, so we can point to a respectful treatment. Now a construct can be interpreted in two ways. It is given a *realistic* interpretation if there is some distinct descriptive property with which it is identified or (more often in complex cases) if there is some discoverable structure with which it is identified. It is given an *instrumentalist* interpretation if it serves some theoretical purposes in organizing data or facilitating inferences. Thus early positivism (Ernst Mach), taking the view that concepts were instruments for organizing the flux of sensations, held that the scientific idea of an atom is a convenient fiction; for that matter, the idea of a table or a chair is also a convenient fiction. Yet many who believed there were literally chairs and tables in existence did not believe there was an existing entity corresponding to "atom." Others took a realistic interpretation of "atom," especially after the discovery of Brownian movements, which were thought to be the consequence of individual particles in motion. Obviously the economic concept of "gross national product" is an instrumental construct; it cannot be put before you in the same way as "the total amount of gold in the country" could in principle be gathered. Interesting issues arise concerning those concepts whose status is uncertain: for example, is "aging" to be taken realistically as the literal diminution of some fund of chemical energies related causally to the various phenomena that are the symptoms of aging, or is it a useful way of referring (as P. B. Medawar has argued) to the increase in the probability of dying?

One final methodological caution: instrumental does not necessarily connote fictitious, nor does it lack criteria for evaluation. There are always purposes of some sort in mind, and some constructs advance those better than others. Whatever the range of conventionalism, there thus remains a hard core of control by the actual processes going on in the world. Hence, while realistic interpretations incline one to ask for truth, instrumental interpretations quite properly allow us to ask for adequacy or fruitfulness. How ultimate the distinction may be is a further matter we need not explore here. Those who argue on metaphysical grounds that all ideas are constructions might say that the difference in the two types of interpretation is only one of degree. Some, like Reichenbach, have treated the concepts of "realistic" and "instrumental" as referring to different modes of speech between which one can decide only on grounds of convenience.

It is time to return to the concept of dignity. I propose that we treat it as an ethical construct, and inquire about its interpretation along both lines suggested.

Certainly one would not expect a simple realistic interpretation. One does not find a man's dignity by locating a substantial fire within him, burning with a hard gem-like flame, as an ancient stoic might have thought, nor a soul precipitating distinctive movements in a pineal gland. Where then would a realistic component be sought?

One may look first for the phenomena of the inquiry. While some ethical concepts may start with behavioral phenomena (e.g., helping a man in distress), questions of dignity are more likely to offer a foothold in phenomenal qualities, and in the discernible qualities of human feeling in interpersonal relations. A phenomenological psychology could well undertake the task of locating and analyzing the gestalt we find in those undoubted cases where we experience human dignity as present. In the case of interpersonal relations the approach is perhaps easiest from the point of view of the "recipient" who senses whether he is being treated with respect or "as a person." But it is often quite clear also to a third party observing the "transaction."

There is no dearth of illustration. Step into any classroom, and after a few moments' observation you will be able to tell whether the teacher is treating the students with respect or as raw materials to be stamped or manipulated. Listen to any conversation, and you can sense whether it is a mere formality or a genuine meeting of mutually respecting parties treating one another with dignity; even worse—for the lack of respect there is perhaps easiest to detect—it may be an aggressive pushing of verbal counters, or concurrent monologues with intersecting moments. The central theme of Martin Buber's analysis of authentic human relations may be seen as the identification of dignity, the difference between being related to you as a Thou, and being related to you as an It. It is not a simple question of sensitive differentiation of feeling: I can have all sorts of variegated responses to you, but if my focus is on my own sensations you have receded into a cause of my sensations, not a participant in a genuine meeting. Buber rightly contrasts authentic interrelation both with such sensationism and with the use of the other as a means to social-institutional ends. (We have to separate in Buber the particular small-group social philosophy from the very insightful delineation of the phenomena of human dignity.)

We need scarcely go on. The reader will think immediately of all he has suffered in bureaucratic action—not through inefficiency, for the action may sometimes be fully efficient, but through feeling himself treated as an item or a case. Or perhaps even worse, he may sense the falsity of a brittle interest which itself so often becomes a counter in commercial relations. In addition, it is important to note that not all examples come from face-to-face interpersonal reactions. There is dignity and lack of it in individual action, even in physical isolation. Observe a man through a one-way screen, or catch him in an unguarded moment. You will see that there is a way of bearing pain which has dignity and a way which lacks it, and similarly with the reception of joy. So too, fear is not incompatible with dignity, though fright or panic is. A man engaged in rational decision may have dignity, though pompous ratiocination lacks it.

In general, I am suggesting that there is a large mass of phenomena to be identified for the study of human dignity. There may be mistakes in particular identification, localisms in which the standards of a particular culture or class are imposed as the criteria of dignity—as Aristotle insists that the proud man walks only with a slow step and never raises his voice or talks quickly, or traditional aristocracies could not recognize dignity unless it were dressed in the right clothes. But certainly the phenomena of human dignity and respect for man are as identifiable as the phenomena of intelligence were in the early days before the initiation of psychological study and intelligence testing. In fact, we might do well to keep in mind the history of the study of intelligence—the diversity of measures, the disputes over the unity of the quality, the correlation of results, the debates over inherent intelligence, the revision of the concept—as a paradigm for a comparable study of dignity.

So far we have looked at the realistic interpretation of the construct in terms of the mass of phenomena denoted. But is there a structure also to be discovered, either within the phenomena or underlying them? This is the claim so often found in the conviction elevated into a metaphysics—that respect and dignity are somehow deeply rooted in the nature of man, that they betoken inherent properties of the human being as such, that no man wholly lacks the quality, at least in the sense of an ability to respond to respect, though much in the way of distortion and mishap as well as systematic conditioning can obstruct its view. Such hypotheses purport to be about what men "essentially" are like, not initially proposals about how they should be treated, although the logical jump is often too quickly made. How can hypotheses of such broad scope be submitted to verification?

It is well to admit at the outset that we do not presently know enough about man to settle such questions. Nor are the terms in which the hypotheses are usually posed very clear. Man's dignity is said to lie in the fact of his rational powers, or in the fact that he is able to entertain a morality, sometimes that he can bind himself by law or operate with rules, sometimes that he has the capacity for outgoing sympathy and mutuality, sometimes merely that he is a conscious being capable of self-consciousness. Some of these need trimming down; certainly rationality cannot win respect if it is just scheming cleverness, and yet the schemer has self-consciousness. Although we cannot be sure what it is that is to be verified, we do have the feeling that some lines of verification point to a hypothesis that is to be built up. For example, the minimal meaning might be that every man, while he is alive, remains a potential source of good or evil—no man is to be "written off." Evidence would lie in the remarkable cases of men who have pulled themselves up from near-despair and have shown a never-die character in their effort; an extensive field for such investigation unfortunately is the psychology of people in prisons and concentration camps. Such investigation can help describe the phenomena; it is premature to expect it to determine how widespread dignity in fact is, or to preclude the view that dignity can be not merely covered, but wholly eradicated. Like a great many other disputes about inherent powers and properties of man, the one about inherent dignity allows of several antecedent alternatives: it may be a property that always remains active, no matter what the degree of distortion; or it may be a mere general potentiality which requires cultivation to mature, and can be permanently shut off quite early in the development of the person; or it may be wholly an outcome, where it occurs, of certain types of social relations, having no determinate base of its own in the human makeup; or it may be a characteristic in one or another of these respects in some men and not in others. Whatever the convictions of an ethical theory, it is well to remember the wide range of interpretation still possible with the kind of evidence that is usually offered today.

There may, however, be attempts in one or another form to show the universality of certain types of responses in human beings that would fall within the hypothesis that man as such has dignity. Much of the older dispute, as in the attempt of British moral sentiment ethics of the eighteenth century to show that Hobbes' egoistic predatory conception of human nature was wrong—for example, Adam Smith's view of inherent sympathy—heads in this direction. The form of such hypotheses may be stated thus: in some form not wholly clear as yet, man calls to man and man responds to man.

Consequently, there are many directions in which inquiry may go, and different emotions and feelings of the interpersonal situation which it may explore. A fascinating study of this type, dealing with the reactions of wounded war veterans to sympathy on the part of others, and the forms that sympathy could take, was carried out by Professor Tamara Dembo and her coworkers in the years after World War II. Professor Dembo worked on the assumption that sympathy from the recipient's point of view would always be felt as a value, and attempted a careful phenomenological and situational delineation of the relation, as well as pointing to explanatory concepts from the psychology of personality.[1]

Another fertile field for study is the social and historical experience of mass movements, especially where human exploitation and indignity have been central. Slavery and slave revolts, peasant movements and peasant revolts, the rise of trade unionism, and passive resistance all constitute areas in which data for hypotheses about human dignity might be found by the analytic historian. In our own day, the revolts against colonialism, the prevalence of resistance and guerrilla movements in occupied countries, and the emergence of passive resistance in civil rights struggles furnish a widespread field in which understanding of human dignity becomes a very practical problem.

So far we have treated the belief in the dignity of man purely on its descriptive side: it indicates that there exists a field of phenomena and that the clarifications of meaning and the principles of interpretation are difficult but by no means impossible to achieve. The entire question of human dignity is so deeply enmeshed in theories of personality of individual and social psychology, in the complexities of political and social phenomena now at the center of controversies in the social sciences, and in philosophical disputes about the nature of man, that we cannot expect a definitive solution short of tremendous advances in the psychological and social

[1] "Adjustment to Misfortune—A Problem of Social-Psychological Rehabilitation," in Tamara Dembo, Gloria Ladieu Leviton, and Beatrice A. Wright, *Artificial Limbs*, Prosthetics Research Board, National Academy of Sciences (Washington, D.C., 1956).

sciences. But we cannot reject the search, assert the irrelevance of inquiry, or even ignore the evidence that has been gathered up to the present.

If we turn from the search for a realistic interpretation of the construct of human dignity to an instrumentalist interpretation, the nature of our inquiry is considerably altered. Dignity is now regarded as an ideal, like justice or well-being, and it is evaluated by the type of life it makes possible, the human purposes it helps achieve, and the human problems to whose solution it contributes. These purposes and problems constitute its psychological and social base; its function is the articulation of principles and the mobilization of multiple human energies and feelings, furnishing a direction for the achievement of purposes and the solution of problems, both perennial and contemporary. As an ideal, human dignity obviously is an ideal of interpersonal relations and social organization. Whether it is a distinctive ideal or merged in a contributory or ancillary way with others depends on how distinctive is its psychological and social base, whether there are unique needs and problems related to it, or whether it simply makes its contribution to solving general problems—as it clearly would to helping achieve peaceful human relations, a desideratum on numerous grounds. The ideal of dignity may acquire on its way a human devotion of high intensity, but this could be a mark of great efficacy rather than of a distinctive base.

The ideal of human dignity as a normative program requires, today especially, that it be woven into concrete areas of human life. As a dynamic ideal it is united in a powerful way with the ideals of well-being, justice, liberty, equality, and in the efforts to remove the major discriminations and exploitations that have beset mankind. If the appeal to human dignity can play a large part in such enterprises it earns its keep quite easily. Yet for this large-scale task it is not important what is assigned to justice and what to dignity. For we are dealing here with the opportunities for the good life, not the detailed form of the good life. But there are increasing areas in which dignity will have to stand on its own feet, and make demands in its own name, and become a ground for decision itself—areas in which to say "It's an indignity" will mean something beyond "It's unjust" or "It deprives one of liberty." This is not a simple issue. We are so accustomed to using the concept of human dignity in the processes of justification—for example, as equivalent to individuality in the justification of lists of human rights—that it has not occurred to us that it may have a place of its own in processes of decision and among the lower-level phenomena themselves. There are many ordinary expressions that seem to embody such a recognition; for example, "You can't treat a human being that way," "I wouldn't do it to a dog." And there are the well-known moral crises in which a man feels that he simply could not live with himself if he behaved in a certain way—for example, if he were an informer. What seem to be intuitions without justification in terms of external reasons may turn out to be instances of the ideal of dignity.

Increasing areas now raise this problem explicitly. For example, in law, rights of privacy raise questions of dignity, and so do issues of wiretapping and spying. Increased control over men makes the problem more pressing. It is suggested that in the administration of justice men may have to choose between dignity and truth, when instead of a jury reckoning, the truth can be discovered by hypnotic or drug-induced revelations.[2] For example, in the treatment of helpless patients and the dying, the *impersonal* element has come increasingly under psychological as well as moral criticism. Florence Nightingale long ago remarked—I have heard it said—that it was a sin to whisper in the room of a dying man. Whispering is a form of shutting out, and her sensitive remark hits directly at the crux, that the psychological basis of dignity may lie in the phenomena of acceptance and rejection—simple acceptance, not qualified or conditional acceptance. Again, not only medicine, but education, now so vast an enterprise, has the problem of treating the student with dignity.

I am well aware that I have been making but probing suggestions, and the work of analysis and investigation is still to be done. Human dignity is an ethical construct. It may have some

[2] Cf. Bernard Botein and Murray A. Gordon, *The Trial of the Future* (New York: Simon and Schuster, Inc., 1963), Chap. 2.

realistic interpretation, but there are serious difficulties in the complexity of the scientific inquiry. It does have sufficient indices to identify phenomena, and to adhere to something when other, better identified aspects are stripped away. It has already a clear meaning in the normative program of removing major discriminations and exploitations. It is increasingly becoming pertinent to problems of individual as against impersonal treatment in a largescale and highly organized society with growing powers of controlling—and crushing—the individual. Dignity is tied to individualism, but it is not equated with it. It is tied to securing well-being, but is not equivalent to it. Its psychological base is perhaps unconditional acceptance and self-acceptance, its phenomenological quality is respect for a person. Its emotional expression is sympathy, its practical expression is care and concern. In the long run it may turn out to be a bundle that can have its strands untied. But in its potential importance in the present state of human problems it seems to be a clue to a vital element in human ethics, an element that may well characterize the humanist emphasis in any philosophical framework.

MORAL THEORY AND MORAL EDUCATION

H. J. Blackham

1 THE MORAL HEMISPHERES

Public Means to Private Ends

In the centuries before Christianity, when the Greeks thought about morals they recognized clearly that private life and public affairs make two distinct though interdependent moral spheres. Private life is a realm of choice, for unless personal beliefs and ideals are one's own they are a sham. Public affairs impose obligation, for unless members of a society are bound by its rules and are not free to evade or break them at will there is no society. This realm of choice and this realm of obligation, the moral hemispheres, are interdependent, for I cannot live outside a society and my society stands to benefit by giving me independence. Personal independence is based on mutual interdependence. The simplest model of this is provided by traffic on the highway. There is a network of public roads and an official highway code which enable me to make journeys for my own purposes whenever and wherever I like. The rules of the road create and impose a common public standard of convenience and safety for all these private journeys. Forgetting the sore problem of traffic in towns, there is here relatively little conflict between private aims and public requirements: there are publicly provided means for privately chosen ends. Social obligation serving personal choice, as means to ends, is one type of moral ideal or moral theory. It is the ideal recommended in this paper as the humanist view of the proper relation of public and private interests, social and personal values. The main structure of a moral theory should be, it is assumed, the relationship between the public and private moral hemispheres.

A friend has told me of a leaflet that came into his hands issued by the Roman Church to Catholic motorists. The validity and authority of the highway code was being impressed on the Catholic motorist in this leaflet with quotations from St. Thomas Aquinas. This absurdity was only possible because there still survives, especially in the Roman Catholic community, the idea of Christendom as a uniform society, sharing the same religious beliefs and practices and the same political order and ordinances. This uniform society left no room for the distinction between personal choice and social obligation. Ideals and duties were all fused in the total sphere of Christian faith. The Church had closed the philosophical schools, and after the fall of Rome the Christian bishops created the First Europe. Therefore, so long as Christendom lasted there was no full recognition of the realm of choice, and the realm of obligation was given the sanction of an acknowledged religious authority. This uniformity was breached by the Reformation. Although most Protestant communities maintained the unity of Church and State, the jurisdiction of the magistrate over conscience was challenged, and at length the right of the individual to form his own beliefs and seek salvation at his own risk was acknowledged. Religious liberty was in due course followed by democratic liberty, expressed not only in political terms (the right to share in government), but also in personal terms (the right to a private life). "The only part of the conduct of any one for which he is amenable to society is that which concerns others. In the part which merely concerns himself, his independence is, of right, absolute. Over himself, over his own body and mind, the individual is sovereign." In these words John Stuart Mill in the mid-nineteenth century staked the claim of the individual to an acknowledged independence based on an acknowledged interdependence. This was a return in thought after more than twenty centuries to Periclean Athens.

We have, then, to look first at the realm of social obligation and then at the realm of personal choice, and to make clear the relations between them.

Social Obligation

Social obligation is necessary to the existence of any society. The highway code shows this in the simplest and most direct way, but these are only conventional rules with a limited application. Nobody minds very much what they are, so long as everybody knows what they are and observes them. But many of the rules, laws, procedures, customs, and mutual expectations which regulate society are not so directly seen to be serving a common interest. Indeed, in many societies there is no common interest. Society may be organized force and fraud, a privileged few oppressing the unfortunate many. A society in which the rules are determined by the rulers exclusively to serve their own interests, and are enforced by coercive measures, is one possibility. At the other end of the scale would be a society in which the rules were fully agreed upon and affected all interests equally, approximating to the model of the highway code. Most societies stand somewhere between these extremes, but approximating to the one or the other.

The more fully agreed upon the rules of a society are, the more they are morally binding, for then everyone is party to them and responsible for observing them: they create and serve a common interest acknowledged in the agreement. By contrast, if they are merely imposed by arbitrary authority, people will be likely to feel justified in evading them if they can. However, it is impossible to reach full agreement on all the rules required to regulate the complex interests of a populous industrialized society. Some of the rules will be conventional, like the rules of the road, some customary, like the rules of etiquette, some technical, like the rules of debate, some expressing a principle, like the rules of the law courts or electoral procedures or the rights designated as civil liberties, some compromises, like most statutes, some mutually expected but unwritten and non-enforceable at law, like truth-telling or promise-keeping. All these rules and norms regulating behavior in a society have a moral ground and impose a moral obligation, as distinct from legal grounds and sanctions, to the extent that they equally affect all and are equally determined by all. Since this is an ideal which may never be fully realizable, the effective ground of moral obligation in social rules is the availability of recognized procedures for changing the rules. Insofar as the rules are, in this sense, provisional and progressive, open to revision to bring them nearer to agreement, they are morally binding. In other words, political democracy, with equality before the law and a trend toward equal conditions for all, provides the moral basis for the rules for living and working together.

The moral obligation of social rules derives also from the universality of the principles they embody. The rule itself is not moral just because it is agreed upon; the agreement is a moral undertaking to observe the rule. Agreed rules, whatever they are, have this moral implication—that the people concerned have accepted an obligation to observe them. But the rule itself may be morally binding; and it is so if it embodies a universal principle. The rules which provide for civil liberties and democratic procedures have this character, for they express politically the fundamental equivalence of human beings as human beings—and this is the most universal moral principle. That every human being is an end in himself and not merely a means to another's ends; that every human being is a subject like oneself, and not merely an object to oneself: this is the underlying rule of coexistence and cooperation, which justifies the practical rules which regulate a society. When Jeremy Bentham and the Utilitarians enunciated the maxim "the greatest happiness of the greatest number," with the corollary "everybody to count for one and nobody for more than one," they thought they were providing a rough and ready end and rule for testing all laws, institutions, social policies, and social conduct. This particular test may be too rough and not ready enough for a workable application, but in principle it proposed the most universal standard in a form relevant to social needs.

The moral obligation of social rules, then, depends on the extent to which they are agreed upon and the extent to which they embody universal principles. The reality of both these moral conditions depends largely on equality of social conditions. Rules are not likely to be agreed upon unless they serve the interests affected. If they are instruments of exploitation they belie the most universal of moral principles. Thus it is in a genuine and progressive democracy that conditions for the moral obligation of social rules are most fully realized.

To show that moral rules are social rules which depend for their moral obligation on social conditions, consider the rule against stealing. This could hardly apply to anyone who had no property of his own and no legitimate means of acquiring any. He would have no interests to be protected by the rule; he would be outside the society which required the rule. Even the ultimate moral rule which requires the treatment of another as an end in himself and never only as a means cannot be unconditional, for it is reciprocal and does not override self-preservation. If I am persistently exploited by somebody in spite of protests, he forfeits his claim to be considered as an end in himself, however I treat him in fact.

Society, then, may be an organization of public means to private ends, with social obligation subserving personal choice. Society then has no other final end than to provide means for the personal lives of its members. This of course is itself an ideal, a social choice, since a society may be organized on quite different lines and for the sake of a social purpose which overrides personal ends. This particular social choice, public means to private ends, independence based upon interdependence, is justified by a high valuation of personal life. This social ideal assumes personal life as the highest value. Personal life, of course, is unthinkable outside society, and the relation between the two is intimate and without parallel, not adequately described as means to ends. Interdependence is the cradle of independence. Society is rather like a mother, whose offspring are destined for independence and who has a character and integrity of her own. The relationship has difficulties and may be disastrous, but can be splendid.

Social rules, insofar as they are in principle agreed upon, are morally binding. Even so, there may be a conflict between the conscience of the individual member of a democratic society and what he is morally required and has, so to speak, undertaken to do. The classical case is the pacifist's refusal to accept the social obligation to take part in war—which may be required for the defense and survival of all the good embodied in the society. In such a case, the individual may for the sake of conscience be prepared to take all the penal consequences of defying his society, defaulting and defecting as it will seem to his fellows, forfeiting the rights and benefits of his membership, constituting himself an outlaw, so to speak. Society may be tolerant, and find some way of accommodating the dissenter. And insofar as it is a society based on agreement it will do so. For agreement cannot be forced. Nevertheless, setting one's conscience against the judgment and decision of one's fellows is an extremely serious matter. Occasionally, the dissenter may be a pioneer of better ways which his fellows will learn to recognize and accept. But this possibility does not justify the refusal to be provisionally bound by the judgment of the majority in a matter which touches all.

Travel on the roads has been taken as a simple model of the use of public means for private ends, and as in essentials the model for the relations between social and personal life. In this case society is not represented merely nor mainly by the rules of the road, for the provision of roads and of vehicles, and of all the associated goods and services, is primary and is equally a case of interdependence and social cooperation. This practical cooperation provides concrete freedom, "practicability of purpose," without which there is no occasion for rules of the road. Perhaps it is better to regard all rules regulating interdependence and social cooperation as aiming not only at maximum social stability and dependability but also at higher productivity, so that practicability of purpose is continuously increased. More people are enabled to do more things; more choices are made available to all. Independence based upon interdependence is not only socially allowed but also socially endowed.

Personal Choice

The independent personal life which is allowed and endowed by loyal collaboration in the realm of interdependence is regulated by a different ethic, not an ethic of obligation and of rules, but an ethic of choice and of ideals. There may be a basic personal obligation to make a job of one's life; one may owe it to one's fellows not to be a waster, to set an example. There may also be an obligation to form one's opinions and beliefs on the basis of adequate information, and not arbitrarily or at random. And there may be an obligation to treat with the utmost respect, if not fully and finally to accept, the consensus of mankind in the realm of values. Nevertheless, in all these respects this is a realm of alternatives, of choices, not of conformity to a norm or rule. Excellence here does not consist in performing faithfully and rigorously what it is the duty of all to do, but in becoming oneself, in being a self, authentic and unique. Such excellence is achieved through forming one's own convictions, selecting values and ideals for cultivation and pursuit, forming initiatives, and learning from the experience one creates. To become in this way one's own person, author of a style of life and a pattern of good, is to crown human living with the sovereignty to which it aspires.

Here, however, is the main difference between the humanist and the religious believer. The believer is already committed to a way of life, to following an exemplar. Christ is the model, or Buddha. There is no other way: holiness, sainthood, salvation indicate the final and only goal. There are no alternatives here, and therefore no choice, only obligation. For the believer sees as the only alternative to the way of salvation the broad road that leads to destruction. Ultimately, there are no rival goods, no plurality of ideals. The one God, or undifferentiated Being, forbids the entertainment of other ideal possibilities. By contrast, the humanist accepts no universal exemplar of the way of life for all men. Holiness is only one way of life—and not one he is likely to choose. The choice of one pattern of good may necessarily mean the rejection of another equally good. There are different vocations, there are different temperaments, and there are differences in the personal choice and cultivation of values. Prudence and generosity, or self-assertion and submissiveness, as keynotes of character denote different types of personality and different styles of life, each of which has its own excellence and its own liability to lose approval by excess.

The realm of personal independence is far from being a realm of irresponsibility. But the responsibility is not to society. If it is not an acknowledged responsibility to God, it is responsibility to oneself, autonomy. Self-criticism is part of self-creation. In personal life one is responsible as the artist is responsible rather than as the motorist is responsible. Ajax and Ulysses, T. S. Eliot and Winston Churchill, the end products of self-choice and cultivation, are incomparable, as works of art are incomparable. All the same, standards are formed only by making comparisons. Everybody as a person is both his own standard and subject to comparisons.

Summary

Rules of a democratic society of all kinds, from rules of the road to rules of the courts, from statutes to contracts and promises, imply good faith and public spirit. They are not to be thought of as commandments or taboos, but rather as instruments of coexistence and cooperation in a free society for the sake of self-realization for all. The rules are therefore subject to revision by agreed procedures, and they stand less for a fixed order, a code of any kind, than for a drive toward fuller agreement and more equal conditions. This realm of social obligation supports a realm of freedom enclosed only by ideals personally chosen. Independence is founded upon interdependence.

A society reproduces itself through its schools. When society was founded on an unquestioned Christian faith, the schools were Christian foundations. In a secular democratic society, the proper foundation of the school can hardly be religious: it is moral. In such a society education should include education in social obligation and education for the choice of life.

2 MORAL EDUCATION

Induction and instruction are the two interdependent methods of moral education. By "induction" here is meant not, as in the dictionary sense, a ceremonial initiation or formal installation of any kind, but a guided and developing experience of membership of a group: induction into the family, into the peer group, into the school, into the neighborhood. One learns the requirements of the group and becomes adapted to it as an acceptable member. There is imitation and there is an element of instruction from adept and authoritative members of the group, but the young person under moral education does not merely adapt in deference to the adept, for the element of instruction includes also guidance informed by universal principle which transcends the group.

Induction into the family means, ideally, that a child is dependably cared for, firmly controlled when necessary but never punished, weaned at the right times physically and morally, enabled to become competent and competitive, and thus self-dependent, dependable, and cooperative. It means exposure to the ideas and ideals, the traditions and ways, the standards and values of the particular family.

The values of the peer group, their approvals and disapprovals, and their interests are different from and independent of those of the authorities, including parents. The role of authority in the phases of moral education is neither abstention nor intervention, but a judicious (rather than judicial) aid to developing people. In the school, particularly, peer groups of different kinds are thrown together, with authority omnipresent. In this situation, suffering at the hands of peers and/or authorities can be disastrous. For some, their school days have been life's worst handicap. The principal task of moral education in school is to create out of this situation a moral community bound together by and called out by and enthusiastic for their educational tasks and ideals. To prize excellence in various forms, to accept diversity with parity of esteem, to be engaged in enjoyed activities which evoke a spontaneous public spirit that protects the order they require, to form together community approvals and disapprovals generated by common interests and aspirations and by a generous respect for the individual, and to examine and discuss such approvals and disapprovals: moral education means experiences of this kind in a community which values them.

The school, however, is not left free to do what it will under the best educational guidance. The school cannot educate against society, for society reproduces itself through its schools, and therefore imposes upon them its own conditions. "Parity of esteem" for different types of excellence within the school is hardly possible if in society only those are highly esteemed who excel in performances measured by academic criteria. I remember in the early fifties in a school in Harlem watching the Negro teacher build up a solitary Puerto Rican in the class, so that by her suggestion it was made to seem mighty fine to be a Puerto Rican. Indirectly and powerfully, she was using her moral influence to resist and reverse the current prejudiced estimate of those in lowest social esteem; but this moral influence was practically nullified by the need of the Harlem Negro community for a scapegoat, about which the school could do nothing. Similarly, education for an open society can hardly take place in a church school. Moral education in schools does make a marginal difference to society in changing its ways and influencing its values, but it cannot be expected to do the job of, nor to beat, the family, the neighborhood, and society at large.

All the same, the school remains the focus of moral education, for it is in some ways a self-creating community which can form its own standards and choose its own ideals, and is not merely a subservient instrument or a reflective mirror of the society it serves. Induction into the neighborhood, for example, should mean in practice that at one or more of the stages of the school course the pupil would participate in a group which explored the neighborhood in a more or less systematic way to get a picture of its life and character, learning something of what was amiss and what was missing, and which responded with an acceptance of responsibility issuing in an initiative, a thought out and informed project designed to improve in some way the local conditions.

Finally, moral education should include induction into the company of moral exemplars, historical and perhaps legendary or fictitious representatives of ideal types and outstanding achievement. At least from a humanist point of view, this should be induction into a mixed company, offering different patterns of being human, contrast and variety of example. There is here a repudiation of every *absolute* religious ideal embodied in a revered founder.

Turning now from induction to instruction, the first simple but all-important point to make is that instruction should be based on dependable knowledge. Little enough research has yet been done on moral education, but at least there is some established knowledge of the phases and stages in the development of the child. This knowledge indicates what is to be expected and what is to be done at each stage, and what should not be attempted: for example, the age at which and the manner in which a child should be morally weaned, enabled to be self-dependent; or the age at which the ritual observance of rules begins to give place to a sense of their purpose, so that the child can and should be given reasons for what is required. Instruction is blended with induction in guided group experience, and both are dependent upon spontaneous activities and responses normal to the child at the given age. Basic knowledge of the needs and characteristics of each stage of child development, which should govern the whole course of moral education, is part of the professional equipment of the teacher, but is by no means to be expected of the parents who manage the child during its most impressionable years when habits, attitudes, and life styles are formed in enduring patterns of behavior. Social services which help the family cannot make good parental inadequacy. Attempts have to be made in time and at the right time to equip parents with the basic knowledge about child care—which will include not least the handling of adolescents.

Basic knowledge underlies all instruction, but some forms of instruction also require special skills. Counseling is obviously one of these, and young people, perhaps without exception, need the help at some time of a counselor, who may not be, and sometimes should not be, either parent or teacher. Counselors may be on the staff of the school or attached to a club or in some other way available, but available they should be, for they have a necessary part to play in moral education.

Discussion in class of moral questions also demands a special skill, as Socrates demonstrated. Every school should have this forum, whatever the arrangements may be. School approvals and disapprovals and school rules should be examined and discussed. Children should be allowed and encouraged to bring their own problems up for discussion. Topical outside problems and questions provide further material. Besides being encouraged to think about principles through the discussion of actual judgments and concrete problems, children should be helped at the right age to think about techniques. How to make a decision or choice, what to do about failure, how to set about solving a problem, how to plan and manage one's life: techniques concerned with such matters are of not less moral importance than moral principles. To put more moral resolve into what one does becomes demoralizing if one is going about what one is doing in a way that is doomed to failure. Young people need to be shown how to use their minds and manage themselves, and introduced to the resources they have for self-help. If this is left out of the moral education course, there is little left that is worthwhile, for then the limited but supremely important power of self-creation is a birthright which is more than likely to be unclaimed. Regimental *esprit de corps* is an emasculated version of moral education.

Without induction, which is moral experience, there is no moral education; and without instruction, which leads to the conscious possession and evaluation of moral experience, there is no moral education. Moral experience and reflection upon it is an encounter with reality and a projection of ideals. Or this is what it may and should become under the guidance of instruction. Induction into the family, into the peer group, even into the school, is hardly likely to be experience of a model community. The blend of instruction with induction is required to lift experience to the plane of conscious possession, so that the actual is seen in the light of the possible. The pupil is not morally educated if he is left to live at the level of imitation and conformity, doing what others do and what is effectively required. With regard to society, there is the natural tendency to imitation and conformity; with regard to oneself, there are the usual lusts and ambitions; with regard to others, there is some natural fellow-feeling mixed up with envy and strife and all uncharitableness: if moral education is to transform this wilderness into a garden, the pupil must be enabled to learn to see the actual in the light of better and worse possibilities and to want to enlist on the side of the better. This he can hardly do if he is himself disadvantaged and in any manner excluded from the benefits of society—and therefore of being human. Thus, coaching a backward child in the three Rs or broadening the curriculum to give scope and merit to the non-academic may be the most appropriate form of moral education in a given case.

Conclusion

Acceptance of these moral hemispheres as the preferred moral order—personal ideals and choice resting upon social rules and obligation; independence supported by interdependence—solves one of the severest practical problems, for it subordinates society to conscience and personal values in the only way in which a pluriform, highly organized and industrialized modern society can be kept subordinate. Education in the public school can show how one and the same community may be educated in obligation and for choice. The open school is a preparation for and a model of the open society.

In this preferred moral order relating and regulating private and public life, religion and its alternatives belong to the private hemisphere. Religion is taken away from society as its common foundation and common end. This does not necessarily diminish its importance. In the private hemisphere, religious believers can organize and demonstrate their faith and declare and press its absolute claims, in rivalry with alternative views of the world and permissive ways of life. This very rivalry is guaranteed by this preferred moral order, and is itself a guarantee that personal rather than institutional values shall remain paramount. In some areas we cannot afford to agree and in some we cannot afford not to. History shows how rarely mankind is willing to get this right.

HUMANISTIC ETHICS AND THE CONFLICT OF INTERESTS

Marvin Farber

A humanistic philosophy is a philosophy within nature; it does not recognize and it has no place for anything transcending nature. Physical reality, infinitely extended in space and in time, constitutes for humanism a domain that is large enough for all meaningful purposes. As a philosophy of human existence, humanism provides the necessary setting for a theory of ethical value. In estimating its merits, one must bear in mind that values are essentially restricted to human beings. There can be no advantage to a generalized theory of value extended to all of existence, for that would amount in effect to interpreting existence *as value*. Although the concept of value may be extended to all organic existence, the result would be too thin to provide a solution to the valuational problems of mankind. The scope of a philosophy of values, however, must include all human beings, and must be based upon the principle that it is sufficient to be human for full status in the system of ethical values. The unqualified recognition of all human beings as centers of value, regardless of the accidents of birth, creed, color, or historical conditions, is the greatest merit of the humanistic approach to a philosophy of values.

1 WHAT ARE THE FACTS FOR THE PHILOSOPHY OF VALUES?

It amounts to a truism to state that in any process of reasoning, one must always take account of the facts. An appeal to facts suggests finality, in the sense that a judgment is true if it expresses a fact. That 7 is a prime number is a fact in an ideal mathematical system; that the sum of the interior angles of a triangle is equal to two right angles is a fact in a Euclidean system; that the average age at death of human beings is approximately seventy years is a fact within a limited spatio-temporal region of reference. There are, however, numerous warnings against error, deception, and dogmatism which must be considered. Do the following judgments express facts: "Success under a capitalist economic system is the result of superior ability, and therefore those who are superior are sure to be the wealthiest"; or the statement by an American Nazi, that "A Jew is not a man"; or Hitler's assertion that "A Negro is a half-monkey"? Does a reported "experience of mystical ecstasy" express a fact? Are facts established by arguments such as the ontological and the cosmological proofs of the existence of a Supreme Being, or by Spinoza's reasoning concerning substance, interpreted as God, in his *Ethics*? Such diverse cases illustrate the need for caution in making an appeal to alleged facts.

Statistical generalizations express facts. Probability statements are statements of facts that may be superseded by additional evidence; accordingly, the relevant conditions must always be indicated in any probabilistic assertion. For example, in 1968 the chance of a safe journey by an airplane in the United States may be expressed by a numerical ratio, and it is understood that the ratio may be changed at any time, as new evidence becomes available.

When proper safeguards and cautions have been observed, descriptions may be said to express facts. The source of possible error may be technical in character, it may be due to the personal background or circumstances of the observer, it may be ascribed to difficulties presented by the objects under description, or in the final analysis it may be attributed to the social system. Purported descriptions may be based on misleading reports, expressions of vested interests, or organized prejudices. They may be vague statements about man and his nature, framed on an abstract level of generality, and concealing a complex of special assumptions—in short, they may harbor wishful fantasy or express an assumed "philosophical anthropology."

Without dwelling any longer on the preliminary problem of the determination of facts, let us consider the nature of the facts involved in the discussion of ethical values and principles. Difficulties may occur at every step, for one cannot claim certainty in ethical knowledge. Antecedently accepted ideas and theories continue to play a role; and there are always cultural traditions and conflicting interests to be considered. Disinterested objective inquiry is an ideal.

Granting the complex difficulties that face us, let us indicate briefly the nature of the facts that apply to ethical inquiry. One may describe the individual human being, his abilities, aptitudes, psychological traits, economic status, social and family relations, needs, desires, and what may be called, in objective language, his interests (whether he is actually "interested" or not). Individual differences must be noted, but not at the cost of class or group characteristics. Both types of fact, referring to individuals and to classes or groups, are irreducible, and it is important to recognize this factor. In so doing, one does not leave the order of unique and passing events for a static order of permanent structures. The characteristics of a class or group are also unique and passing. They are seen in family organizations, with their composite needs and interests; in economic classes, such as workers or capitalists; in cultural organizations devoted to music, art, or literature; in national and international organizations; and in special groups, both conflicting and harmonious, in various countries.

There are variable features of individuals and classes of individuals as well as relatively stable features, which may be regarded as constant for all practical purposes. Thus the need for food, shelter, and clothing is constant. This is manifested in many different ways, so that what qualifies as suitable nourishment for one individual may be harmful for another. There is a great diversity of individual tastes and preferences, with regional and national differences. Despite the diversity, there are always general requirements for existence that must be met. The food requirement may be satisfied maximally or partially, with many individual and group differences. But a need for food or for a sufficient number of energy units is a constant condition for survival. The range of variation in satisfying this need goes all the way from roots and nuts to cannibalism, from farm produce to the use of solar energy. There is an ideal maximum of satisfaction, and there is a physical minimum, below which life would not be possible. This minimum, determined by the conditions necessary for the survival of an organism, is somewhat different for different individuals. This is to be distinguished from the degree to which one participates in his social system. The "iron law of wages," which was once supposed to define the limit of need below which wages could not go if workers were to be able to function, was not based upon facts. Wages have indeed gone below the level needed for subsistence, and, viewed historically, it is seen that there is no "lowest limit." Furthermore, there has been no lowest limit in dealing with the problem of poverty and unemployment. To illustrate the extremes to which conditions may degenerate, it is sufficient to point to the Trujillo regime in Santo Domingo, which "solved" the problem of unemployed and destitute Haitians by a program of extermination. There is a lower limit for survival, but that lower limit has not been universally respected in human society. On the contrary, masses of unfortunate human beings have either been liquidated or allowed to starve by more powerful groups in society.

Class needs refer to all that is necessary to preserve or advance a given class as such. If it is profitable for an industrial system to have an available reserve supply of labor, immigration is encouraged. In order to protect foreign commercial interests, military strength is regarded as a need. Class needs involve cultural activities and institutions as well: an educational system may be committed to the preservation of the existing order of society, with the press induced to be "cooperative," and a spirit of loyalty on the part of the representatives of the leading religious traditions encouraged. With the rise of labor unions, there was a marked preference for company unions, which were considered to be more tractable. If strikes occurred, "scabs" or "finks" were viewed as a necessary response to a class need. The specialist strike breaker (well portrayed by E. Levinson in his book *I Break Strikes*) is now outmoded, for a pattern of strikes, whether actual or threatened, as a prelude to wage negotiations (and, on occasion, as a relief to overproduction) has superseded it. The preservation of an economy dominated by the profit motive is the basic need of a capitalist class, and that underlies all other needs. It has reached such intensity that many of its defenders apparently prefer the risk of nuclear extinction, rather than face the prospect of limiting if not finally eliminating the profit motive from human affairs.

One may approach needs factually, though this must be done critically. It is a fact, for example, that the British or French capitalist classes regard themselves as threatened by American competition. There is, they argue, a need for currency regulation, and for economic as well as political alliances to offset America's economic interests. The needs of Britain and France may be viewed in a different manner, however, with respect to the interests of *all* the people in them, and not simply the dominant economic classes. The account is still factual, but the selection of facts is now not limited by the set of dominant interests and historically conditioned economic, legal, and moral practices which are firmly embedded in the social system. The account now requires a degree of detachment, sufficient to survey the potentialities of the social system with a view to its possible reconstruction. If a case of class preservation, involving the profit system, requires the defense of an entire complex of legal, military, and other social relationships, it is also true that the advancement of the interests of all members of the same society will require fundamental changes in human relations. Selected facts can be adduced to support both alternatives. Thus, a general appeal to the "facts themselves" may be satisfied in a number of conflicting ways: one may consider as basic the preservation of the existing economic and social system, or one may take as central the need to modify the system in terms of an "enlightened" individualism or a newer socialistic organization. An unqualified or general appeal to the facts is thus too tenuous to be of any use. The appeal to facts must be combined with proposals, theories, and principles. Every such appeal must be selective and directed; if it is not, it loses its force through empty generality.

It is a fact—or it is not a fact—that labor is the source of all economic value; that capital makes labor possible (or is "the mother of labor," according to Thomas Huxley), or vice versa; that the possession of capital is the result of thrift; that workers have nothing to lose but their chains (as Marx expressed it); that labor unions frequently emphasize the thesis that in order to be loyal to his union, the laborer must disregard certain duties to the community at large (as Josiah Royce maintained); that we are gradually drifting toward a form of socialism (as asserted by William James); that the profit motive is essential for progress in the satisfaction of human needs; and that inequality of opportunity is a cause of social unrest and conflict. There are facts about organic, economic, social, and cultural needs; about the physical conditions of life; about the ethical ideas of various individuals and classes in a given society; about the behavior of human beings, individually and in groups, including statistical generalizations; about the consequences of programs of conduct, or plans of organization; about the premises of a given line of reasoning, or of a proposed line of action (logical facts, that a given conclusion or argument involves one or more premises); that one nation was the aggressor in a conflict with another nation, or vice versa, whereby it might be argued that both may be aggressors in different ways, in keeping with the claims of both sides; that ethical value has been defined in various ways, and that it is therefore not "indefinable" (unless indefinableness is assumptively read into its very meaning); that a so-called life of pleasure is usually self-defeating; or that pleasure is not a universal motive of conduct.

There are also facts about facts—for example, that our knowledge of facts enables us to choose between rival valuational and practical views. Thus there are facts about the effectiveness of the appeal to facts, and about incorrect as well as correct appeals to facts. There are truths about abstract principles, about idealizations and ideal objects of thought, about transcendental and natural facts, about sense and nonsense. If it is a fact that makes a judgment true or false, there must be countless types of fact, in accordance with the unlimited number of types of judgment. In the context of values, there are facts about the experience and realization of values, the judgment of values, the choice of value systems, the justification of values, and fallacious thinking about values. There may be correct reports about the ways in which people apply or fail to apply value systems; and there is the relevant evidence when the formally based principles are applied to human experience.

In any appeal to the facts themselves, then, it must be made clear whether primary truths of experiences are in question, or formally conditioned principles. In all cases, the evidence must be made clear. A truth about a group is not necessarily applicable to an individual, who may go counter to the group. The final test is provided by the evidence. But the types of evidence are as varied as the types of fact, and it is necessary to distinguish between judgments dealing descriptively with experience and judgments of value. Included under the judgments of experience are all the actual valuations that are illustrated in human history; and included under the judgments of value are all the tests of human values, and all the types of justification, involving special definitions and premises, that have been employed. Thus there are two orders of facts—the existential and the formal. But there are also existential facts about formal relationships; and all existential facts may be represented formally in systems of judgments and arranged in a deductive pattern.

2 VALUES AND CONFLICTING INTERESTS

One knows what values are by describing the ways in which they are realized. Values may be realized in ways not actually desired, as illustrated by the education of the young. For example, children are compelled to take medicine, and it has value for them, even though they may not desire it. In a negative sense, value is realized if a person is imprisoned, or if he suffers capital punishment. But fulfillment, although good in the sense of a limited positive value, may nevertheless be ethically bad because of its consequences; and frustration, although bad in a limited sense of negative value, may be judged to be good from a more general point of view. The realization of value may accompany desire; it may be independent of desire, so that one could speak of a neutrality of desire on the part of those directly concerned; or it may go counter to desire. Again, some persons affected by an action may desire it, and others may oppose it, so that there are conflicting desires. In all such cases there is a realization of value, positive or negative, as determined by fulfillment or frustration.

The actual moral appraisals of people are important, for they express the desires, interests, and conceptions of particular people under existing conditions. An avowed desire, however, may not be a genuine desire, for reasons well known to analysts and psychologists; and an asserted appraisal may not necessarily be the actual judgment of a person. An appraisal may be forced or compelled, and one may conform with the prevailing moral judgments of his society. Frequently people accept the guiding precepts of their cultural tradition, even though their conduct would hardly be said to exemplify the acknowledged moral ideals. Such appraisals, however, may be recognized as reflecting a definite cultural tradition. There are many reasons why a person may not speak as he feels, desires, or thinks: fear, self-interest, the wish to please or not to displease, and illogical or confused thinking are among the most prominent.

It is good procedure to replace a question that cannot be answered conclusively by one or more questions that can. Thus Aristotle turned from the general question "What is happiness?" to the question concerning the peculiar happiness of man. What a person desires may be really as indeterminate in its way as the question of happiness in general. Objective questions that can be answered are preferable to subjectively directed questions, important though the analysis of the latter may be for the understanding of human beings. A descriptive account of the realization of value through the satisfaction of interests provides definite knowledge about human existence. Whether or not one desires food, he has an interest in surviving, so that the satisfaction of the need for food is a positive realization of value. How far can one go in this way, never leaving the objective facts of existence? Many features of human existence will come into play, but by no means all, on the present level of scientific inquiry.

Without detailed clarification, the concepts of desire, need, and interest can only be used roughly. They have physical, biological, and cultural aspects, and they may be individual or social in their reference. In relationship to a concrete social problem, as illustrated by the demands of a group of strikers, it is not too difficult to indicate the interests involved. The interests can be identified, and their relative importance or weight can be determined.

In making estimates of importance or weight, there must be a basis of undifferentiated units on which to operate. If the units are held to be uneven in weight, the difficulties encountered in ethical reasoning are greatly increased. Let us say, then, that all the interests of a person are on the same plane of importance, as expressed by the statement "An interest is merely one interest, and is not in itself weightier than any other interest." The phrase "in itself" leaves it open, however, for an interest to have ulterior effects on the fulfillment of many other interests, so that its long-range importance is greater. Such interests are value-conditioning for other interests, and are found to be more important, or to have greater weights, from the perspective of a larger system of interests. But there is no inherent superiority or inferiority on the part of any interest whatsoever, whether it be in nutrition, family life, or cultural activities. By virtue of their role in the lives of individuals, however, some interests outweigh others because they condition the amount of value to be realized, if not the very survival of the individual in question. The same reasoning applies to groups, with additional considerations involved because of the greater complexity. It is therefore not even paradoxical to state that interests, taken as undifferentiated in themselves for the purposes of a calculus of interests, nevertheless differ in importance or weight when their conditioning effects on other interests are considered. The two statements are compatible: no interest is inherently superior to any other, whether it be an interest in food, music, or sex; and one interest may have greater weight than another because of its consequences for the total system of interests involved. The interest in food clearly conditions all other realizations of value. It can also happen that one experience of listening to a musical performance has a decisive influence on an entire life-plan. If existence occurred all at once and had limited duration, it would be possible to consider an interest as final in itself. For human beings, however, planning for the future is essential, if other values are to be realized. This does not introduce a totally new factor into existence, for the factor of relative importance or of value-conditioning is present when organic beings have evolved. Human beings can only exist if sufficient attention is given to the satisfaction of prior interests, or if due allowance is made for future interests by the adjustment or redirection of present activities. Reforestation, birth control, and the extension of social security are obvious illustrations of the issue.

When an individual is considered in isolation, the idea of undifferentiated units of interest is harmless. This idea is helpful for ethical analysis, but its limited truth must be subordinated to a larger view of human existence in action. The principle of the inherent nonsuperiority of interests to one another thus is not misleading, unless it is taken out of its context and misinterpreted.

Many additional factors must come into play when a social group is considered.[1] The complexity of interests is much greater for a family, a community, or a nation. The unit of a social group is an individual human being. Just as different indices of weight attach to interests, so must the units of society be considered different with respect to potentialities, interests, and achievements. The principle of inherent nonsuperiority also applies on the level of social relations. There are no existential facts that would justify a human hierarchy, in the ethical sense of a greater inherent right to the realization of value, although there is a great diversity of individual differences of interests and aptitudes. Racist arguments amount to prejudice or libel, and are readily exposed as such. They cannot be sustained by facts. The facts about individual differences or group differences do not support an order of ethical preference. They merely enter into the subject matter for ethical analysis, adding to the knowledge of human beings. One can say with Lessing that it is sufficient to be a man, or, in the language of the present discussion, that it is sufficient to be a human being, with no inherent basis for subordination or superordination. That does not preclude differences of physical, social, economic, cultural, or moral achievement. One individual's achievements may outweigh the achievements of many

[1] Cf. M. Farber, *Basic Issues of Philosophy* (New York: Harper & Row, Publishers, 1968).

others, although the same gifted individual may have quite a low rank on a number of other scales of achievement necessary for the values of a social system. This is again not to intrude a new factor into existence arbitrarily. The differences of human individuals are there objectively, both at a given time and when viewed from the perspective of the achievements of a generation. All of this is descriptively true.

There is a complication in viewing an individual on the social scale, however, which must be considered. If he is a member of a society as simple as Captain Smith's group in colonial Virginia, then the social relationships are readily observable and its achievements are easily determined. In order to eat, a person had to work, and there was recognition of the basic equality of all members of the group. In a complex society, a distinction must be drawn between real and apparent weight. The achievement of one person may consist in getting others to assist him in amassing wealth. It may consist in acquiring slaves, or in gaining ownership of large areas of land and natural resources by any available means. The achievement of a predatory entrepreneur—that is, the use of other men merely to advance one's own interests—cannot be accepted at face value in any rational ethics. It is an apparent and not a real achievement, in terms of the realization of positive value. Such practices must be recognized as prominent in any attempt at a genuine portrayal of human existence. They are conspicuously present in a succession of forms from the slaveholders of antiquity to those profiting by the inequalities of the twentieth century.

So long as one talks simply about an interest in food and shelter in order to satisfy one's basic needs, or in general terms about participation in the cultural enjoyments provided by a social system, there are no great difficulties encountered in estimating the values realized in such activities. The incompleteness of such a selective approach to human values, however, must be understood. Its limitations may be removed by a greater attention to concreteness. On the individual level, attention must be directed to such facts as aptitudes, desires, and aversions. The need for economic sufficiency is bound to assert itself, and so will the fact that the broader interests and happiness of an individual normally involve other human beings, and thus society in general. On the social level, the need for concreteness is all the greater in those developed societies which are marked by a division of labor and distinctions of class. Men are viewed as workers, employers, artists, or teachers—always in terms of their concrete roles in the social system. But it is necessary to examine the actual contributions through work by all members of society. The real value of what is contributed may be quite different from the apparent value.

Some descriptions of human activity, supported by the conditions of our existing society, have been appraised highly—for example, planned murders with economic incentives. The bizarre and the illicit aspects of human experience have also had their repercussion in the literature of philosophy, with Sartre's description of a man looking through a keyhole a high point. Titles such as the "rational man," the "*homo faber*," the "small businessman," and the "large-scale entrepreneur," exemplars of our capitalistic society, should be added to by designations such as "man the rogue," "pickpocket," and "brigand," extended to a national and international scale. There is more than a grain of truth in the rejoinder of Diogenes to a person chiding him with once having been a counterfeiter: "What I was then, you are now; and what I am now, you will never be." If it is not the currency that is being falsified, we quite generally enter into gambling arrangements with disarming names—frequently investments for future security—in such a way that we may profit or perhaps lose through the admitted weaknesses and inequalities of the economic system. Most people are partners to some extent in processes of falsification, even though care is taken that they be legally sanctioned. The rational man alluded to but hardly approached by Diogenes is still in the future. Thus the narrow interests of individuals and classes in a competitive economic system are open to criticism. How, we may ask, are we to appraise conflicting interests in a corrupt economic system?

The ideal to be approached progressively requires an understanding of the nature of man in all important respects—natural, historical, and cultural. It also requires a genuinely humanistic ethics, with all principles and criteria supported by the facts of experience, and based upon the conscious rational choice of all human beings. However imperfectly this goal may be realized in present and future social systems, the ideal must be held up as a standard for critical judgment. One can only speak of a moral quest, and not of a settled state of affairs. The process of satisfying interests and desires is endless, and it can be expected that there will always be conflicts to be resolved for an individual and for a social group. Soundness of judgment in expressing moral preference is the answer to this general need, which is coextensive with the entire process of experience. Ethics is therewith embraced to science, and the rational moral man is a man of science in the literal sense of that term.

DEMOCRACY AND THE PROBLEM OF WAR*

John Somerville

The aim of the present paper is to approach the problem of war, in its relation to democracy, from the standpoint of humanist ethics. Since this standpoint may have different meanings to different persons, a brief statement of what it means to the present writer should perhaps be given at the outset. It might be summed up as the recognition of three factors: (1) a naturalistic, as distinguished from a supernaturalistic foundation for ethics; (2) the need for a rational or scientific method in working out ethics; (3) the attainment of the maximum welfare of all human beings as the goal of ethics.

Thus, from this standpoint, ethics or morals is a field of knowledge created by the mind of man operating in terms of humanly understandable logic; it is not a set of commands issued by a supernatural, humanly incomprehensible God. It is interesting, and historically somewhat ironical, that a statement of this kind, made today, has a rather radical, nonconformist sound, and is usually identified, in the minds of those who are not professional scholars, with recent trends in modern thought. Actually, it represents the most classic approach to the subject, set forth in ancient times by Aris-

* A shorter version of this article appeared in *The Humanist,* XXVII, No. 3 (1967), 77–80. Reprinted by permission of *The Humanist.*

totle, who was a political conservative. What he did in ethics is very significant, though it included great mistakes; and it affords an excellent framework in which to set the present point.

Using the language of today, we should have to say that Aristotle approached the whole subject of ethics as a social science, though we make it difficult for ourselves fully to appreciate this fact by publishing and studying the work we call his *Ethics* separately from the work we call his *Politics,* whereas he conceived of them as one connected work, which he called *Politika.* He meant by this term, judging from what he put into the work, not only politics and government in the restricted sense, but elements of what we call social science in the broader sense (sociology, social psychology, etc.).

Aristotle's treatise begins: "Every art and every inquiry, and similarly every action and pursuit is thought to aim at some good; and for this reason the good has rightly been declared to be that at which all things aim." [1] Reading this with "modern" habits of mind, one is at first tempted to assume that the words "is thought to aim at some good" signify that Aristotle accepts the kind of contextual associations that usually go with such language in our world. That is, since different persons have different ideas about what is good, the whole thing boils down to a matter of subjective choice—"each to his taste." But, as we read on, we see that the situation is actually the opposite. What Aristotle is saying is that the term good has as objective, empirical, and understandable an origin as the term "health." It is neither mystical nor arbitrary. And, as what is healthy for man can be determined by observation and analysis of man, so what is good for man can be determined in basically the same way—by observation and analysis of man's needs, wants, organs, attributes, potentialities of development, and preconditions of development. It is neither arbitrary nor mystical that man prefers pleasure to pain, health to illness, joy to misery, sufficiency to poverty, knowledge to ignorance, development to stultification—in a word, happiness to unhappiness. All this is built in. It goes with being a human being, and is the objective root of all ethical values. Thus ethics is a rational study of how to be happy.

[1] Aristotle: *Nicomachean Ethics,* Book I, trans. W. D. Ross, in *Introduction to Aristotle* (New York: Modern Library, 1947), p. 308.

It must also be a social study, for it is at once clear that man is a social (political) creature, that he could not be man at all except in and through society, social institutions, and that he could not be a happy man except in and through a society whose institutions were of a kind to permit and facilitate the attainment of all that goes into the happy life which is the good life because it is the happy life in the most inclusive sense. This calls for a careful study of social institutions, not just in general (that would be to forget what the whole thing is about), but in relation to the attainment of human happiness.

On all these important matters I think that Aristotle was right, and right in the humanist sense. Where he went seriously wrong was in a number of empirical conclusions which he accepted without sufficient evidence: that only a minority of human beings possessed, or ever would possess, sufficient potentiality of rational development to be able to manage their own lives successfully, take part in running the state, solve their problems, and attain genuine human happiness; hence, that slavery was forever justified; that only men counted; that the state should forever be paternalistic; and that society should forever be divided into a small ruling class of educated aristocrats and an uneducated mass of slaves and manual workers. In short, Aristotle was naturalistic in his basis, scientific in his choice of method, humanistic in his focus, but mistaken about key facts, and, worst of all, lacking in a theory of socio-historical development. We can retain the basis and the method, correct the facts, supply a theory of history, and enrich the humanism. This should be done first and foremost in regard to the problem of war in the modern world.

In view of the changed character and consequences of war today, there is urgent need to rethink the problem, not only in relation to humanistic ethics in general, but to the concept of democracy in particular.

Throughout human history up to the end of World War II, armed conflict between powerful nations did not effectively threaten the existence of the planet Earth or the continuity of the human race. This threat is now upon us. War is capable of wiping out not only all existing human values, but the very possibility of creating any further human values to replace them. It is clear we are dealing with a qualitatively new phenomenon, which perhaps should be called by a new name. In fact, in order to indicate the new power and scope of the death-dealing possibilities inherent in the weapons of contemporary war, a new term already has had to be added to the vocabulary of killing. To supplement the terms homicide and genocide, which stand merely for the killing of a man, or of groups of human beings forming a nation or a race, we have had to invent the word "biocide" to designate the killing off, at one stroke, of all forms of life—plant, animal, and human. Such is the technical possibility which has now emerged in the development of thermonuclear weaponry.

Clearly, a new moral evaluation must be undertaken. New questions must be faced: Is there any longer the same meaning—or any meaning—in the traditional distinction between a just and unjust war, if wars are fought with thermonuclear weapons? What concept of human justice would be compatible with the total annihilation of all actual and potential human values? Has not the world now reached the point where the responsible philosopher must unambiguously declare and uncompromisingly teach that, where such a likelihood enters the situation, armed warfare between sovereign states has become unjust and immoral, something which can never again be regarded as the lesser of two evils, which henceforth must always be regarded as the greatest of all evils? To take this view demands courage and may invite reprisals; but is there any other view that is humanly defensible in the year 1969?

It is important to note that war as we are speaking of it is not an activity of individuals as individuals. It is not even the activity of large groups just as large groups. The sovereign state, through its government, is the only kind of large group which possesses the resources, power, and authority necessary to carry on the kind of war which constitutes our problem. It is even more important to note that war can be carried on only if individuals as individuals agree to participate. In a sense, it is first a matter between the individual and his conscience; then it is a matter between the individual and his government.

Considering these facts one need not be simply fatalistic or pessimistic about war. It is far from being a phenomenon which is beyond the control of human beings, like the gradual cooling of the sun or the expansion of the universe in space. Although war is a social phenomenon, it is also individually voluntary in a very high degree, and in a way that makes it humanly controllable. In point of fact, it is more controllable than government itself. In large part, government is something done to me rather than anything I do; something often silent, elusive, of which I may not even be conscious. It does much of its work through the accepted routines of normal life, by inertia, as it were. The individual, as worker, consumer, or citizen, may never be aware of myriads of enforced regulations, standards, and prohibitions which enter into and determine in so many ways the warp and woof of his daily living conditions in regard to the buildings in which he dwells and works, his supply of water and other utilities, all that goes into buying, selling, education, entertainment, travel, and the whole social and economic spectrum. To a large extent, I can be governed without knowing it, but I can never fight a war without knowing it. Government without consent of the governed is relatively easy to bring about. War without consent of the warriors is impossible. Conscience, if it has the courage of its convictions, can remain in control.

Under the impact of the modern democratic tradition, the concept of human rights has become firmly established as a standard for regulating the relations between government and the persons being governed; as a standard for determining, among other things, the limits of governmental power, the limits beyond which the government has no legitimate authority to exercise power over the individual. The modern democratic tradition is very clear and explicit in its insistence on the principle that, insofar as the government is something having authority over the people, such authority is never absolute. It is always subordinate, in the final reckoning, both morally and empirically, to the authority which the people have over the government. This is the irreducible meaning of the sovereignty of the people. First come human rights, then comes government.

It is no accident that this logical and moral order was laid down by Thomas Jefferson when he wrote the Declaration of Independence, in which he structured with clarity and economy the argument of democracy. He says, in effect, that we begin with axioms. One of these is that people have "unalienable rights," and that among these rights are "life, liberty, and the pursuit of happiness." In other words, we begin with human rights, and the first of these is the right to life. Government has not yet come into the picture. It is not government which brings these rights into being. On the contrary, it is certain necessities involved in the fulfillment of these rights which bring government into being. The only moral justification for government is the service it can render in this regard. Thus, Jefferson continues: "That to secure these rights, governments are instituted among men, deriving their just powers from the consent of the governed. . . ."

Ethically speaking, I suppose that few philosophers today would differ with Jefferson's order of values: governments exist for human beings, not human beings for governments; the use of power must be judged and controlled by relation to human rights; the primary right, the precondition to the enjoyment of any other human right, is life, the right to live out one's natural span. It follows then, both logically and morally, that wherever thermonuclear weapons may be involved:

1. The warmaking power can no longer be considered as among the legitimate powers of government.
2. No government can legitimately request or require any individual to participate in war.

If anyone should feel that such conclusions, even though justified by the premises, are entirely outside the realm of practical possibility, and thus represent merely an exercise in wishful thinking, let him reflect on the history of slavery. There was a time when slavery was the common practice of the most powerful countries in the world. It was the chief source of economic power, embodied in the civil and criminal law as something to be protected and enforced. It was justified by the leading theologians as morally acceptable in the sight of God, and by the leading philosophers as logically acceptable in the light of reason. In such an apparently impregnable context it lasted for centuries. Yet the time came when the slave-making or slavery-enforcing power was recognized as *per se* in violation of human rights—not something which could be considered as just under certain conditions, and unjust under others, but as something unjust and immoral by definition. If the slave-making power could thus be removed from the powers legitimately exercised under the laws of state, why should it be considered impossible for the war-making power to be brought to the same end?

I am not assuming a naïve theory of history in which the chief causal factor in the movement of human events would be simple moral feeling. The removal of human slavery as a basic social institution might well have been impossible if technological developments had not rendered its continuance unprofitable. I am suggesting that technological developments in the field of thermonuclear weaponry have now rendered war totally unprofitable.

In relation to the thesis here being developed a number of questions must be answered. What about the right of self-defense? Does not a nation invaded or attacked always have the right to take up arms against the invader? What about a nation enslaved, or placed under colonial subjection by another? Would it not be justified in using war as a means of national liberation? What about revolutionary wars, the right of revolution against a tyrannical government? Did not Jefferson also include that among the self-evident truths in the Declaration of Independence?

In the past, the democratic tradition gave an affirmative answer to all these questions, an answer that was justified by the existence of certain facts. These facts could be summed up as follows: After the revolutionary war, or the war of national liberation, or the war of self-defense, we can be sure that our motherland will still physically exist, and that at least a part of our nation will still survive to inhabit it, and to live the life we cherish. However, suppose that Jefferson, or any other democrat of the past had been unable to make that statement. Suppose the facts had been such that the most likely consequence of a decision to enter into a state of war would have been the termination of all life whatsoever. Would such a decision still have been justified?

To think of someone maintaining that it still would have been justified seems almost equivalent to doubting his sanity, because we all realize upon reflection that there is a moral calculus attached to the exercise of any right. That is, if we exercise a right we do so in order to attain a situation which will be more advantageous, or more just, than the present situation. In New York City I have a right, which I have frequently exercised, to play with my children in Central Park. But if the physical and chemical conditions of the park underwent change to such an extent that to continue to play there would probably result in the death of my children and myself, everyone would tell me not to continue. Some would put it that the right no longer existed; others, that the right continued to exist, but that it was now unwise to exercise it. In any case, all would agree that I must change my pattern of action.

It should perhaps be emphasized that this line of reasoning does not represent an abandonment or a weakening of the moral and political principles underlying the right of forcible revolution against a tyrannical government or the justifiability of a war fought for national liberation. The moral and political principle underlying the justification of revolution and liberation is of course the sovereignty of the people. The present line of reasoning has to do with the effects of certain means of implementing that principle under certain new conditions which have emerged. Everything depends on what the effects are most likely to be in the concrete case in question. Even in an age of thermonuclear weapons there may well be instances of civil wars, revolutions within a country, or wars of national liberation, which, for various reasons, are not likely to lead to thermonuclear conflict. But we confront the further question: once thermonuclear weapons exist, do they give a sort of absolute power to those who possess them? They certainly give more military power than any other weapons give, but this fact is to a degree counteracted by two further facts. First, thermonuclear weapons are possessed by both sides in the worldwide ideological competition which is the decisive feature of the present period, so that, to an extent, mutual restraints come into play. Second, though governments can form policies, people can control governments, especially in the matter of carrying on large-scale war, as pointed out above. The power of any government ultimately depends on the cooperation of the people. Governments need people more than people need governments.

But aren't there times when death is actually preferable to life, when death would be preferable to going on living under the given conditions? Did not Patrick Henry, a contemporary of Thomas Jefferson and a fellow revolutionary in the same cause, pronounce the words that have become famous: "Give me liberty, or give me death"? Though Jefferson and Henry were among the "reds" of their day, the saying of some anti-reds of the present has a similar logic: "I would rather be dead than red." What is important to notice is that these are individual choices. One may consider death preferable to living under a red regime, and another may consider death preferable to living under a white, a black, or a brown regime. As I see it, a man has a right to make that choice for himself. But he has no right to make that choice for himself in a way that would foreclose every alternative choice for everyone else, present and future. In other words, "I would rather be dead than red" is not an argument that could justify thermonuclear war. The most it could justify is my own suicide or death in battle, or the suicide or death in battle of a particular group. Even individual suicide or killing is considered by many to be morally unacceptable in any circumstances. This is a debatable matter. But surely the least arguable of all value judgments is that any human group living at any one time ever would have the right to prevent the creation of any further human values. Even if it could be shown that a majority of people living at one time wanted to do that, there would still be the new and unique problem of whether any present majority has the right to destroy the future. Majority rule might be justified as a way of playing the game. Can it be justified as a way of preventing any game at all from being played?

However, it seems very unlikely that we shall ever be faced with a situation in which the majority of people living at a given time have declared themselves for the annihilation of the human race and the planet Earth. What we are actually faced with is of an opposite character: contemporary democracy has not yet found a solution to the problem of applying the concept of majority decision to the question of war. I mean a solution that works in practice. In the United States there is a clear constitutional theory, with explicit legal provisions, to the effect that the decision to enter into a state of war shall be taken only by the legislative branch of the government, the national Congress (elected officials from every section of the country), by majority vote of its members after having had the opportunity to discuss and debate the issue of war. Clearly, there is wisdom in this procedure. War, being a matter of life or death, represents the gravest course of action which any nation can undertake. If there was ever a matter on which the people should be consulted, it is this, because at stake are not only their property, their liberty, and their convenience, but their very lives.

Facts show, however, that this excellent theory has not worked. But its failure to work has not been because the procedures established by the Constitution were impossible to follow in the face of sudden attacks which placed the country in such immediate jeopardy that there was no time to assemble the Congress and put the matter before the members. Abstractly, problems of this kind might have been expected. Concretely, however, in those cases where the attack upon us came suddenly and without warning, as in World War I and World War II, it was still feasible for the Executive to send a message to the assembled Congress explaining the reasons why a declaration of war seemed justified, and for the Congress to deliberate and vote.

The actual problems revolving around evasion and violation of the constitutional provisions concerning the entering into war arose in a different way, through situations in which there was no direct attack upon us, and no action by any power large enough to give rise to fears for our immediate security. This was the way in the Mexican war of the 1840s, the Korean war, and the present war in Vietnam. In these cases there was ample time for Congressional deliberation, or even a national plebiscite, as to whether what was at stake was worth a war or not. But the pattern followed by the Executive was to order into action military units of so small a size and on so limited a scale that the operation could be referred to as a mere police action, or as a mission of advisers, in short, as part of the conduct of foreign policy short of war. Then, when our soldiers began to be killed, it was asserted that they must naturally be protected in the performance of their duties by sending reinforcements. As the casualties increased, the scale of operations increased, until everyone had to admit it was a war, although it had never been declared, nor discussed as a war, before the sacrifices of life were ordered. To speak plainly, this is fraud practiced by the government, for in each case the Executive knew that the effect of its orders was to place the country at war, and that the Constitution required that it ask the Congress for a declaration of war before issuing such orders. The Executive, with good reason, probably feared that the Congress would not see sufficient grounds to declare war, but would support a war if it was presented to them as a *fait accompli.* In his day, Henry David Thoreau made this penetrating observation on the first page of his *Civil Disobedience:* "Witness the present Mexican war, the work of comparatively a few individuals . . . for, in the outset, the people would not have consented to this measure." The legislature of Massachusetts had backbone enough to censure the federal administration for carrying on an undeclared war. Today it is a mystery why the federal courts cannot rule upon the question whether the present administration is carrying on an undeclared war in Vietnam in violation of explicit provisions of the U.S. Constitution (I,8,11).

This whole problem of war is a continuing problem, very much with us today. We may not have much time in which to solve it. We ought to put it in the center of our work.

V
DEATH

THE CRISIS CALLED DEATH*

Corliss Lamont

No philosophy, religion, or overall way of life can be judged complete or adequate unless it includes a definite position on whether or not the human personality can surmount the crisis called death and continue its career in another and immortal realm of existence. Without being dogmatic about it, naturalistic humanism does give an answer on this issue.

Humanism, in line with its rejection of belief in any form of the supernatural, considers illusory the idea of personal immortality, or the conscious survival of the self beyond death for any period of time whatsoever. The basic reason for regarding a hereafter as out of the question is that since a human being is a living unity of body and personality, including the mind, it is impossible for the personality to continue when the body and the brain have ceased to function.

The sciences of biology, medicine, and psychology have accumulated an enormous amount of evidence pointing to the oneness and inseparability of personality and the physical organism. And it is inconceivable that the characteristic mental activities of thought, memory, and imagination could go on without the sustaining structure of the brain and cerebral cortex. The only possible way for a

* This article was published originally in *The Humanist,* XXVII, No. 1 (1967), 19. Reprinted by permission of *The Humanist.*

man to achieve immortality is to carry out its original meaning, "not-death," by keeping alive his natural body forever. Although such an outcome is extremely improbable, the average span of life, at least in the United States, has been increasingly extended during this twentieth century. I can imagine my own this-earthly "resurrection" taking place some twenty years hence at about the age of eighty-five, when I shall go for a week or so to the hospital and have my tiring natural heart replaced by an inexhaustible mechanical heart.

Paradoxically enough, traditional Christianity supports the humanist position on the unity of body and personality by insisting that man can gain immortality only through the literal resurrection of the physical body. The promise of this resurrection was, according to the New Testament, the wonderful, world-shaking message that Jesus brought. Undoubtedly the best chance for personal survival after death is precisely through this resurrection route of old-time religion. The trouble here for humanists is that they cannot possibly accept the resurrection doctrine.

Since the humanist thinks that his one and only life is in the here and now, he aims to make the best of it in terms of attaining happiness for himself, his family, his countrymen, and all mankind. Accordingly, the humanist is a militant fighter for social justice, racial equality, higher living standards, and world peace. And he remembers that faith in immortality has often cut the nerve of effective action for improving the lot of humanity on this earth.

For example, during this crucial era when the folly, horror, and tragedy of international war continue to afflict mankind, we find the following gem of supernaturalist apologia in *The New York Times* of Sept. 11, 1950, at the height of the Korean War: "Sorrowing parents whose sons have been drafted for combat duty were told yesterday in St. Patrick's Cathedral that death in battle was part of God's plan for populating the kingdom of heaven." A Catholic prelate, Monsignor William T. Greene, offered this extraordinary form of consolation, but both Pope John XXIII and Pope Paul VI would surely have winced at it.

The humanist faces his own death and that of others with more equanimity than the average person, because he realizes that in the processes of Nature death is a necessary corollary of life and has played an indispensable role in the evolution of the higher animals, including man. Death has rid the earth of unprogressive species and has given full meaning to the Darwinian doctrine of the survival of the fittest. Without our good friend death, the race of man would never have come into being at all.

Biologically speaking, Nature's method with the more complex forms of life is to discard the old and faltering organism at a certain stage to make way for newborn and lustier vitality. As the American novelist Anne Parrish says, each one of us "must die for the sake of life, for the flow of the stream too great to be dammed in any pool, for the growth of the seed too strong to stay in one shape. . . . Because these bodies must perish, we are greater than we know. The most selfish must be generous, letting his life pour out to others. The most cowardly must be brave enough to go." So it is that death gives the opportunity for the largest possible number of human beings, including our own descendants, to experience the joys of living. And in this sense, death acts as the firm ally of future and unborn generations, through the simple procedure of making room for them upon this planet.

To philosophize about man's mortality, as I have been doing, or to take seriously religious promises of an afterlife, may soften slightly the impact of death; but in my opinion nothing can really counteract its bitter sting. The humanist believes that death is a blow of such magnitude and finality that it is always a tragedy, either for the deceased or the survivors who were close to him, or for both. Even when dying puts an end to a painful and incurable illness, it remains tragic that extinction of the individual should be the only cure. Of course, the tragedy is greater when a person dies in youth or the prime of life.

But it is always too soon to die, even if you are three-score years and ten, even if you are four-score years and ten—indeed, no matter how young or old you may be. Hotspur's cry in *Henry IV* resounds down the ages, "O gentlemen! the time of life is short." I myself am almost sixty-five and have the familiar experience of looking back on my life and finding that it has all gone by with appalling swiftness. Days, years, decades have slipped by so quickly that now it seems I hardly knew what was happening. Have I been daydreaming all this time?

Today, more than ever, I feel the haunting sense of transiency.

If only time would for a while come to a stop! If only each day would last 100 hours and each year 1,000 days! I sympathize with everyone who ever longed for immortality and I wish that the enchanting dream of eternal life could indeed come true. So it is that as a humanist I deeply regret that death is the end. Frankly, I would like to go on living indefinitely, providing that I could be assured of continued good health and economic security. And I would be most happy if anybody could prove to me that there actually is personal survival after death.

Humanists try to look death in the face—honestly, courageously, calmly. They recognize that it is one of the basic tragedies inherent in the great gift of life. We do not agonize over this fact, nor are we preoccupied with it. Our main antidote for death is *preoccupation with life,* with the manifold enjoyments that it brings and with creative work that contributes to the progress of our country and the welfare of humanity. We know there can be no individual immortality, but we have hopes that once global peace is permanently established, international cooperation and the steady advance of science will secure the immortality of the human race in this infinitely varied and beautiful world of Nature.

HUMANISM AND DEATH

Maurice Natanson

"There is a loud noise of Death
Where I lay . . ."
Samuel Greenberg[1]

Medieval manuals of death—*Ars Moriendi*, the art or craft of knowing how to die—may in the latter part of the twentieth century find their black or underground counterparts in "survival" guides for those who seek a meaningful end to their lives. What needs to be learned, chiefly, is how to retain or achieve personal identity and dignity in situations which threaten the individual's right to die with at least a modicum of self-respect and social respect. The majority of deaths in the United States occur in hospitals, and it is there as well that the care of the dying is centered. The locus of death appears to have shifted from the home to the institution, and with that change there comes about a related transformation in attitudes toward dying. The question is no longer, How can the individual meet his death appropriately and honorably in familiar surroundings? but rather, How can he find his own way to death in the midst of a medical bureaucracy whose design often involves the management of the dying by institutional standards over which the individual has relatively little control? The "Art and Crafte to

[1] From "To Dear Daniel" in *Poems by Samuel Greenberg*, edited by Harold Holden and Jack McManis, with a Preface by Allen Tate (New York: Henry Holt, 1947).

Know Well to Dye" in a revised version for our own time might well be, or at least include, a strategy of deceit, intimidation, cajolery, and bribery. The larger question, however, is that of how the meaning of death for the person is to be understood, how each of us can, in principle, come to terms with the fact of mortality, and what significance our death has for our fellow men. Whatever the concrete situation in which dying and death occur, the place of mortality in the human estate is relevant to the moribund as well as to those who survive him. In an age when dying properly demands strategy, philosophy remains the matrix within which all strategies find their vindication or their condemnation.

The concrete situation of the dying person is the beginning point for any consideration of the meaning of mortality. And that situation varies fantastically. However obvious it may be, it is necessary to remember that the dying person may be a premature infant or a centenarian, Socrates or a half-wit, a schizophrenic or a saint. The democracy of roles permits every one of us, in time, to become a dying patient; only sudden, accidental, or atypical deaths escape this condition. Given the extraordinary range of dying individuals, it would seem impractical if not impossible to list and examine the details of their lives and the history of their outlooks. A typology of the dying would overwhelm us with detail and threaten to trivialize the momentousness of death. The burden of range must simply be borne here by the investigator and the reader. Consider the distance between the situation of a famous and wealthy septuagenarian entering a distinguished institution (General Eisenhower going into Walter Reed Hospital, for example) and an indigent old man admitted to a large, crowded, understaffed charity ward in a metropolis—the kind of place Dr. Cherkasky had in mind when he recalled: "A story that used to be told about one of our major municipal hospitals—only possibly apocryphal—was that a man was found dead there, and that it was obvious he had been dead for a week because there were seven glasses of orange juice by his bed." [2]

[2] Martin Cherkasky, "The City Should Get Out of the Hospital Business," *The New York Times Magazine*, October 8, 1967, p. 53.

Quite apart from the fame or status of the patient and the hospital, there is also the question of the medical condition of the individual. Again, what may well be taken for granted as obvious should be considered carefully. Some dying patients are fully conscious and in command of their faculties; others are sedated to the point of dullness or are comatose. There are some who are relatively poised and cheerful; others are apathetic or melancholic. The variables mount: age, sex, race, education, occupation, economic status, profession, religious views, church ties, family, friends, interests, values. And added to these are the medical elements: the patient's disease, the specific form it has taken in his case, the stage of the disease, accompanying illnesses (a man dying of cancer of the pancreas can also be seriously troubled by a toothache!), past illnesses. Further, there are the patient's physician or surgeon, his nurses, orderlies, and other members of the staff, the hospital itself. Finally, there is the time of confinement, the moment in public affairs when the individual is dying, and the historical horizon in terms of which dying and death are experienced and judged. It is necessary to liberate ourselves from this thicket of variables.

I said that the concrete situation of the dying person is the beginning point for any consideration of the meaning of mortality. With all honor to the differences in the situations of the dying, it is still possible to attend to what is fundamentally common to them. By the "situation" of the dying person I mean the integral conjunction of limiting features of human action. Following Jean-Paul Sartre, we may say that man is always in a "situation," whose elements restrict his choice and yet whose meaning is interpreted, qualified, reconstructed—Sartre uses the term "chosen"—by the individual. The larger "situation" all men share involves historical, cultural, linguistic, and economic as well as biological factors. But these elements are seen by Sartre in their dialectical character. The individual is *inserted* in history, and that means that his existence is projected toward goals which are selected and enlivened or weakened by the continuous involvement or withdrawal of the individual. Interpretation and action are integral in the situation of man in the world. Thus, Sartre writes:

> For us, man is defined first of all as a being "in a situation." That means that he forms a synthetic whole with his situation—biological, economic, political, cultural, etc. He cannot be distinguished from his situation, for it forms him and decides his possibilities; but, inversely, it is he who gives it meaning by making his choices within it and by it. To be in a situation, as we see it, is *to choose oneself* in a situation, and men differ from one another in their situations and also in the choices they themselves make of themselves. What men have in common is not a "nature" but a condition, that is, an ensemble of limits and restrictions: the inevitability of death, the necessity of working for a living, of living in a world already inhabited by other men. Fundamentally this condition is nothing more than the basic human situation, or, if you prefer, the ensemble of abstract characteristics common to all situations.[3]

Interpretation, on this account, may be considered to be a mode of action, for being in a situation means creating as well as responding to the significance of history, language, and concrete relationships with fellow men. Out of the larger notion of situation we are able to clarify the meaning of the small human parcel of attitudes and responses which we have called the "concrete situation" of the dying man.

Let us put matters very simply and directly: in each instance, a dying person is bringing to a finish *his* life, a human career which can be repeated in its typical or general characteristics but which remains unique in its historical actuality. The term "unique" is used here in a quite neutral sense. No value judgment is offered about the quality of the concrete existence in question. That each person's life is *his* is not a redundancy but a pointing toward the texture of individuation in the domain of autobiography. The "concrete situation" of the dying man is a function of that which may properly be said to be *his:* his parents, his childhood, his education, his own family and friends, his career, his commitments and values are brought together through *his* life as a concatenation of awareness and intent, as a fabric of attitudes. Thus, to speak of the concrete situation of the dying of a child is already to presuppose not only age, sex, and a host of other categories but more essentially the

[3] Jean-Paul Sartre, *Anti-Semite and Jew*, trans. George J. Becker (New York: Schocken Books, 1948), pp. 59–60.

particular microcosm of that child's individual existence in which being twelve rather than thirteen years of age may make a profound difference to the twelve-year-old who desperately wants to be thirteen, a difference incomprehensible to "vital" statistics. To turn to the concrete situation of the dying person, then, is to attempt to uncover the focus and center of *his* identity as the source of his interpretation of life and the clue to his comprehension of death.

A central implication of turning to concrete existence is that awareness of dying, i.e., the patient's understanding that he is dying, is an essential feature of the individual's comprehension of death and a major component in the formation of what we have called the sense of identity. The question of the individual's awareness of dying brings us also to the ethical dimension of our theme, for it is evident, especially in the cases of death occurring in hospitals, that knowledge of his state may be and indeed very often is kept from the dying patient. The ethical problem is most often formulated through the question: Should the patient be told that he is dying? I intend to explore the question in the "situational" context provided by existential thought. Indirectly at the outset and directly at the end, we shall also be examining the implications of an existential humanism for a philosophy of death. It may be prudent to note immediately that in medical and hospital practice, much more often than not, the patient is not told that he is dying. "One of the most difficult of doctor's dilemmas," write Glaser and Strauss,

> is whether or not to tell a patient he has a fatal illness. The *ideal* rule offered by doctors is that in each individual case they should decide whether the patient really wants to know and can "take it." However, 69 to 90 per cent of doctors (depending on the study) favor not telling their patients about terminal illness, rather than following this "ideal" individual decision. So it appears that most doctors have a general standard from which the same decision flows for most patients—that they should not be told. This finding also indicates that the standard of "do not tell" receives very strong support from colleagues.[4]

[4] Barney G. Glaser and Anselm L. Strauss, *Awareness of Dying* (Chicago: Aldine Publishing Co., 1965), p. 119.

The fact, then, is that most often the dying are not told about their condition. The underside of the fact is that the appeal to judging individual cases may be used as a rationalization for what is not a patient-determined decision but a general policy "not to tell." In blunter terms, the dying patient is told a lie by his doctor, though the lie may vary from a direct and categorical "You do not have a fatal disease" to skilled avoidance of any direct response through strategies of silence, changing the subject, introducing technical jargon, claiming uncertainty, pointing to the possibilities of new research and therapy, leaving the problem to be handled by nurses, clergy, family, friends, or other patients on the ward or floor.[5] The lie, of course, is not without its apologists. For some it is a necessary lie, a desirable lie, a noble lie. Whatever else it may be, it is at least a lie which demands scrutiny.

Exactly what are we asking in the question, Should the patient be told? Let us start with the doctor and assume we have an instance in his practice when the diagnosis of a fatal illness is absolutely certain and when the patient involved is a reasonably intelligent and responsible adult who does not know or suspect that he is dying. Let us assume further that an operation has just been performed on this patient which revealed an advanced and incurable cancer. At the most, he has a few weeks to live. When the physician visits the patient, he may or may not be asked directly about the outcome of the operation and the patient's medical outlook. How should the doctor proceed? What are his responsibilities? There are at least three relevant domains to be considered: the distinctively medical aspect of the patient's condition and hospital circumstances; the legal, religious, and social responsibilities and relationships of the patient; and the existential reality of the dying person. Any attempt to answer the ethical question in the first two

[5] Cf. Glaser and Strauss, *op. cit.* Also see Jeanne C. Quint, *The Nurse and the Dying Patient* (New York: The Macmillan Company, 1967); K. R. Eissler, *The Psychiatrist and the Dying Patient* (New York: International Universities Press, 1955); John Hinton, *Dying* (Baltimore: Penguin Books, 1967); Robert Fulton, ed., *Death and Identity* (New York: John Wiley & Sons, Inc., 1965); Herman Feifel, ed., *The Meaning of Death* (New York: McGraw-Hill Book Company, 1959).

realms without reference and appeal to the third results in a failure to honor the humanistic possibilities of dying and death. Conversely, respecting the existential reality of the person in considering the medical and social orders constitutes a humanistic approach to the reality of the dying person. The three realms need close inspection:

1. The medical and hospital factor: The physician is in a privileged position in judging the narrowly medical aspects of the patient's condition. But even if he is correct in his judgment that the patient has no more than a few weeks to live, that judgment is caught up in the more complex value orientation of medical practice within whose orbit a decision is in fact made to try to extend the patient's life as long as possible or to allow the patient to die as quickly as possible. The decision to extend or shorten life is not based on medical judgment in the same sense that predicting the course of disease is based on medical judgment. Whether the patient will live for one week or one month has nothing to do with whether the doctor believes the patient ought to live for a longer or shorter time. Yet the doctor's value judgment does in fact have a good deal to do with how long the patient stays alive, for he may keep him alive by artificial techniques or he may choose to avoid extraordinary means for prolonging life. If it is simply assumed or taken for granted by the doctor that his responsibility is always to prolong life and if that conviction is held to be implied in a general code of medical ethics, then all dying patients will be viewed and treated in the same way. Since it is often maintained that telling the patient he will die is medically as well as psychologically destructive, i.e., produces shock, upset, and melancholy, it would appear that a commitment to extending life as far as possible is incompatible with telling the patient he will die. Certainly, a more moderate position can easily be formulated. The doctor's commitment is to extend life in the case of the dying patient as long as pain can be controlled, the will to live sustained, and the relative resources of the person kept intact and stable. Being honest with the dying person is not incompatible with these criteria; indeed, honesty may help to establish or support the well-being of the dying. The doctor's decision to "tell" must take into strong account the concrete situation of the individual person. Without such recognition, the decision stems from an artificial and often ill-considered claim regarding the responsibility of the doctor to sustain life. The decision, in fact, may come from the procedures of a particular hospital rather than the judgment of an individual physician. Similarly, the decision always to "tell," never to tell, or to tell sometimes may be required or determined by hospital policy. Rather than some medical code of ethics, it may be that the doctor's decision is affected by questions of hospital management—maintaining quiet on the wards, avoiding "scenes" with troublesome patients or their families, or arranging the schedules of doctors and nurses so as to make efficient use of their time. When the decision to tell is dictated by formal policy, by general codes, or by managerial considerations, the patient has been denied acknowledgment as an existential reality. If the doctor has lied to his patient within this context, that lie comes from the refusal of the person, whatever gloss is introduced to account for the action.

2. *Legal, religious, and social factors:* The dying patient is a member of the social order and retains responsibilities in that order. Whether or not he has made a will, needs to change provisions in his will, should rearrange his financial or business affairs, or take other steps in his personal affairs are clearly serious matters which turn in good measure on the question of whether the individual is aware that he is going to die. In the domain of religious and church involvement, the dying man has what is generally recognized as a right to receive the appropriate ministrations by clergy. And in family life, the dying person bears a special relationship to those who will be with him during his dying and will survive his death. The legal, religious, and social factors pose the question, Should the doctor tell? in quite a new way. We are no longer in the focus of the expert knowledge of the practitioner diagnosing disease nor are we in the field of hospital management. After all, the individual does retain certain legal rights even when he is dying, and he does have a right to see his minister or priest, and, it would seem, he does have a right to resolve his family affairs. Yet, in fact, the decision as to whether putting those rights into practice will be recognized as necessary or desirable may well depend on the doctor's decision to tell. The issues become extremely complex here. For

example, telling the patient may or may not be a way of telling the family. We are dealing only with the problem of whether the dying person should be told, but it is evident that one way of telling him or not is by first telling his family or denying them information—by lying to them, too. Suggesting that the patient should set his affairs in order, see his lawyer, speak to his minister may be tantamount to telling him he is going to die. A doctor who believes dying patients should not be told may nevertheless recognize that it is important for a businessman to settle his financial affairs before he dies or for a devout Catholic patient to be permitted to receive the sacrament of the Church. The principle of not telling begins to be compromised by a variety of conditions and particular circumstances which have less to do with the individual patient than with categories of economic and professional status, church affiliation, and civic involvement. The less obvious exceptions to general treatment come from the cultural and value orientation of the doctor. In effect, the decision to tell a businessman he is going to die may be made by a doctor who considers the world of finance of preponderant importance. The same doctor may withhold that information from a medically analogous patient whose occupation is carpentry. Telling on the basis of category tends to involve a double effect: first, discrimination takes place against those whose economic, societal, or religious status does not require special consideration or whose status is not deemed to be of sufficient significance within the value orientation of the doctor; second, those who are considered worthy of being told are discriminated against because they have been treated as members of a class or category rather than individuals. In some instances, a doctor may decide not to tell a patient he is dying despite the fact that the question of changing a will is of pressing importance.[6] The existential needs and possibilities of an individual may outweigh the urgencies of law. The physician who makes the decision to tell assumes responsibility for that decision. His patient, however, bears the consequences of his doctor's choice.

3. *The existential reality of the dying person:* We return, finally, to the concrete situation of the individual and *his* world. To attend

[6] See K. R. Eissler, *op. cit.*

to the existential reality of the person is to try to discover the principal themes and commitments which point to the self and which indicate the particular way in which the person has organized and built his life. The components of such organization include the individual's attitude toward death. One way of avoiding the power of the concrete, one way of precluding individuation or submerging it, is to assume that the period of dying is a "left-over" from life which is to be gotten through as painlessly and as swiftly as the case permits. The patient who dies in a hospital finds himself surrounded by a medical establishment with its own views of dying and death, and the patient may be considered "difficult" who insists on fulfilling and exploring his own way when it conflicts with hospital norms. But there is strong psychiatric evidence to add to philosophical insight which argues for the liberation of the patient to permit his dying to be not only an integral part of his life but even a remarkably fulfilling event. Liberation does not necessarily mean telling the patient. It does necessarily mean attending to him in the most humanly attentive way, listening to him, responding to him, and indeed challenging him to realize whatever possibilities he has. The existential reality of the person involves the uniqueness of the self, the specificity of realizing oneself as *this* human being among others. Where scientific analysis calls for the analysis of the behavior of the individual, existential analysis turns to the response of the person as the form and unity of his life's meaning. Behavior is judged by an observer; response is granted to a participant. It might be suggested that the juncture between behavior and response, between science and existence comes in therapy, for there the physician is both observer and respondent. The importance in remembering that medicine is an art as well as a science is that recognizing typical features of disease is a necessary but not a sufficient condition for treating—*attending*—the diseased person. The sufficient condition is provided by the art of the physician who not only acknowledges individual differences because they are relevant to scientific practice but who honors those differences because they announce the person he is treating, *caring* for. In these terms, the existential reality of the person is neither a mysterious and unfathomable attribute nor a trans-empirical essence. It is the individual in his full humanity, located in the response of a fellow man who turns to him as the source and center of a world of attitudes and recognitions, as a project and a freedom. If this being is forgotten or ignored or slighted or patronized in the doctor's decision, then whatever the outcome of that decision—to tell or not—the dying patient has been denied a primordial right, the right to die meaningfully.

When all three domains of the medical, the legal, and the existential are taken into genuinely interpenetrating account, a humanistic context for understanding the problems of death is established. Of course, no problems have been resolved, but they can at least be formulated and approached in a new way. Should the dying patient be told? Negatively answered, we can say that no decision should be reached on the abstract basis alone of medical ethics, of hospital policy, of his legal, religious, or familial status or circumstances. Positively put, any decision about telling must confront in full honesty the concrete existence of the person and attempt to respond to him as an integral being. Although there is considerable agreement that there can be no simple and definitive answer to the question of whether to tell, it has been pointed out that the formulation of the question is defective. Hinton writes:

> The frequently debated question, "Should the doctor tell?", tends to carry a false implication that the doctor knows all about the patient's approaching death and the patient knows nothing. The resultant discussion and controversy is therefore often irrelevant or, at least, tangential to the real problem. Doctors are far from omniscient. Even if they have no doubt that their patients' condition will be fatal, they can rarely foretell the time of death with any accuracy unless it is close at hand. Furthermore . . . patients are not necessarily unaware of what is happening; many have a very clear idea that they are dying.[7]

This is fair enough as a caution, but the "real problem" merely proves to be more complex than a discussion can indicate which takes as its procedural paradigm the doctor knowing and patient not knowing. To be sure, very often the patient knows, more often suspects that he is dying. Perhaps universally his "knowing" is an

[7] Hinton, *op. cit.*, p. 126.

unconscious foreboding or a marginal and oblique recognition which parallels consciousness but barely intersects its shadow. Whatever the degree or quality of knowledge (and there is a margin of tormenting error on both sides: the physician may be wrong in his diagnosis and the patient who thinks he is dying may not be dying at all), the more penetrating complaint about the form of the question, Should the patient be told? is that it severs the bare information at issue from the situation in which dying occurs. The question does have to be answered but, as I have suggested, it should be answered in full recognition of the existential reality of the dying person. Once that is granted as a *desideratum,* related questions must be raised: When, how, and by whom should the patient be told?

There are no instructions for treating the dying anymore than there are blueprints for death. We are properly caught in a web of concretions, in the procedures of medical art as practiced by human beings who are as frequently inadequate to their tasks as the dying are to the potentialities of their condition. Nevertheless, certain things can be said. The "when" of being told should be soon enough to give the patient time to recover from what is often the initial shock of learning about dying, and soon enough too for the patient to be able to plan his future. Though it may be odd to speak about the "future" for a person who has none, it must be realized that the time structure of the dying person is not that of the rest of the human community. The future may be limited to two weeks or two years, but the days and months involved have their own horizon of significance for the dying person. They may be time enough to complete some course of action already initiated in normal life or time enough to begin the exploration of a new relationship or problem which the individual might otherwise never have considered. The sooner the "when" of telling can be managed appropriately, the greater the possibility of the person to explore what remains to him as someone enabled, freed to begin a radical adventure.

The "how" and the "by whom" cannot be separated, for the way of telling is created and made possible by the one who tells. Similarly, manner and content are integral. A blunt, unequivocal announcement made by a doctor who knows, has cared for and respected the patient over a period of years may be a more suitable way of proceeding than an indirect, euphemistic, and seemingly kinder telling by a nurse who has known the patient for a few days.[8] Finally, the "how" and the "by whom" are not restricted to the initial act of confession. The patient often grows in his understanding of the telling as well as of what is told, and one way in which that development may take place is by coming into relationship with the one who tells him. The open horizon and possibilities of learning about death are among the final gifts we can give to the dying as well as the final humanistic recognition we can take of their existential reality.

"Humanistic recognition" means a turning to what can be directly ascertained in the situation of the concrete individual. All that is given in that situation is worthy of scrutiny and philosophic respect because an image of what is possible for man is created in the expression of all action. Events and interpretation are not removed from the human arena of analysis and understanding but are celebrated as the themes for self-comprehension. In this way, even the appeal to the divine, to revelation, to prophecy, or to the forebodings of eschatology are centered in a humanistic frame when they are counted as human productions and achievements. Setting aside their transcendent claims to truth is not to strip them of their legitimacy but to choose them in their givenness to us, the human beings who must come to terms with their claims and demands. An existential humanism of the kind I have pointed to here permits and encourages these conclusions:

[8] In *Death Be Not Proud*, John Gunther relates the way in which a great surgeon gave his judgment as a consulting physician of the condition of Gunther's young son, who was suffering from a brain tumor. In this case it was the parents who were told, not the patient. Gunther writes: "Penfield spent an hour on the slides; always, in a thing of this hideous kind, the possibility exists of mistaken diagnosis, and the tumor might have changed for the better or worse. We waited, and then with everybody listening Penfield cut through all the euphemisms and said directly, 'Your child has a malignant glioma, and it will kill him'" (Modern Library edition, p. 74).

1. Men transcend their spiritual hesitations and frailties by confronting themselves and each other with as much honesty and directness as are compatible with compassion and trust.

2. It is less than human to lie to the dying and refuse them the right to choose for themselves how they are to define their death.

3. Yet it is less than humane to tell the truth to the dying regardless of the individual case simply because of some general attitude or policy.

4. It is less than honorable to tell the rich but not the poor, to confide news of mortality to the Catholic but not the Protestant, or always to shield the child on the uncertain and indiscriminate grounds of his innocence.

5. If we are driven at last to insist on the variegation of human situations and needs, we are still not freed from the existential mandate of affirming the freedom of the dying person, for locked in his difference and distance from us is the furious or sullen intimation of our own death.

NOTES ON CONTRIBUTORS

JOHN P. ANTON is Professor of Philosophy and Associate Dean of the Graduate School at the State University of New York at Buffalo. He is author of *Aristotle's Theory of Contrariety* and has edited *Naturalism and Historical Understanding.*

KURT BAIER is Professor and Chairman of the Department of Philosophy at the University of Pittsburgh. He has taught at universities in Australia and is author of *The Moral Point of View.*

H. J. BLACKHAM, former Chairman of the British Humanist Association, is author of *Humanism, Religion in a Modern Society, Political Discipline in a Free Society,* and has edited *Six Existentialist Thinkers* and *Objections to Humanism.*

ABRAHAM EDEL is Professor of Philosophy at City College of the City University of New York. He is on the editorial board of *Revue Universitaire de Science Morale* and is author of *Ethical Judgment, Science and the Structure of Ethics, Method in Ethical Theory,* among other works.

MARVIN FARBER is Professor of Philosophy at the State University of New York at Buffalo. Former President of the American Philosophical Association (Eastern Division), he is founder and editor of the journal *Philosophy and Phenomenological Research.* Among his recent books are *Phenomenology and Existence, The Aims of Phenomenology,* and *Naturalism and Subjectivism.*

HERBERT FEIGL is Professor of Philosophy at the University of Minnesota and Director of the Minnesota Center for the Philosophy of Science. Former President of the American Philosophical Association (Western Division), he is also an original member of the famed Vienna Circle. He has edited the volumes *Minnesota Studies in the Philosophy of Science,* and is a member of the Publication Committee of *The Humanist.*

CHARLES FRANKEL, formerly Assistant Secretary of State for Cultural Affairs, is Professor of Philosophy at Columbia University. He is author of many books, including *The Case for Modern Man, The Democratic Prospect,* and *Faith of Reason.*

ROLLO HANDY is Professor of Philosophy and Provost of Education at the State University of New York at Buffalo. He is co-author of *A Current Appraisal of the Behavioral Sciences* and author of *Methodology of the Behavioral Sciences.*

SIDNEY HOOK, Professor and Chairman of the Department of Philosophy at New York University, is a founder of the Congress for Cultural Freedom and former President of the American Philosophical Association (Eastern Division). Among the books that he has authored are *The Paradoxes of Freedom, Religion in a Free Society, Education for Modern Man,* and *Reason, Social Myths and Democracy.*

PAUL KURTZ is Professor of Philosophy at the State University of New York at Buffalo. He is editor of *The Humanist* and co-editor of the *International Directory of Philosophy and Philosophers,* and on the editorial board of *Revue Universitaire de Science Morale.* He is author of *Decision and the Condition of Man,* co-author of *A Current Appraisal of the Behavioral Sciences,* and has recently edited the book *Sidney Hook and the Contemporary World.*

CORLISS LAMONT has taught for many years at Columbia University. He is a former Director of The American Humanist Association and Chairman of the Emergency Civil Liberties Committee. He is author of *The Philosophy of Humanism, The Illusion of Immortality,* and *Freedom of Choice Affirmed.*

A. H. MASLOW, past President of the American Psychological Association, is Professor of Psychology at Brandeis University. He is a recipient of the "Humanist of the Year" award. A founder of the *Journal for Humanistic Psychology,* he is also author of *Religions, Values and Peak Experiences, Toward a Psychology of Being,* and has edited *New Knowledge in Human Values.*

ERNEST NAGEL is John Dewey Professor of Philosophy at Columbia University. Former editor of *The Journal of Philosophy* and *Philosophy of Science,* he also is past President of the American Philosophical Association (Eastern Division) and the Association for Symbolic Logic. He is author of *The Structure of Science, Sovereign Reason,* and *Logic without Metaphysics,* among other works.

MAURICE NATANSON, Professor of Philosophy at the University of California at Santa Cruz, formerly taught at the University of North Carolina. He has edited the books *Essays in Phenomenology* and *Philosophy of the Social Sciences.*

KAI NIELSEN is Professor of Philosophy at New York University. He is author of two recent books, *The Quest for God* and *Ethics Without God.*

CARL R. ROGERS, formerly with the University of Wisconsin, is now with the Western Behavioral Sciences Institute. He is author of *Client-Centered Therapy* and *On Becoming a Person.*

B. F. SKINNER, noted behavioristic psychologist, is Professor of Psychology at Harvard University. He is a member of the Publication Committee of *The Humanist.* He is author of *Walden Two, Science and Human Behavior,* and *Verbal Behavior.*

JOHN SOMERVILLE is Professor of Philosophy at Hunter College of the City University of New York. He is editor of *Soviet Studies in Philosophy.* He is author of *The Philosophy of Peace* and *Methodology in Social Science,* and has co-edited *Social and Political Philosophy* and other works.